Richmond upon Thames Libraries

Renew online at www.richmond.gov.uk/libraries

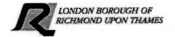

MY STORY

From Foster Care to Footballer

MARK BRIGHT

with

Kevin Brennan

CONSTABLE

CONSTABLE

First published in Great Britain in 2019 by Constable
This paperback edition published in Great Britain in 2020 by Constable

1 3 5 7 9 10 8 6 4 2

Copyright © Mark Bright and Kevin Brennan, 2019

The moral right of the authors has been asserted.

A CIP catalogue record for this book
is available from the British Library.

ISBN: 978-1-47213-078-5

Typeset in Bembo by Hewer Text UK Ltd, Edinburgh
Printed and bound in Great Britain by Clays Ltd, Elcograf S.p.A.

Papers used by Constable are from well-managed
forests and other responsible sources.

MIX
Paper from
responsible sources
FSC® C104740

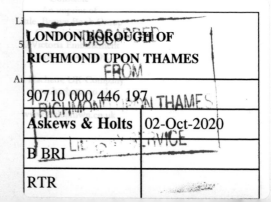

To Alice Irene Davies, better known as 'Gran'.

I will never get my head around how a parent can give up a child. Luckily there are people in this world willing to take on someone else's responsibility, and more importantly, give a child a chance in life.

Contents

Foreword by Gary Lineker   ix

1 What Do You Want to Do?   1
2 The Note   9
3 Nana Parton   17
4 The Lollipop and the Stick   35
5 Gran and Grandad   47
6 A Different Apprenticeship   59
7 Goal Bonus   79
8 Big Boots to Fill   97
9 Christmas Jeer   113
10 Headline Writer's Dream   129
11 Angry and Hungry   143
12 The Night a Team Was Born   161
13 Ecstasy to Agony   183
14 All Good Things   205
15 Familiar Faces   227
16 Vegas   243
17 Alpine Adventure   257
18 Happy at the Valley   269
19 Feels Like Home   283

Acknowledgements   299
Index   301

Foreword by Gary Lineker

'What a waste of money, what a waste of money.' That was the chorus that reverberated around the decrepit stands of Filbert Street, and their target was me. My first appearance for Everton was at my old club Leicester City, in my hometown. My humiliation at walking into the wrong dressing room at half-time with us trailing was bad enough, but by the end of the game not only had we lost but my replacement at the Foxes, a certain Mark Bright, had scored two goals, one of them an absolute pearler into the top corner – something I hadn't achieved in my more than two hundred appearances for the club. 'What a waste of money,' sang my family and friends when I got home.

Given this history, and knowing Brighty's sense of humour, I am pretty sure that's why he asked me to write this foreword. He knew I would have to mention it. The ignominy continues. To be honest, they were about the only goals he managed that season with Leicester (never peak too soon, Brighty) and he was soon on his way to Crystal Palace. There, of course, he made his name as the straight man in a truly wonderful striking partnership with Ian Wright.

Wright and Bright were unstoppable. Wrighty provided the flair, the speed, the goals. Brighty provided the . . . erm . . . work rate, the . . . heading, yes, heading . . . and hold-up play, definitely hold-up play. Do you have to be kind when writing a foreword to someone's book?

I jest, of course. Brighty was the sort of striker every Wrighty wanted to play alongside. A man to fight your battles, a man to do the hard yards, a man with the intelligence in his game to make things easier for you. Sounds selfish, but strikers, well, our kind of strikers, are selfish and rely on partners like Mark Bright to make us look good, to make our goal-scoring statistics better.

Brighty did all these things and more during a career that really started at Port Vale, his hometown club. But he also scored goals himself, plenty of them. His career record is mightily impressive, scoring better than a goal every three games. At Crystal Palace he netted 91 goals in 227 league matches and at his next club, Sheffield Wednesday, he maintained that ratio with 48 goals in 133 league games. How much would that cost you these days? He even managed to notch a few for Charlton at the end of his career when he was about forty-nine years old (slight exaggeration).

The highlights in an outstanding career, though, were many. A Second Division Golden Boot with Palace in the 1987–88 season with twenty-four goals. Promotion via the play-offs came the next season. A season of stability in the old Division One was followed by Crystal Palace's best ever season in the top flight when they finished third (a confession, I had to double check that stat). There was an epic FA

Cup semi-final victory and an all-important goal against the then dominant Liverpool, and another FA Cup goal in the all-Sheffield semi-final.

After football Mark became a regular on our television screens, where his endearing personality, intelligence and understanding of the game shone through. These days he's back at Crystal Palace and is frequently seen alongside their chairman, Steve Parish. You could say he's become the best man-to-man marker the game has witnessed since Des Walker.

In all seriousness, though, Brighty is more than just a footballer, he's one of the good guys. Having played with him, played against him, worked alongside him in television, I feel proud to count him as a close friend and have forgiven him for one of the worst days of my professional life. 'What a waste of money.' Well, almost.

The dressing room was huge and the fact that I was sitting in it sent a tingle of excitement down my spine. I always thought that, one day, playing in a final at Wembley was realistic for me. I believed European Cup finals were really for the elite, the great players, but getting to a FA Cup final always seemed like something I could achieve, something I could strive for, a goal that could one day come true. That day arrived in May 1990. I was twenty-seven years old and had worked hard to make sure I used every ounce of ability I had as a footballer since I had become a full-time professional seven years earlier. Against all the odds I was part of a Crystal Palace team who were about to play in an FA Cup final against Manchester United. I knew that it was, without doubt, the biggest day of my footballing life.

What Do You Want to Do?

As a kid I knew I had enough about me to play the game at a decent level, even if some people questioned that along the way. I was naturally athletic and always loved kicking a ball about. Like so many other kids I wanted to be a professional footballer, wanted to earn my living from playing a game I loved. It was always a dream, but turning the dream into reality proved to be a lot harder than I could ever have imagined. I wasn't the sort of player who had fantastic natural gifts. Yes, I had talent, probably more than a lot of other would-be footballers when I was young, but I think I realised pretty early on that you had to work hard in life if you wanted to achieve things, and the main thing I wanted to achieve was to have a career as a footballer. I had enough self-confidence and belief to think it could happen and, as I got older, I became more single-minded about the whole thing.

At school I wasn't the sort of pupil who mucked about too much or was a disruptive influence in class. Academically I suppose I was average, although I always used to do pretty well in English, but it was always sport that was really my best subject. In school reports PE was where I got my best marks and the most praise from my teacher. There was one particular report in which my sports teacher used a line about me that I have never forgotten.

'A budding athlete, if ever I saw one,' he wrote.

I was lucky enough to have the physical attributes I needed to play sport well, and apart from playing football whenever I could, I would also work hard at making sure I was fit enough to compete in matches, and give myself the chance of getting to where I wanted to be. I never saw it as something that was out of my reach: I thought it was there for me, it was just a case of working out the best way to get the chance I wanted. The chance to break into the professional game. I was desperate to get an opportunity to show what I was capable of and to let people see the potential I had. By the time I became a teenager, I was pretty confident I had the ability to get what I wanted. The whole idea of being a footballer was never really far from my thoughts. I not only worked at improving myself as a player, I also used to spend a lot of time thinking about what it would be like when I finally achieved my goal. Unfortunately, I never quite showed the same obsession I had for football when it came to my school work. I remember being in a French lesson once, just staring out of the window and imagining myself playing for Port Vale or Stoke City, who were my two local teams, and my teacher, Mr Llewelyn, came over and banged the window pole on the desk in front of me, asking what I was doing.

'What was the last thing I just said, Bright?' he asked.

'*Bonjour*, sir?' I sheepishly replied.

Of course, it was a complete guess because I'd been in a world of my own, and the answer did me no good at all. He sent me out of the class, which wasn't good, but it did allow me to carry on day dreaming as I stood in the corridor.

Another teacher at the same Maryhill Comprehensive School in Stoke was Mr Arkle, who took us for geography and, like a lot of other teachers back then, he also taught other subjects as well, in his case woodwork and metalwork. He was a big man who loved his rugby and was one of those guys who genuinely cared about the kids he was teaching. He took a real interest in all of us and cared about our futures and the lives we were going to have when we left school. I think he liked me, but probably also thought I could be a bit cocky and lazy in the classroom at times. One day after a lesson he made a point of going around everyone in the class and asking us all the same simple question: what did we want to do when we left school?

'Bright, what do you want to do?' he asked.

'Play football, sir,' I told him, as everyone in the class began to laugh.

'Bright, what are you going to do?' he asked again, only this time there was a definite sign of irritation in his voice.

'I'm going to be a footballer, sir. I want to be a professional footballer,' I replied.

'And what's plan B if that doesn't work?' he said with a slightly amused smile on his face.

'Plan B, sir? There is no plan B!' I told him.

Once again there was laughter from the rest of the class, and Mr Arkle clearly thought I was enjoying playing the cheeky kid in front of my classmates, but that wasn't what I was doing. I wasn't trying to be cheeky, I wasn't playing the class clown and I wasn't trying to make my classmates laugh. I was being deadly serious with him. He dismissed the rest of the class and asked me to stay behind. I thought I was in for a telling off at the very least but, as it turned out, that wasn't the case. Instead, he sat me down and told me how concerned he was about me, and my expectations, which he obviously thought might ultimately end in disappointment.

'I'm worried about you,' he said. 'I look at you in class sometimes and I think you're a bit of a dreamer. When I was your age, I wanted to be a doctor, but I wasn't good enough or clever enough to do that job, so then I decided to focus on becoming a teacher. The fact is, life isn't always the way we planned it or wanted things to turn out. I'm really worried that if you don't achieve your goal of playing football for a living, you don't really seem to have given any thought to what might happen, or have any idea about what else you might do.'

'Sir, you don't have to worry, I'll be all right,' I told him. 'I know I'm going to be a footballer.'

I think he probably felt frustrated by the fact that I appeared so naive. He knew that very soon in my young life I would have to leave school and face the outside world, when I would be hit by the reality of actually having to find a job and work for a living, but at the same time I think he realised it was pretty hopeless to try and get me to consider any alternatives. The fact of the matter was, I was absolutely certain that I was going to be able to make it. I had a one-track mind as far as a future career was concerned, and as I left the classroom and Mr Arkle that day, I walked out continuing to dream about becoming a professional and earning my living as a footballer. It wasn't just that day: I thought about it every day. I thought about what it would be like, how it would feel. I even began practising how I would sign my autograph. I was obsessed with the whole notion of becoming a professional footballer.

Happily, that dream did eventually become a reality. It was by no means easy for me, but through a mixture of ability, hard work and persistence, I eventually made it, and getting to that FA Cup final with Palace seemed to make it all worthwhile. I'd had the dream of getting to Wembley and realised I was one of the lucky ones who would be able to say their dream came true. On that day in 1990 I was about to take part in one of the showpieces of the English game, which was also a global event that was going to be watched by millions of people in different countries around the world. As I sat in the Wembley dressing room desperately trying to take in everything that was happening around me, I suddenly noticed a pile of what looked like yellow envelopes on one of the tables. Someone was going through them and started handing out little bundles to individual players. I wasn't sure what they were at first, but soon realised they were good-luck telegrams sent to us by family and friends, wishing us well for the match. Little messages that meant a lot because they gave you a nice mental boost before what was going to be the most important game of your life. These days players would be getting texts or emails from well-wishers, but it was very different then. There weren't too many mobile phones about in 1990. If you did happen to own one, they were about the size of a brick, with a screw-in aerial that was about six inches long, and they were for making calls, nothing else. How times have changed!

The pre-match ritual of getting good-luck telegrams was traditionally all part of the big day for the players who were taking part. Although the FA Cup is still a big deal today, I think it's fair to say that twenty-nine years ago it was a lot different. The final was something that was eagerly anticipated, even by people who hardly watched a football match throughout the season. The build-up for the game went on all week leading to the match on the Saturday, and the interest and excitement seemed much greater then. The players who played in the match were all of a generation that had grown up watching the final on television, and dreaming about playing in one. It was the showpiece game in an era when there were very few live matches shown during the course of a season. The FA Cup final dominated television from the morning of the game right through until the result had been decided. I was determined to try and enjoy the whole experience and take everything in.

There was a lot going on in the dressing room, with each player going through their personal preparations, just as they would on any other matchday, but at the same time, we all knew this was no ordinary match, and no ordinary day for any of us. You get used to your own ground and the home-team changing room, and there's also a familiarity about a lot of the other dressing rooms you use throughout the year when you play at different grounds, but Wembley was different and so was FA Cup final day. The telegrams were one of the things that made the day so different and special. Just like all the other players, I began to go through the yellow envelopes that had been handed to me. It was great to get all the good-luck messages, and then I opened one which made me feel incredibly emotional. Even to this day, it has the same effect when I think back to the message it contained.

'Mark. I'm the proudest man in Stoke-on-Trent. I'm glad you realised your dream. Be a winner.'

The telegram came from Mr Arkle. I was immediately transported back to that classroom and the conversation I'd had with him the day he'd asked me what I wanted to do when I left school. I was so pleased I had been able to make it as a footballer, and equally pleased that he had followed my career and wanted to let me know on such an important day that he was back in Stoke willing me on to do well in the biggest game of my career. It meant an awful lot. I had been a kid with dreams when he taught me and, as I sat in that Wembley dressing room, I realised I was about to turn one of those dreams into reality.

2

The Note

I was too young to actually know about what was happening at the time, but I later found out that it was a note pinned to a door that was the trigger for the direction my life was to take from a very young age. I had a brother and a sister, a mum and a dad, just like so many other kids, but the note signalled the end of any real hope there might have been for all of us to have anything approaching a normal family life.

The note had been left by my mum, and it was read by my dad on the night of Saturday 21 November, 1964, less than two-and-a-half years after I was born. My parents weren't exactly on the best of terms at the time and were living apart, and they had already separated on and off not that long after I was born. I had little idea of what was really going on with their marriage. I was just a young kid and so was my brother Philip, who was about a year older than me, and our sister, Marie, was a year older than him. The three of us never really had a clue about what was happening, and we certainly had no idea of what was to come our way. How could we have at such a young age?

On that Saturday we were being looked after by our dad while my mum went to a wedding. At the time the three of us were living with her at our maternal grandmother's house. That day the arrangement was that he would return us at 10 p.m. to our grandmother's house, but when he turned up and knocked on the door there was no answer, and there was no sign of our mother either. Instead, there was a note, and in it she basically told our father that she'd had enough. She was fed up with her life, and was going away, telling him that he would have to look after the three of us, which was clearly a non-starter as far as he was concerned. At the time, he rented a place with one small room downstairs and a bedroom upstairs. He worked as a labourer for a local clay company, driving a fork-lift truck, and the thought of having to take care of three children on his own completely panicked him.

Things moved pretty rapidly after that. He left the three of us with a friend on the following Monday, and he went off to see the local authorities, asking for help and telling them that there was no way he was going to be able to cope on his own. They apparently agreed with him, because four days later my brother Philip and I found ourselves in a new home, being looked after by a woman who was a complete stranger to us. She was very nice and extremely kind, doing as much as she possibly could to welcome us into her house, the place that was going to be our new home. It was the start of a completely different kind of life for the two of us, and for our sister who didn't go with us, but would instead end up living with our dad. It was a crazy situation for all of us to have to cope with, but even before all of this happened, our lives could hardly have been described as normal, mainly due to my parents' troubled relationship.

My mum and dad were from Stoke-on-Trent, or at least my mother was. My father was originally from the Gambia and had travelled to this country in the 1950s. It was probably partly for the adventure of going to another country, and perhaps it was partly the fact that he thought he could find work in England. I'm not entirely sure how a guy from the Gambia ended up in Stoke instead of somewhere like London, but that's what he did and that's where he met my mum. Being black in Britain at that time could not have been easy and I've heard all sorts of stories about how landlords wouldn't even allow black people to rent rooms or flats. I'm sure it was not the easiest of times for a black man, and it must also have been very difficult for my mother, who was a local white girl. I've been told that the two of them had to endure things like openly being taunted by people and spat at in the street when they went out together as a couple. My mother was actually chased around the house by her own brother when he became aware of her relationship with my father.

'You're not going out with a black man!' he screamed.

I'm not sure how you deal with incidents like that. It must have been pretty horrible for her and I'm sure the sight of a black guy with a white woman wasn't exactly a common thing back then, but to have your own brother reacting so strongly to the relationship probably shows just how difficult it must have been for her to carry on seeing my dad. Things are not perfect even now, but times have changed an awful lot, and I can't really say I ever experienced that level of intolerance. Throughout my life, the relationships I've had have not been dictated by the colour of a girl's skin: it has always been about the person, what their personality is like and the mutual attraction we've had for each other.

Perhaps the easiest thing for my mother to have done, all those years ago, would have been to walk away from the relationship and in doing so avoid all the prejudice and hassle that came her way because of it, but despite the problems they encountered, their relationship endured, and so on 28 November 1959, Maureen Clarke married Edwin Bright at Stoke Register Office. This was despite a pretty stark warning of what life might be like for my mother if she went ahead with the marriage, because on their wedding day a woman apparently turned up at the door with her daughter and told my mum that the girl's father was Edwin Bright, the man she was about to marry. The visit by the woman that day didn't stop the wedding, but it was certainly an indication of what was to come and of how difficult and complicated life might be in the years that followed.

I can see that it might have been difficult for them to maintain their relationship, particularly when you consider how different their backgrounds were. My mother came from a very ordinary white working-class family in the Potteries. My dad had come from the Gambia and was apparently called Eddie Oakes-Bright, but the Oakes part of his name got dropped when he somehow made his way to England. The fact that they got together at all in the climate that existed at the time when it came to mixed relationships is pretty remarkable, but they did and by the time they got married my mum was already pregnant with

Marie, who was born in May 1960, six months after the wedding. Phil came along a year after that, and I arrived thirteen months later.

In the first couple of years of my life I was simply too young to realise what was going on, and I don't have any strong memories from that time. I don't recall exactly what life was like before that note was left on the door of my grandmother's house. As a child I think I was always very self-contained. By that I mean that from a very early age I seemed to be able to accept what was happening around me and just get on with things, even if I didn't fully understand what the true situation was. It was part of my personality and probably helped me when it came to coping with the circumstances I had to face so early on. Even though my early years may have been confusing, it was as though I never let the problems totally intrude on my life. As a kid I think I was pretty happy and quite outgoing. Stuff happened, good and bad, but I just got on with life and sort of steered a course through it all. I can't say the break-up of my parents had no effect on me, it must have, and certainly from a practical point of view my future was set on a different course because of their split, but I wasn't the only one affected by it.

Whatever was actually happening in my parents' relationship when I came along, it seems clear that things were crumbling. The fact that they separated for about a year when I was very young is an indication that they clearly had problems long before the note on the door. Before then, my mother left my dad after she found out he'd gone off with another woman, and during the time they were apart she lived with another man. Even though she eventually returned to live with our father, it seems that the move was just papering over the cracks, which were getting bigger by the day. The truth is that neither of them were exactly faithful to each other, and when my mother returned to live with my father, she told him she was pregnant with a baby she had conceived with the other guy. Initially, it seems that he was willing to accept what had happened and the two of them stayed together, but the relationship with the other man continued, and eventually my mother and father split up. Marie, Philip and I went to live with him, and with the help of an Italian couple who owned the property where he rented rooms, he somehow managed to look after the three of us. My mum refused to get back together with our father, and by the summer of 1963 she was heavily pregnant and living at her mother's house. In July of that same summer our dad was sent to prison for twelve weeks for non-payment of debts, which triggered a new upheaval for Marie, Phil and me. Suddenly we didn't have anyone to look after us and the authorities had to get involved in order to make sure we would be taken care of. They spoke to our mum and she agreed to have us move in with her and stay at our grandmother's house until our dad returned from prison, but that arrangement was cut short after just a few weeks when she gave birth to a baby girl ahead of her due date. With my mum in a maternity home with her new daughter, my gran was simply unable to cope with three young children on her own, and we had to go to a residential nursery for a few days before going back to our gran's once our mother had returned with our new baby sister, Sharon.

The period that followed the birth of Sharon was a relatively stable one for all of us. I was only fourteen months old when she came along and have no real recollection of any of the events I described, but through looking at official documents and piecing together what went on with the help of my family, I have been able to get some idea of what was happening and when it happened. After the birth of Sharon, it seems it was my mum who had the main responsibility for us, and that lasted right up until the date of the note, 21 November 1964. As kids none of us really knew what was going through her mind when she wrote it but, clearly, she found the situation she was in overwhelming. She'd had enough and was quite possibly depressed. Whatever it was, there were consequences for all of us and, at the age of two years and five months, I found myself suddenly having two families. The one I had been born into, and a new one, with a woman I had never seen before.

3

Nana Parton

The childcare people acted quickly when our dad went to see them on the Monday after finding the note from my mother. It was decided that Phil and I would be put into the residential nursery again, while they looked for a suitable foster home for the two of us. The nursery was the same place Marie, Phil and I had been sent to the previous year when our dad had to go to prison for twelve weeks and mum had given birth to Sharon. While we went to the nursery, Marie was put in the care of our dad and went to live with him, and Sharon stayed with my mum. The only strong memory I have of that time is of being with Phil: it was just the two of us, we were on our own. I don't have any great recollection of the nursery itself, what it looked like, the sounds and smells, nothing at all. I don't think I've deliberately tried to block the whole episode out of my memory because it was too painful or traumatic. I believe it is simply a case of me being too young to think it all through. It was that trait of being able to accept what was going on around me and get on with my life, even if I was just two years and five months old. I knew we were no longer living with my mum and sisters, but Phil was with me and, as young as we were, I suspect we became a source of comfort to each other. Even at that young age we instinctively felt we were there for each other, and it's something that has stayed with the two of us throughout our lives.

You hear about kids who end up spending their entire childhood in a care home, but thankfully that didn't happen to us. We were only in the residential nursery for a matter of days in November 1964 before we were on the move again, once the authorities had found the foster home they had been looking for, one they believed would be suitable for us. The person they chose was a woman called Mrs Helena Parton, or Nana Parton, as the two of us would affectionately come to call her.

Nana Parton was lovely. She was white, in her fifties and lived in a place called Stanfield. She was short and quite stocky, with light-coloured hair that was swept back neatly in an unfussy way. She had a kind, reassuring face that would often break into a warm smile, and from the very first time we were taken to meet her I felt comfortable being around her. I'm sure the final decision on whether we would be placed with Nana Parton wasn't down to us. We were too young to make decisions like that, but social services obviously wanted to make sure that the idea of staying in her home wasn't upsetting for us, and they also wanted to make sure that she was comfortable with taking us on. She had three older daughters, Margaret, Jean and Lena, who were happy to help their mother out with looking after us. Mrs Parton obviously knew the circumstances of us being taken into care better than we did at the time. She was experienced in fostering kids and understood just how frightening the experience could be for some children.

The fact that we pretty quickly felt at home and part of her family speaks volumes for the sort of person she was. She certainly didn't have to put herself forward and take on the responsibility of looking after two little black kids. Let's face it, the attitude towards black people throughout Britain in 1964 wasn't great, as I've already mentioned. Stoke wasn't the most open-minded of places at the time and, if you were black, you were very much in the minority. For an all-white family to provide our foster home was a pretty big step for her and the three daughters to take. The great thing was that Nana Parton didn't think anything of it at all: she was just concerned about providing a caring, loving environment for the two of us, and after we moved in and got used to our new surroundings, we were very happy there. It had a really homely feel to it and I remember the lounge being dominated by what seemed like a big wooden cabinet, which had glasses stored on the shelves along with a clock. The sofa had cushions that you sank into. It seemed enormous at the time, and when I first sat on it my feet were lifted off the floor. It must have made an impression on me because I can remember those details to this day, but I have no real recollection of anywhere else that I lived before moving to Nana Parton's.

The house was on a corner and very close to Port Vale's football ground. In fact, if you walked to the end of her road and crossed a field, there was the ground. Little did I know at the time, but not that many years later I would be playing on the pitch that I used to look at through locked gates whenever I went past the ground.

Although we were both very young, we were a bit of a handful, according to some of the childcare reports I have since read. Nana Parton had been used to having girls around the house and I'm sure they were a lot easier to look after than we were. We had bags of energy and liked to play and charge around. Luckily, the house had a decent-sized garden because it was on a corner, and we loved playing in it whenever we could. We shared a room at the back of the house and bedtimes were a nightmare for her at times as we insisted on jumping on our bed and switching lights on and off. The longer we stayed with her, the bigger and bolder we got.

Meanwhile, there was another twist to the complicated nature of my own family about eight months after we went to live with Nana Parton, when my mother gave birth to another baby girl, who she called Maureen. The father was our dad. He apparently paid a visit to our grandmother's house one day to see our mother. I think in some strange way he might have believed they could still get back together, and that was never likely to happen, but they did spend some time together. It seems as a result of that visit she gave birth to a baby girl, my youngest sister, in June 1965.

Over the years, my sister Marie has told me about what was happening and, as an adult, being able to read some of the documents from the files of the care workers who were in charge of Phil and me has also helped to give me an understanding of what was going on around me. I was three years old when Maureen was born and obviously knew nothing of what had happened or how I suddenly had another sister. My world at that time was very much about being looked after by Nana Parton and living alongside Phil. I think it was also a case of him taking on the role of older brother, even though we were so young and he was only a year older. I can't remember thinking about my everyday life too much, or the fact that the two of us had gone to live with Nana Parton and were not with our mum, our gran or our sisters. I wasn't particularly unhappy, and on the whole I think I was contented, but I also think I got reassurance from having Phil with me. It was always the two of us, I wasn't on my own, he was always there for me and I always had someone to play alongside and share my life with. I also think Nana Parton was able to do exactly what the local authorities had hoped she would do by providing a secure and loving environment for the two of us. The fact that we were so young when we went there might have been a good thing, in a way, because our own life experiences were very limited at that point. There were no great references for us to draw on: we'd been moved around from one place to another for most of our lives, so turning up at a new home was probably something we'd become used to. Now that I have a better idea of the order of events and what had gone on, I realise that virtually from the time I was born, I never really had any sort of stability in my life, and also that I never really had a period of time when my mum and dad were together. The times they spent with each other after I had arrived on the scene were fleeting. The only normal family life I had was the comfort I got from having Marie,

Phil and, for that short period, Sharon around before being fostered out to Nana Parton.

There was no time frame put on our stay when we arrived because the authorities didn't know how things would pan out. They didn't know if my parents would get back together and they didn't know how Phil and I would adapt to our new home and lifestyle. They would come and see us to make regular reports on how things were going. They'd ask us a few questions and then talk to Nana Parton and her daughters about us and how we had settled in. It was an ongoing situation and if things changed dramatically, then it would obviously affect us. We were growing boys with bags of energy and I know it must have been difficult at times for her, even with the help of her daughters, but they were committed to looking after us and providing all the basics two little boys of our age needed.

Although a lot of memories from those times are a bit hazy, one that is vivid is our first day at infant school around Easter time in 1966. It was a big day, just like it would be for any kids of that age. A room full of children who had never seen each other before, everyone feeling a bit nervous, some more than others. The great thing for the two of us was that we had each other, we were brothers, and that made things different for us. I never thought much about it at the time, but the other thing that made things different for us on our first day was the fact that we were the only black kids in the class. Being black wasn't something I gave much thought to as a four-year-old, and the truth was that most of the people I had been surrounded by in my life up to that point were white. My mum, my gran, Nana Parton, her daughters, the people from the childcare authority, they were all white. My dad was black, so was Phil and so were my sisters, but nothing seemed strange in any of that – it was just the way things were. On our first day at school, Phil and I were probably aware that we were the only black kids there, but then there weren't really black kids around at all in the area. I don't remember anybody saying or doing anything that was horrible because of the colour of our skin, but I'm sure there was a bit of curiosity. It just wasn't like today; times were different then and being black meant you stuck out. It was inevitable.

Although we lived with Nana Parton, we did still get to see our real gran, sisters and mum on some occasions. I think my gran in particular wanted to make sure there was contact with us, and perhaps in her own mind she hoped there would be a chance for all of the children to live together some time. She used to come and see us at Mrs Parton's, but the visits were never regular. As time went on things started to change for our parents and sisters. There was never any real hope of my mum and dad getting back together and although he initially looked after Marie when Phil and I were fostered out, during the time we were at Nana Parton's she moved out and went to live with our mum. It was a strange set-up, with us still being fostered out while the girls lived with our mum. The reason given to the local authorities was that looking after five children would have just been too much for her to cope with. Meanwhile, our dad pretty much disappeared off the scene with nobody, including the authorities, really knowing exactly where he was for a time. He eventually turned up in Manchester and by that time his marriage to our mum was well and truly over. That fact became a legal reality when my parents finally divorced in the summer of 1968 and, towards the end of that same year, my mother married a guy called Tom Davies.

As Phil and I had bags of energy, football began to play a big part in our lives, just as it did with a lot of the other boys where we lived. Playing in the garden was one thing, but playing out on the streets was the normal thing to do in those days – all the kids did it. There was a guy who used to live a few doors down from us named Phil Bert. He was a bit older than the two of us, and he used to take it upon himself to organise lots of little football activities. They weren't matches, it was more about setting challenges with the ball. We played things like Kerby, which meant chipping it with your left foot, and then with your right, from one side of the street to the other, each time trying to hit the kerb. Even at that early age, taking part in games like that helped improve my skills with a football. All thanks to Phil. We'd also go down to the fields and there was never any shortage of kids who wanted to take part in matches.

We were growing up fast and during 1969, when I was seven and Phil was eight, Nana Parton found it increasingly difficult to cope with us. She had heart problems and had dizzy spells, and the other problem she had was that her daughters got married and that meant they were not around to give their mother the kind of support she'd had when they were living at home. Having her daughters around to help with caring for us must have been important for her, but once things began to change, she found it harder to cope. You need a lot of energy to cope with young kids, and she simply didn't have that any more. She was always kind and caring, but we probably took everything for granted, not realising how physically tough it was for her, and also having to deal with the emotional side of looking after us. We'd been there for quite some time and it meant we were able to have a period of relative stability in our young lives. The fostering system at that time meant you could often stay with the same family, as long as they were happy with you and the authorities felt the arrangement was working as it should do.

I know Nana Parton loved and cared for us throughout our time with her, but because of her failing health and the fact that she found herself on her own, she decided to contact the childcare people and explain the situation. It seems that she did so reluctantly, but she realised that things were only going to get more difficult for her. It must have been a hard decision to make. We had been part of each other's lives for four years. We felt secure and comfortable in her care. She didn't have to take us in and then look after us for that length of time, and I think it takes a special sort of person to do what she did for the pair of us. At that time, we saw nothing of our mother, and I believe Phil became quite upset by the fact that she did not visit. He even told one of the childcare workers that he didn't like our mum, and when she asked why that was the case he simply replied, 'Because she never comes to see me.' There wasn't a great age difference between Phil and me, but I'm sure he was much more aware of what was happening to us and probably more sensitive to everything than I was. Over the course of being in care there were times when we became confused about what was happening around us. We were young and had no experience of life. We didn't even have the normal things that most kids have like sharing a home with your parents, brothers and sisters. Our family had been broken up and, in one form or another, all of my family were living their separate lives. We didn't have a family that was together. Phil and I were fortunate to have someone like Nana Parton looking after us, but our existence was a bit different to other kids, because we had things like regular visits from the authorities to see how the fostering arrangement was working out. I'm sure that at the back of our minds was the thought that at any given moment things could change and we might be on our way again, which was exactly what happened in the end. We weren't aware of the background to our fostering, which was probably why, years later, Phil and I wanted to read some of the files the authorities had compiled on us. They helped fill in some of the gaps from our childhood.

As I remember, we were told that Nana Parton needed to have a rest, and because of that we might have to leave, but I don't think either Phil or I thought it was going to be anything other than a temporary thing. That may have been the interpretation we put on it, but I think we both thought we'd be back with her when she felt better.

Once it was decided that we would have to move from Nana Parton's, the next problem was finding a suitable new home for the two of us. After our mum remarried, she and Tom, or 'Tommo' as we would come to call him, set up home in a house in Bucknall, a suburb of Stoke, and the two of them also had the three girls living with them. He worked for the Corporation Transport Department, and she had a job working part-time at Bucknall Hospital. A childcare officer went to see them and asked about the possibility of Phil and I going to live with them. Apparently, my mother said that if they were in a better financial position, they would not hesitate to have us living with them, but they felt it would be too much of a burden and the authorities agreed with her. So that was that.

However, something positive did come out of that meeting, because having been absent from our lives for what must have been a couple of years our mother suggested that we visited her along with Nana Parton. I don't think Phil was too keen when we were told about what would be happening, but we went and had tea with her and also met Tommo for the first time. I can't remember what the atmosphere was like, but it was a chance for Nana Parton to meet our mother and I think the idea was that there would be further visits, and in the next couple of months, that's exactly what happened.

We managed to see a bit more of her after that as well, because the problem of where we would be fostered next after leaving Nana Parton's was solved when our maternal grandmother agreed to look after us. It seemed a good arrangement. She lived near to where our mum's new home was, we would be able to see more of her and our sisters, and we would also be living with a blood relative and not be sent to the home of a complete stranger. Having to move once again was clearly not an ideal situation for us, but I think it was thought that moving in with our real gran would help smooth things and make it much more comfortable for us. Both Phil and I thought it was a great idea and it was also exciting to think that we would see more of our sisters, and I know they loved the prospect of seeing more of us.

From my gran's point of view, I think she was genuinely pleased at the thought of having us live with her. She would have liked all five of her grandchildren to be together, and the move at least meant we would be a lot closer than we had been. There were a few anxieties on our part, the main one being a change of school and making new friends, but the overall feeling that I remember was just being excited by the whole thing. We ended up going to Abbey Hulton Junior, and for a time Marie, Sharon, Phil and I would all meet up in the mornings and walk off there together.

For Nana Parton it was quite a sad time. She knew she could no longer cope, but seeing the two of us leave was quite upsetting for her. Our gran promised her that she could come over and visit whenever she wanted to, but there were tears shed by everyone as we left the house that had been our home for what by that time had been five years.

Marie was pretty much living with Gran rather than with our mum and Tommo, and she loved the idea of having her two little brothers around, and we had a lot of fun together. I remember it being really cold weather when we went there, but that didn't stop us playing outside. Marie was our big sister and she led the way in a lot of what we did. One day it was incredibly cold and Phil and I were desperate to get back home to our gran's house and warm up. Marie told us that if we sang a song, someone would stop and give us a lift home. So there the two of us were, singing at the top of our voices, convinced that we'd get a lift home, while Marie couldn't help laughing at how she'd managed to trick her gullible kid brothers.

We moved into our gran's at the end of November 1969, but just over two months later we were on the move again. We'd really enjoyed living with our gran and being able to spend much more time with our sisters – we must have all enjoyed that period because we still have fond memories of it. Our gran had the best of intentions when she agreed to take us, but the truth of the matter was we were just too much for her to cope with. She obviously wasn't a young woman and although we didn't do anything outrageous while we were there, she found it hard to keep up, particularly at bedtime. Phil and I shared a double bed at the back of the house and most nights we would play around, bouncing on the bed and generally making too much noise for our gran to tolerate. She would come climbing up the stairs to complain, telling us to be quiet, and the more she did this the funnier we thought it was. We weren't aware of the effect it was having on her, and I'm sure she tried hard to make sure the move worked out for us, but it was probably a bit of a shock for her. She was a kind person who always wanted the best for her family. She knew how badly wrong it had gone for her daughter with us, and I think she wanted to make sure we still had a family link, which she thought she could provide. We were her grandchildren and she genuinely wanted to look after us and provide a happy environment, but after about six weeks of staying with her it became clear the experience was not exactly what she had hoped for. So once again the childcare authorities had to start looking for a new foster home for us.

Once our gran had voiced her concerns to the childcare officer who came to visit, the wheels were set in motion. The authorities again asked our mother if it would be possible for her to take us, but they got the same answer as before: our mum and Tommo simply couldn't afford to support us.

Phil and I were aware that we would be moving on once more, but I'm not sure if we realised that we would not be going back to our gran's at some later stage. In fact, I think we both thought any move would be a temporary one. We were still just kids and despite the fact that the authorities would talk to us when they visited, it was hard to get a proper grasp on all the events that were going on around us. Their visits usually took the form of an interview, when they would ask us certain questions and we would give answers. There was always an element of uncertainty in our minds because we were too young to understand what was going on. The authorities tried to keep everything on a basic level, giving us bite-size chunks of information. Looking back, I suppose they were trying to do their best for us, but it meant we were never aware of the bigger picture when it came to our lives and being fostered.

One day we were told by the childcare officer that they were going to take us on a visit to Kidsgrove, which is a town just to the north of Stoke. We were going there to have tea. The idea behind it all was that we would be introduced to a couple who might potentially be our new foster parents, but the authorities obviously wanted to take us on a short visit first, just to see how we reacted to them, and also to see what they thought of us. I suppose they wanted everyone involved to be introduced in a gentle, step-by-step way, in order to find out if it might work out. The couple the authorities had in mind were tried and trusted foster parents with an incredible amount of experience. In fact, by the time we met them, Bob and Irene Davies, who were in their mid-fifties, had already fostered more than fifty kids, as well as having their own family. They were a white couple, and when we arrived, I noticed that there was already another little black kid being fostered by them. He was younger than Phil and me, but obviously the prospect of looking after and caring for the three of us didn't worry the Davieses in any way at all. Although we knew nothing about them, the childcare authorities did, and they must have thought that going there would be right for us. The Davieses had been down the road of long-term fostering, but they were also used to having kids for short stays, which meant looking after children who had been taken away from their mothers and fathers for whatever reason. It was often because one or other of their parents were ill and were unable to have children around for a few weeks or months.

Their house was in Victoria Avenue, and it was in a mining community. It was work that had originally brought them to Kidsgrove because Mr Davies worked as a miner at Chatterley Whitfield Colliery. The homes on the estate were all pretty much the same and the Davieses lived in a small, neat, semi-detached house. We were introduced to them and had a little chat: they seemed really nice and I felt relaxed in their company. They made an effort to be friendly and wanted to chat with us. I didn't feel uneasy or uncomfortable while we were there, and the house they lived in was very cosy. They obviously wanted us to feel at home and showed us around. The house had an L-shaped lounge and a small kitchen downstairs, while upstairs there was a double bedroom that they used, a bathroom, a small box room and another bedroom that they explained would be ours if we stayed with them. I remember there was heavily patterned wallpaper in all of the rooms and the lounge had a carpet that also had big patterns on it. Looking back, I'm not sure any of it matched, but it somehow had the effect of making the place feel warm and comforting.

I think we came away thinking the house was a real family home and that the Davieses seemed like nice people. Although their own three sons had grown up and didn't live with them any more, Bob and Irene Davies were happy to have the responsibility of taking the two of us on. They were happy to have us be part of their family.

Mr Davies really won us over on the second occasion we went to meet them. We spent a whole day there, and a lot of time he played games with the two of us. It was eventually decided that we would make the move to their home during the school half-term holidays, and when it happened, I think it hit our gran quite hard. Although we'd been too much for her to cope with, she had desperately wanted it to work out. I remember her being quite tearful when we were picked up by the childcare officer, who had arranged to take us to Mr and Mrs Davies' house. The few possessions we had were bundled up, put in a car and off we went. Gran knew she would still be able to visit us, but I don't think she realised how emotional the whole experience would be until the moment came when we physically moved out of her home.

At that time there was no mention of exactly how long we would be staying with the Davieses, which wasn't unusual because nobody knew how things would work out, but I do think I had the impression that we would at some stage be going back to our gran. The overwhelming sense I have of this period is that it felt like we were being lied to by the authorities or, at the very least, let's just say they were economical with the truth. I think we felt this was going to be a temporary situation because of the way things were explained to us. I realise that the authorities had a difficult job, and I don't know at what age they thought it was OK to tell the whole truth to a youngster. Can you handle the truth when you're seven and eight years old, and had our kind of family background? By the time we met the Davieses, we'd already spent periods of time with our dad, mum, Nana Parton and our gran, not to mention those brief stays in the residential nursery. Not exactly a settled existence.

Perhaps the childcare people were just trying to do their jobs and protect us, but I can't help feeling let down by it all.

At the time it had become an accepted way of life for the two of us, although perhaps Phil gave it more thought than I did. In the end, there was no choice for either of us really. The decision was made by the childcare authorities. They wanted to do the best they could for us, and at least we were fostered out to a family. It must have been a lot worse for kids who grew up not having that opportunity, and who spent their young lives living in care homes, never getting the chance to experience family life, even if it was a family that was not theirs. We were not going to be able to live with our mum and our sisters, and that was upsetting, but Phil and I were together. We had each other, and in the Davieses we seemed to have found two people determined to make sure they provided a loving and stable environment for us.

4

The Lollipop and the Stick

When we went to the Davieses' I had no way of knowing exactly how long we would be staying with
them. It was yet another home we had been placed in. There
had already been a lot of chopping and changing in our
young lives up to that point and, as we had done before, both
Phil and I just got on with things. We'd had that period of
relative stability with Nana Parton, but then our time with
Gran had lasted a matter of weeks, so when we arrived in
Kidsgrove we didn't know what to expect. I wasn't sure how
long we would be there, but I ended up staying with them
for over a decade. I was seven years old when I arrived at
their house and eighteen when I moved out.

As you can imagine, a lot happened to me during that
time. I went from being a kid to being a young man, from
owning a toy car to owning a real one, and of dreaming
about being a footballer to actually playing for a local professional club.

We had no way of knowing when we first arrived, but
Bob and Irene Davies would have a big part to play in our
lives. They were kind but firm and we soon started to refer
to them as Grandad and Gran. It was funny really, but they

were sort of part parents and part grandparents. They were obviously used to fostering and everything it entailed, and didn't seem the least worried about having three lively little black boys to look after. Phil was almost nine when we went there and Carl Wright, the little kid we'd met on our visits to the house, was about three years younger than me. The colour of our skin was clearly of no concern to the Davieses: it was all about us as children, about caring for us, and about giving us the love and support we needed as we grew up.

Colour may not have been an issue for them, but we soon learned that was not the case for some of the children we went to school with. The move from Abbey Hulton to Kidsgrove not only meant a change of house, it also meant another change of school for us, and pretty soon we found ourselves attending Dove Bank Primary. It was only a few hundred yards from the house, and we would walk to the school each day, but it wasn't long before the walk home became the walk of fear, simply because we were the only black kids in the school.

We very quickly realised that our colour singled us out. It wasn't the first time I'd noticed this because apart from an Asian family who lived nearby the Davieses' house, everyone else was white, but we never thought too much about it at that age. When we joined the school, our head teacher spoke to the other kids and introduced us, clearly with an eye on the fact that we were black. It may seem strange these days to think of something like that happening, but the make-up of schools back then was very different to how it is now. There simply weren't that many black people around and that meant we were a very small minority when it came to joining the school. He told the other children that we were to be treated exactly the same as any of the other kids, but as well-meaning as his comments were, they certainly didn't have the desired effect.

Although Phil was older than me, they decided to put us both in the same class, keeping us together so that we would feel more comfortable. It was a nice idea but the flipside of it was I struggled to keep up with a lot of the lessons, because everyone else in the class was about a year older than me and more advanced in all the subjects. I found it tough, especially in the first few days, but it was nothing compared to what began to happen on a regular basis whenever lessons stopped and the day was over.

The school had two sets of gates, the ones at the top led to the posher houses nearby, and the ones at the bottom were used by all the kids who, like us, came from the mining estate. Our daily walk home soon became the source of a new game for some of the other kids. They would lie in wait for us, knowing we would have to go past them and, when we did, they really let us have it. They would get hold of whatever they could get their hands on and aim an assortment of objects at the two of us. We knew they were coming, but couldn't do anything about it except run as fast as we could through the hail of missiles that were being launched in our direction. About twenty yards from where they would wait for us was a small, winding path and, at the end of that, was a lollipop lady. We used to try and get to her as quickly as we could without being hit, because we knew they wouldn't try to throw anything at us in front of her. We knew we were safe, at least until the next afternoon when the whole thing would start over again. One day she must have heard something and looked up to see what it was, just as we were running past the kids lobbing all sorts of things at us. She asked me if we were all right, but both Phil and I were too frightened to say anything to her. We just ran across the road as fast as we could, and the kids who had been throwing the stuff at us stood there waving at us from the other side of the road.

'See you tomorrow!' they shouted, and we knew we were in for more of the same the next day.

The mornings were fine because the kids would be taken to school by their parents, so there was never any chance of the same sort of thing happening then, but home time was a different matter. It became a nightmare. I'm not sure exactly how long it went on for, but one day the lollipop lady saw our gran, Mrs Davies, and told her that the other children had been chasing us and throwing things as we made our way home from school. Gran Davies was obviously upset and asked Phil and me if it was true, insisting that the two of us told her the truth. We didn't want to say anything, but at the same time we didn't want to lie to her, and we confirmed what the lollipop lady had told her. She was really upset by the story, so the next morning she marched us up to the school, went straight to the secretary's office and demanded to see the headmaster. Our gran knew why it had happened: it wasn't because we were new to the school, it was because we were different, we were black. It was a difficult situation for my brother and me because she then said we had to tell the headmaster what had been happening to us. He was clearly annoyed by what had gone on, particularly after his efforts to make our introduction to the school as smooth and problem free as he could. He promised our gran that he would immediately address the issue, and that is exactly what he did. However, it was horrendous for the two of us because he did it in assembly that same morning in front of about eighty other kids. We had to sit on the stage next to him while he spoke to the rest of the school. We didn't want to be there but there was nowhere for us to hide. We just sat there feeling uncomfortable and awkward.

'Do you see these two children here with me this morning?' he asked. 'When they first joined the school, I told all of you that they were to be treated just like everyone else, but they've not been treated like everyone else, have they? A lot of you will know exactly what I am talking about and I want what has been happening to stop right now, do you understand?'

'Yes, sir,' the rest of the school chorused.

He never actually said that we were being picked on because of the colour of our skin, but everyone knew that was what he meant. Perhaps he thought saying it out loud might have made the whole thing a bigger issue, but I think he believed he had made his point in front of everyone, and he was probably trying to make the whole situation a little easier for us as well, but it still made the two of us feel really awkward. Neither of us thought it would do any good and Phil and I were looking down at the other kids thinking, We're really going to get it tonight!

During the day there were a few mutterings from a couple of the boys saying we were 'dead' after what we'd done. It was a bit of an exaggeration, but when you are seven and eight years old, it's still not a particularly pleasant experience. In the end nothing did happen that evening. The kids backed off and the headmaster's words worked. They continued to work in the days and weeks that followed, but the fact both of us were pretty good at PE helped as well. Playing sport seemed to bring new friends and a bit of respect – everybody wanted you on their side when it came to picking teams for football. The sporting thing began to break down some of the barriers that might have been there – heaven knows what it might have been like for us if we'd been useless at PE or just not interested. It wasn't necessarily right, because if that had been the case, those barriers might have continued to exist. It wasn't what the headmaster had talked about. It wasn't about them treating us like everyone else, it was really more about us being useful to have around, at least at first. As time went on, I do think the colour of our skin didn't seem to be an issue for the other kids. They saw us for who we were as individuals, not what we looked like because of our colour. It was probably the first major incident of racism that I'd experienced up to that point, but while we were still new to the area, it wasn't to be the last.

From the moment I could walk, I also wanted to kick a ball around. Any spare moment I had would be spent with a ball at my feet. I played in my brother's year for the football team at school and when we got home to the Davieses' we'd climb over a fence to where there were some pitches and kick a ball around until it was dark. I was always looking for places to play football, and I was also keen to explore the area when we first moved to Kidsgrove. One evening I went out to see if there was a game going on – it was quite normal for kids to be playing out on the street or on any patch of grass they could find – but on this particular evening nobody was playing and so I started to make my way back home. On the way to the house I had to walk up a narrow dirt track that wound its way up to where the Davieses lived, and as I turned a corner a kid appeared, standing still with a German shepherd dog on a lead. In his other hand he had a long stick with a piece of washing line tied to the end of it, like a homemade whip.

'What are you doing?' he asked me.

'Nothing,' I said. 'I was just looking to see if anyone was out playing football.'

'See him off!' he shouted at the dog, who then started barking and pulling on the lead.

The dog's sudden movement and the loudness of his barking frightened me and I jumped backwards, but there was a fence, and it didn't give me any room to get out of the way. I stood there, frozen by what was happening and worried that the dog was going to be let off the lead and allowed to come charging at me. The kid was laughing at the sight of me cowering against the fence, clearly enjoyed the sight of his dog terrifying the life out of me, even though I was just a kid. I didn't want to run and have the dog chase me, because I knew there would only be one winner and it wouldn't be me. I was wearing shorts and the kid flicked his stick and hit me across the legs with the washing line that was attached to the end of it. He did it about two or three times, and I started crying. Luckily, someone came along and distracted him, which gave me the chance to run away as fast as I could. I had been really scared by the whole incident, the way he looked at me and the way he seemed to be enjoying everything that was happening.

I didn't tell anyone about what had gone on, I just wanted to forget about it. It was a nasty experience and I certainly didn't want to relive it by talking to someone and making a big fuss, but the memory stayed with me. In an odd sort of way, I did manage to get a bit of revenge a couple of years later when I was bigger and stronger and went to my senior school. One day I looked across the room and saw a boy whose face looked very familiar. I was puzzled and convinced I knew him from somewhere. Then the realisation dawned on me: he was the guy who had frightened me with his dog and then hit me on the legs two years earlier. I went over and asked him if we knew each other, but he told me he didn't recognise me. Then I asked if his family had a dog.

'No,' he said. 'We don't have a dog.'

He was clearly uncomfortable with me talking to him, especially when I asked about having a dog. I knew there was something not quite right about the way he'd answered me and later that week I discovered he'd lied. One evening when we were all leaving school his dad turned up to collect him, and he had a German shepherd dog with him. From that moment on I made it my business to make the kid's life a misery. If I walked past him in the corridor, I would clip him around the head, or give his ankle a kick. If we played basketball, I would smash him in the face with the ball. I got into trouble for it and was told by the headmaster that he would not tolerate bullying. Looking back, I'm not proud of my behaviour, it was awful really, but I couldn't help myself. Every time I saw his face, I would think of that episode with the dog and how terrified I was. To this day I still feel uncomfortable with dogs, and I'm pretty sure it is all down to that incident.

Our senior school was called Maryhill Comprehensive and our introduction to it was a bit different to the one we received at Dove Bank Primary. We were obviously older and a bit more confident than we had been then, but starting at a new school is always a bit daunting, and although the 'walk of fear' episode had been a few years earlier, we wondered what might be waiting for us. As I mentioned, Bob and Irene Davies were very experienced foster parents, and one of the families they had in their care for a while consisted of three boys who were sent to them because their mother had been taken ill. They lived on the same estate as us, and the boys were notorious, real hard cases. On our first day at Maryhill, one of the boys, who was about sixteen at the time, came over to Phil and me. He knew we were living with Gran and he knew it was our first day.

'If anyone says or does anything to you, just come to see me,' he told us as we nodded our heads and thanked him.

It couldn't have been more different to those early days at Dove Bank when our lives had been made a misery by the kids who thought it was fun to pick on the two new little black boys. This time we were being given protection by the hardest kid in the school, we had our own 'minder', and everyone knew it. That meant they also knew not to mess with us because of what he and his brothers might do to anyone who did. If it ever got a bit awkward, we would just mention this fact to any of the kids and, not surprisingly, they backed off.

By this time, I was completely aware that being a black kid meant you were very much in the minority, but I didn't experience any real problems at senior school because of it. There weren't too many black kids around on our estate either; there was the Asian family and a black family and that was just about it. The Asian family probably got the worst of it because they actually had stones thrown at their house. I can recall people walking past me in the street and calling me 'Nigger', and these were grown men, not kids. By the early 1970s there was a lot of racism around and maybe as we got older we became more aware of what was happening around us. I tried to ignore it but it's not nice when you saw and heard things on the television that made you feel uncomfortable and awkward. There was a really popular television show called *Love Thy Neighbour* on at the time, which was a sitcom about a white couple who had a black couple living next door to them. The trouble was, I never found it funny. The same was true of *Till Death Us Do Part*, another comedy that just made me feel awkward, especially with some of the comments made by the main character, Alf Garnett, when he would go off on one of his rants. I understand that it was supposed to show what an uneducated bigot he was, but when you're young you don't really pick up on anything like that, and I suspect that was true for a lot of black kids. It just made me feel uncomfortable. Lenny Henry made our lives a misery as well, because it felt like he was taking the piss out of black people with his jokes, but at the time, all of this was pretty normal in society and it was something I grew up with.

Happily, we never really needed to call on our school 'minders' and by the time they had left, Phil and I were part of everything just like any of the other kids. Once again, I think sport helped because everyone wanted us in their teams, and my love of football continued to grow. And the older I got, the more I began to realise I was pretty good at it.

5

Gran and Grandad

Bob and Irene Davies will always be Grandad and Gran to Phil and me, just as Mrs Parton is Nana Parton, and I will always be grateful to all three of them. Nana Parton did a wonderful job helping us to feel comfortable and secure at a very difficult time in our lives. We were so young when we went to her, but she seemed to know just what was needed to help us adjust to the strange circumstances we had found ourselves in. I realise now just how strange those circumstances were. Our sisters lived with our mother and her new husband, but the two of us lived with someone else. We would see them and we would occasionally see our mother, but she never showed any real affection when we did see her. She wasn't nasty, but the relationship we had with her could hardly be called close. As for our dad, we never really saw him at all. I remember one day Nana Parton told the two of us that we had to wear some special smart clothes because our dad was coming to visit us. We sat and waited for him to arrive, but he never turned up. We were obviously disappointed, but at least I was young enough to get over any disappointment I had very quickly with the help of a football to play around with outside in the garden.

I think Phil thought a lot more about what was happening to the two of us than I did. One of the things that used to happen on an annual basis was having a medical, which was then passed to the childcare people. It was such a different world then and I remember my brother and I would have to take buses to get there. Two little black kids holding hands and getting on and off buses. Phil was the one who knew which ones to get before we finally arrived at the medical centre. We never gave it a thought that it might be dangerous in any way, it was just something that we did, and we were no different to a lot of other kids in those days who would regularly take buses to get to different places in the area. On one of these occasions, when I was about eight years old, we turned up at the medical centre, gave our names and then sat in the reception area waiting to be called.

'Shall we run away?' Phil suddenly asked me, and I could see he meant it.

'Where to?' I said.

'We'll find somewhere,' he told me.

'No, don't,' I replied. 'Where are we running to? Who's going to look after us?'

We both sat there looking at the door for a few minutes. I knew he wasn't joking but I really didn't fancy the idea. The thought of it worried me, and thankfully the idea of running away soon passed and the subject was never mentioned again. Instead, we had our medicals, got on the buses once more, and went home to Gran and Grandad. I don't think Phil was unhappy about being with the Davieses. It was just one of those moments where he perhaps wanted to be able to leave everything that had happened behind and start again. Phil sometimes felt the sadness of what had gone on; he thought about things much more than I did, and I don't think he could ever really get his head around the fact that the two of us had been fostered out.

Whenever either of us had a birthday, we would get a card from our mum. It would arrive on the morning of our birthday before we went to school and there would be £5 in it. My brother would open the card, see the money drop out, read whatever she'd written, put the money back and then throw both the card and the money on the fire. He didn't want to have anything to do with it. I would be scrambling to try and get it, but he would always tell me to leave it. When my card arrived, he'd want me to do the same, but I never did. After all, £5 was a lot of money!

Our relationship with our mum throughout our childhood was virtually non-existent. When she remarried, we would see the girls, and she would say hello to us, Tommo would do the same, but that was as far as it went. It was bizarre when I think about it now, and pretty sad as well. I don't ever remember her saying, 'I love you.' It just never happened. I say it all the time to my son when we meet or talk on the phone, it's second nature, but it never happened to me or Phil, and she wasn't the sort of person to give you hugs or kisses. We were both part of her, and yet we had been apart from her for most of our lives. We'd had so much disruption in our young lives by the time we arrived at Gran and Grandad's home, it was no wonder we felt unsettled. We weren't sure how long we would be with them and that uncertainty was always there in the back of our mind. We weren't to know that our stay with them was to be such a long-term arrangement.

The childcare authorities had to regularly check out what was going on. Just as they had when we were with Nana Parton, they wanted to see how we were with our foster parents. It could be a bit unnerving because of the way they would just suddenly turn up and we didn't know they were coming. We would come home from school and there would be someone there to ask us a series of questions. They were all pretty general things and they tried to make it as relaxed as possible, but we still felt as though we had to be careful about our answers. Once we'd been questioned by them, we would go out of the house and play, while they stayed and chatted to Gran and Grandad. Whenever this happened and whatever was said on these occasions, things must have all gone well, because we ended up staying with them for so long. What they ended up giving us was the stability in our lives that we needed, but the two of us were never really sure about what might happen. We both thought things could quickly change, just as they had done in the past, but those fears began to fade the longer our stay with them went on.

They were very good for us, and during our time with them they helped to give us the right sort of values, and helped us develop as people. Grandad taught us to respect other people, to be polite, to work hard and always live up to our responsibilities. I have tremendous respect for both him and my gran. To take on the responsibility of bringing up other people's kids and to effectively be their parents is incredible. They treated us as if we were their own flesh and blood, and not once did I feel anything other than part of their family. Apart from having Phil, me and Carl in their home, they also somehow found time to welcome other kids on a temporary basis when the need arose. One day we came home from school to find little twin girls there. They stayed for maybe a week or less while their parents sorted their problems out and then they were off. One minute they were there and then we came home from school and they were gone. We never saw them again.

My grandad was from Wales and at one time they had lived in Lancashire because he worked in the pits and that was where the mining jobs were for him. They moved on to Kidsgrove for the same reason. He was a typically hard-working, no-nonsense miner, but he was very good with the pair of us in the way he tried to instil the rights and wrongs of behaviour. I would say that he, more than anybody, shaped me as a person. He was tough, and at times it was hard to think that I loved him like I loved my gran. The sort of tough love he showed towards me and Phil kind of made us in many ways. I suppose you could say he was old fashioned in a lot of ways – he ruled the household and you did what he said – but he also had very good values when it came to the way you should live your life and treat others, which he passed on to us and to his own sons. He treated us just as he had treated them. Those values never changed. Later in our stay with them, he came into a bit of money, which he was awarded as part of compensation for an accident he'd had at work. This meant that he had a bit of spare cash and he was quite happy to give out loans, but when he did the amount and date would be noted in a book that he kept, and then when you paid it back, he would tick it off. He would always say that you should never spend what you can't afford, which, these days in the credit card era, some would see as very old fashioned and outdated. It's just a little saying he had, but it's stuck with me throughout my life, and it's a principle I've maintained as an adult.

He smoked a pipe and I have vivid memories of him sitting in his chair in front of the fire, smoking it and then, every so often, spitting onto the flaming coals in the grate. When he did this there would immediately be a flash and a hiss from the fire. It's one of those childhood memories that have stayed with me, because I was fascinated by it, and so were a lot of my friends who would come to the house just to see him perform his party piece for me.

'Go on, Grandad, do it,' I'd say to him, and when he did there was a collective gasp of appreciation from all of my friends. One of them was in awe because he always managed to hit the same spot.

Although we began to feel more secure with Gran and Grandad, there was always the thought that a change in their circumstances would impact on us, and that might mean us having to move on yet again. After a few years with them, neither Phil nor me wanted that to happen. Living with them meant we'd managed to find a constant in our lives, and we didn't want that to change. They might have been a lot older than the parents of other kids our age, but that never bothered us at all. I don't think either Phil or I ever looked at them and saw old people. We just saw a man and a woman who cared about us a lot. They gave us love, affection and security. I hated the thought of having to move out. It took quite a long time until I no longer thought there was going to be a knock on the door one day and someone was going to say we had to move on.

As much as they loved having us with them, my grandad warned us one day that if we ever got in trouble with the police, that would be it. We'd be out and handed to the authorities; the prospect of it was frightening for me and for Phil. It was easy to get into a bit of trouble with the police when you're a kid. Nothing serious, just kids being kids and messing about. I had friends who sometimes were a little bit naughty and might try their hand at nicking petrol. They knew about the warning I'd been given by Grandad, so if they were up to no good, they'd tell me not to go with them because of the risk of getting caught.

One of the things we used to like to do was go to Bathpool Park near Kidsgrove. It had a big manmade lake and we used to love swimming across to an island they had in the middle, but one day the police came along and told us we weren't allowed to go swimming there. They were doing it for our own good because they were worried about our safety and didn't want any of us drowning. Of course, once they'd gone, we all began swimming again, but the police came back and saw all of our clothes piled up at the side of the lake, so they knew we'd gone to the island and they waited for us to come back. They said they were going to take all of our names and addresses and would be going to our homes later that evening to talk to our parents. I was absolutely petrified. If they called in to speak to Gran and Grandad, that would be it for us. When the police had gone, my mates couldn't believe that I'd not only given them my name, but also the right address.

'Why didn't you make it up like the rest of us?' one of them asked, clearly thinking I was an idiot for being so honest.

When I got home, Phil asked me the same question. He must have thought I'd put both of our futures at risk, but he also said he didn't think the police would pay a visit. I wasn't convinced. I stood at the window in the front room waiting for them to turn up. I was so worried I just stood there for ages, with my eyes fixed on the road outside the house, but nothing happened. There was no police car, no flashing lights, no knock at the door. As the evening turned into night, I started to feel a little easier. Phil was right, they weren't going to come and tell Grandad what had happened. We weren't going to have to leave and go into a care home. We were safe.

The police might not have been dealing with a major incident when they came and told us to stop swimming, but there was another much more serious and alarming incident that involved Bathpool. It happened in 1975 when I was a few months away from my thirteenth birthday and the body of a seventeen-year-old girl named Lesley Whittle was found hanging in an underground drainage shaft of a reservoir at Bathpool Park. She had been kidnapped by a man named Donald Neilson in January of that year and he'd kept her there tethered to the side of the shaft by a wire noose. Police eventually found her hanging there dead two months later. It was huge news both locally and nationally, with Neilson being captured in December. He was known as the Black Panther, because apart from what he did to poor Lesley Whittle, he'd worn a black balaclava during post office robberies he'd committed, and also shot three people dead. It was a horrible story and so tragic, but as kids the whole thing also became something of a fascination, with all the police activity and constant reporting in the media.

I was with Gran and Grandad in their caravan when the body was discovered. Caravanning was one of their passions and they had one in Rhyl on the north-east coast of Wales. If the weather was good, we'd often come home from school on a Friday evening and be driven to the caravan for the whole weekend. It was a lovely thing to do, and it still provides me with some happy memories. When they sold the caravan in Rhyl, they bought another one closer to home in a place called Baldwin's Gate, which is a hamlet in Newcastle-under-Lyme. It was only a short drive from the house, but as well as weekend trips, we would also go there for summer holidays.

Our gran and grandad created a very secure atmosphere for Phil and me, and also for Carl, who we got on with really well. Despite a few years' age difference, the three of us would happily play together whenever we went to the caravan. It wasn't just my gran and grandad who helped with the family atmosphere at the Davieses': their three grown-up sons also played a big part in our lives. They were always willing to join in our games, and were good fun whenever they came down to Rhyl. Once Uncle Malcolm decided to take us out on the wide beaches over there and we found a little place that had a bit of a mound to it. We had buckets and spades, a canvas matting, and a load of other bits and pieces that we dutifully carried as we set off to make camp. I was about ten at the time. Phil, Carl and I built our sand castles, put the mat down and were feeling pleased with ourselves. It was only when Phil looked concerned that the mood changed.

'Uncle Malcolm,' he said, looking over our shoulders. 'There's sea behind us that wasn't there before.'

Sure enough, as we all stood up and looked around, we realised that the beach we had walked on to get to our camp was now covered by seawater. In fact, we were surrounded by water. The tide had come in and we were cut off. There was a look of fear on Malcolm's face and then he quickly went into 'don't panic' mode, but still didn't look too relaxed about the situation. He stepped into the water and it came up to his shorts. He quickly tossed all of our stuff onto the mat and then, as he told us to wade through the water, he pulled all of our gear behind him. The water was getting deeper as we made our way to dry land, but we managed to get there unscathed, feeling relieved and at the same time excited by what had happened.

'Don't tell Gran and Grandad about this!' said Uncle Malcolm, laughing with us, although at the same time realising our little adventure on the beach could have gone so horribly wrong.

Along with his brothers, Granville and Victor, Malcolm

played a big part in our lives. They were a lot older than us but they always made an effort to include us. As far as they were concerned, we were just their little brothers and we immediately felt accepted by them.

Those caravan trips that we took as a family were a lot of fun. The only problem I later had with going away at week-ends was that it sometimes stopped me from playing football with my mates, and as I reached my teenage years, football was something that began to consume me. It was what I was determined to do. I wanted to be a professional footballer.

6

A Different Apprenticeship

I can't remember exactly when I had that conversation with Mr Arkle, but by the time it took place I was obviously quite a way down the line to believing that football was not only a game; it was something that I could earn money from: a job. Something I would do when I left school. In one of the visits that was made by a childcare officer when I was ten, I apparently said that I wanted to join the army. I have no idea why I said it. Perhaps I'd heard other kids talking about it, or seen something on television that had sparked my imagination, but whatever it was, the idea didn't last for long.

I was soon back to thinking about playing football, and the idea of doing it for a living always seemed perfectly possible to me. Perhaps when I was younger it was more about hoping it would happen one day, but as I got older, bigger and stronger, I became convinced it was achievable. All the boys liked playing football, and there was never any shortage of games you could take part in. There were some decent players as well, but I knew I was good, maybe better than most. I also knew I had a determination and desire to succeed. The games I played in were never just a kickabout as far as I was concerned. They were about me taking them seriously and trying to improve all the time, to keep playing at a higher level. I would have played football all day, every day, if I could have, and although I was never that keen on the academic side of being at school, I was more than happy to play for the school team.

By the time I was fifteen, I had been recommended to Port Vale, and had started to train one night a week with them so that they could have a close look at me and see how I was developing as a footballer. I knew that if they liked what they saw there was the chance that they would take me on as an apprentice, which was the natural first step on the ladder of becoming a professional footballer. Being 'spotted' by a club scout when you were playing for your school or a local team, or perhaps writing to a professional club and asking for a trial, was often a way of getting your foot in the door. If they liked what they saw, that might lead to you being offered an apprenticeship, allowing you to be paid for playing football while at the same time doing a lot of the manual jobs at the club, like painting the stands, cleaning toilets and polishing the boots of the first-team players. That sort of thing just doesn't happen these days. Young players tend to concentrate on their football and education. The 'jobs' are a thing of the past, but a lot of players who did go through that sort of thing as a youngster will argue that it was a good thing and something that kept them grounded.

I was one of the better players the school had and our sports teacher agreed, because he recommended me for Staffordshire county trials. It was something that happened all over the country: if you were a decent player then you went along to trials that were held on a regular basis and, if you were selected for the squad, you got the chance of making the county team. Once again, it was part of the over-all process a lot of kids who went on to become professional went through. If you were good enough for your county team it was usually a fair indication that you had something about you as a player. It was no guarantee that you would go on to have a career as a professional, but it certainly showed that you had reached a level that might make you of interest to clubs. Their scouts would always be at county matches, and even at that early age, it was something that could put you in the shop window.

I went along to the trials and the guy in charge of them decided that he would play me on one wing in the first half, and then on the other wing in the second. Although I liked playing centre forward and that was probably my best posi-tion, I did sometimes play on the wing. Sometime after the trials, my sports teacher spoke to me and asked how I had got on because he had heard nothing back from the county, which basically meant they didn't want me for the squad. I told him about being played on the wing and he was clearly surprised. He contacted the guy who had been in charge of the trials and asked him what had happened.

'Mark Bright is one of our best players,' he apparently told him. 'Why didn't you think he was any good?'

The guy just said that I hadn't impressed him and didn't warrant a place in the county squad. It was a disappointment to me, because I would have loved to have been picked for the squad, but at the same time I wasn't going to let it knock my confidence. I still had belief in myself and, if anything, getting knocked back in that fashion just made me more determined to succeed and to prove the county wrong. One of the other schoolboy players who trained with me at Port Vale was Mark Chamberlain, who would go on to have a great career and play for England, and is the father of Liverpool's Alex Oxlade-Chamberlain. One evening when Mark and I were training with Port Vale, he asked me why I wasn't in the county squad.

'They just didn't fancy me,' I told him. He couldn't believe it, but there was nothing I could do about it. I had to put it behind me and get on with making sure I proved them wrong. Apart from my school team, I would play for different local sides whenever I could, and most importantly, I was still training with Port Vale and getting some games in their youth side. I remember playing against Nottingham Forest at Keele University and at the end of the match Brian Clough came up to me and shook my hand, telling me how well I'd played. Apart from being a great manager, he had also been a brilliant goal scorer as a player, so his praise meant a lot to me, but one comment like that didn't mean I was going to make it, and I had a very different experience at another match.

One day we played at Lilleshall against a Wolverhampton Wanderers team, who had Wayne Clarke, one of the famous Clarke footballing brothers, in their side. He was a striker like me and I thought I was doing all right during the first half of the match, but Alan Philpott, who was in charge of our team at Port Vale, clearly had other ideas. We got into the dressing room at half-time and sat down on the benches. Philpott came straight over to me.

'Stand up,' he shouted at me. 'Take your top off, take your shorts off, take your socks off. Now, get in the shower. I don't want to see you again for the rest of the day. You will not make a footballer as long as you have a hole in your arse. Now, go on, get out of my sight!'

As dressing downs go it was pretty fierce, and if he spoke and acted the way he did these days, he would probably have lost his job as a youth coach, but they were very different times then. It didn't matter if you were still a fifteen-year-old kid, football was a tough business and the managers of teams would speak to you in exactly the same way as they would have done to a fully grown man. I'm not saying it was the right way to do things, but that's just the way it was. He was of his time and that day I was left in no doubt that he didn't think much of me as a player. I had to go back on the team minibus, and Philpott came over to speak to me again.

'Don't bother coming training again,' he told me, just emphasising how little he thought of my footballing ability. I did turn up for training despite what he had said, and they tried to work on me being more aggressive in my play, but at the end of the season I suffered a huge disappointment when the club decided they would not be taking me on as an apprentice.

It was a blow. I can't pretend it wasn't because I was so desperate to become a footballer. I was coming to the end of my time at school. I was going to have to leave. I knew I hadn't put in enough work and effort when it came to my school work, and I realised my exam results were not going to be the best. Those words from Mr Arkle began to have a lot more meaning in the summer of 1978, because I really didn't have a plan B. I had been convinced I would leave school and start out on the road to becoming a professional footballer by being an apprentice at Port Vale, but it wasn't going to happen. Alan Philpott had made it very clear what he thought of me. Strange as it may sound, I think he liked me and I think he wanted me to do well and succeed, but he genuinely didn't think I had what it takes. He didn't think I'd make it.

Those words he spat out at me might seem harsh, but I wasn't the sort of kid to let them destroy my confidence or belief. In fact, the opposite was true. They just spurred me on, just like the rejection I got from the county team. I wanted to prove them wrong and make sure they saw that I was right. I could become a footballer. It might take a bit longer and I might have to take a different route, but I was absolutely convinced I would still make it. I believed I had ability, and I knew for a fact that I had self-belief and determination. I just had to keep on playing, keep on improving and make sure I gave myself the best shot I could of getting to where I eventually wanted to be.

One of the things I'd noticed was that I found myself having a lack of stamina in some matches. I knew I had to stay strong throughout a game and not begin to fade towards the end of a match, or have trouble recovering if I put in a long sprint. There was a guy called Barry McGregor, who lived a few doors down from us in Kidsgrove, and he was an extremely good cross-country runner. He'd run long distances as part of his training and one day I asked him if I could go running with him. He was happy to have me tag along, even though there was no way I was able to keep up with him at first. He was very good about having me there with him and I'm sure he slowed down a bit when we went on our runs, but the great thing was that whenever I started to flag, he would be in my ear telling me not to quit, to keep going. He pushed me and as a consequence my fitness and stamina levels began to improve.

After not being taken on by Port Vale I knew I had to start looking for a job. I was still living with Gran and Grandad, so it wasn't as though I didn't have a roof over my head and had to pay rent for accommodation, but I wasn't academically equipped to go on to higher education. I'd put all my eggs into one basket as I was convinced football would be my job when I left school behind. How wrong I was. Instead, I had to start writing letters and knocking on the doors of factories to see if someone would hire me. I couldn't wait to leave school, but the realisation that the next thing I had to do was find a job was a bit daunting. My brother had already had to go down the route of finding a job and he was working as a panel beater at a local firm called Rigby's.

One of the guys who was in Phil's year at school was called Rob Langford, and I bumped into him one day in town. I told him I was trying to find a job and asked him if there was anything going at the place he worked. To be honest, I wasn't even sure about what he did, but he told me he worked in a hydraulics factory and he would ask the guy who owned it if he was looking to take anyone on. Rob came up trumps for me because I was invited along for an interview with the owner, and whatever I said seemed to go down well. He offered me an apprenticeship at the company, Staffs Hydraulics. Getting the job was a relief; I was going to be earning some money, even if it was 52p an hour. The downside was that having rid myself of school and full-time education, I was about to be right back in it again, because for the first year of the apprenticeship I would be at college full-time. It absolutely killed me! The good thing was that the college was only about five hundred yards from our house in Kidsgrove, but it was tough. If we went away at weekends to the caravan at Baldwin's Gate, I used to earn a bit of extra money by cleaning the caravan toilets. Not the greatest job in the world, but it was nice to have the cash in my pocket.

I played for a few local clubs and also for a team at Baldwin's Gate when we were there, which really helped my football development because it was a men's team. I played against grown men and it could be quite hard and rough. I was only sixteen but the guy who ran our team told me I was to play under the name of another player who had been registered, and that if anyone asked how old I was, I had to tell them I was eighteen. I think it did me good and although the standard wasn't great, I enjoyed playing the matches and getting the chance to play against men rather than kids who were my own age. It was an experience and, as far as I was concerned, the more matches I played and the more experience I got, the more likely it was that I could work my way back to achieving my ultimate goal.

As always, Phil was there to give me encouragement, telling me that I was a good enough player to make it. He took the whole thing with Alan Philpott more personally than I did. He thought I had enough ability to get an apprenticeship with Port Vale, but when it didn't happen and I had to start looking at another route he was very supportive. Throughout our lives he had always been there for me, and although he was only thirteen months older, it always felt like he was looking out for me in whatever happened in our lives. Both of us realised that when we reached the age of eighteen, we would no longer be in care. We would be considered adults and have to leave Gran and Grandad. It was one of those things that I really hadn't given much thought to by the time I left school and started my apprenticeship at the hydraulics factory in the summer of 1978, but by the end of the year that had all changed because of a situation that had developed with Phil.

He was seventeen and, like any teenager of that age, wanted to be more independent, be able to go out with his mates and not have restrictions about what time he had to be home at night. He wasn't doing anything out of the ordinary, but his behaviour began to cause friction between him and our gran and grandad. Phil was a young man but he was still under the care of the Davieses. He was still living in their home and it was a home where Grandad set the rules. As far as he was concerned, Phil couldn't just come and go as he pleased because he was still under their care, but my brother was getting increasingly frustrated by their attitude. He had been working as a panel beater for about eighteen months, he was not a kid any more, and I think he began to feel he needed his own space. When all of this blew up, I remember feeling a bit annoyed because I thought Phil was putting at risk everything we'd wanted. A home, security and a stable environment to grow up in, with people who cared for the both of us. I knew he loved Gran and Grandad, just as I did, but the atmosphere in the house at this time was not good. After discussions with the care authorities it was decided that the best solution might be for Phil to move out. Although technically he was not yet an adult, it would only be a matter of months before he reached eighteen, and so the solution everyone came up with was that he should leave early and go into lodgings.

It was a big move for Phil but it was also a big move for me. He had been with me for my entire life. We had shared our young lives together; he was there for me and I was there for him. Apart from a music festival he'd been to with some of his mates, I had never been separated from him, but I knew that was all going to change. In January 1979, four months before his eighteenth birthday, Phil moved out. As you might imagine it wasn't a particularly happy moment. Not for him, not for me and not for Gran and Grandad. When the day came, I remember being upset. I went upstairs to the bedroom we'd shared for all those years and cried. Downstairs Gran was in tears as well. At the time I thought Grandad was being horrible, but I don't think that now. He just wasn't going to compromise: it was his house, we were in their care and he set the rules for as long as we stayed there.

Phil's new lodgings were with a couple called Mr and Mrs Baggley. They also had a daughter named Yvonne living with them, and before moving in, the childcare people had arranged for a visit to make sure everyone got on and it was the sort of place that would be suitable for Phil. They turned out to be quite laidback in their approach to having him stay with them and that meant Phil was able to get the degree of independence he'd wanted. I didn't see him for a while, but he kept in touch and once he had properly settled in at the Baggleys' home he came over to see Gran, Grandad and me. I also went over to see his new place, and it felt strange to think of him living there, because I'd only ever known him being by my side. We talked a bit about what I was going to do when the time came for me to leave Gran and Grandad and start living on my own. The time to do just that was fast approaching, and I knew I should start giving it some thought, but I was still very much living for the moment, and apart from completing the first full year of my apprenticeship, my main energies were still focused on football.

Getting that knockback from Port Vale wasn't a pleasant experience but, after the initial disappointment of it, I became even more determined to somehow get to where I wanted to be. The key to it all, as far as I was concerned, was to keep playing football matches and play as many of them as I could. I played for all sorts of local teams, sometimes taking part in games in the mornings and afternoons on both Saturdays and Sundays. I just couldn't get enough football.

One of the most important moments came when I joined a team called Masons Arms. It was a Sunday league football team, but they played at a very decent level, and one of the co-managers was a guy who knew me from my days at Port Vale. His name was Russell Bromage and he played for Port Vale's first team. The other guy who helped run the team was called Paul Johnson, and he played for Stoke City. They were both very good and really encouraging when it came to my game. Russell knew Port Vale hadn't offered me an apprenticeship with them and also knew I was desperate to make it as a footballer. I was about seventeen years old when I started playing for them, and playing Sunday league football did me the world of good. I think Russell could see some potential in me and he also saw that I was willing to work at my game and improve.

Somebody else who thought I could play and had potential was Alan Vickers. He was the manager of Leek Town, a semi-professional team. He knew I hadn't been taken on by Port Vale, but must have seen me play or heard about me. He had a chat with me and said he thought I could still make it, and that playing for Leek could only help me and my footballing development.

'If you come to Leek Town, I'll improve you as a player,' he promised me. 'You'll still have a chance to make it as a professional, and I think you can do it.'

I saw it as a good opportunity for me to be part of a team that played at a high standard. I would be playing with and against some really experienced footballers in a very good league and, as an added bonus, I would also pick up a few extra quid each week for playing because they were a semi-professional outfit. Learning your trade in non-league football could often be a good way of getting into the full-time game. I think it happened quite a lot back then, and it can still be a way in to this day, Jamie Vardy being a prime example of someone who worked his way to the top after playing non-league football. There are probably fewer players taking that route because the whole scouting system is different, and kids as young as seven get identified as being possible future professional players. Playing for Leek didn't stop me playing on Sundays for Masons Arms, so it seemed like a good idea. I was playing and learning all the time, which was just what I needed to do.

John Rudge was a coach with Port Vale and knew Russell managed the Masons Arms team, and one day John asked him to let him know if he saw any young player who he thought might be able to make the step up and play league football.

'I'll tell you what,' said Russell, 'there's a kid I've seen who would definitely score goals if he played with better players.'

'Well, let's get him in and have a look then,' said John.

'All right, I'll arrange it,' replied Russell. 'Oh, I forgot to say, you already know him. It's Brighty.'

I went to play in a game so that John Rudge could see me in action and decide whether I had the potential to play at a higher level. John McGrath had been appointed as manager of Port Vale by this time and there was a feeling at the club that he was willing to give young players a chance, which was encouraging for me, but at the same time he was not the sort to waste his time. If he thought you weren't up to it, you were out. They decided they liked what they saw and asked me to go and train with them, and I also started to play some games for them as part of their B squad. Getting the chance to be around the club again was just what I needed, but I knew there were no guarantees. I wasn't contracted to Port Vale and I wasn't earning much money from football – that still came from the job I had at the hydraulics factory – but it was certainly a step in the right direction for me.

The summer of 1980 was a big moment in my life. It was when I had my eighteenth birthday which, in turn, meant I was no longer in the care of the local social services. I knew that it also meant that I would have to leave Gran, Grandad and the house I had called home for ten years. The Davieses knew it too, but I don't think any of us were fully prepared for the emotions we all felt on the day. The social services people had talked to Gran, Grandad and me in the weeks leading up to my birthday, making sure everyone understood the process.

Unlike Phil, I wasn't going to go into lodgings as he had with the Baggleys, but instead my Uncle Malcolm and his wife Christine had agreed I could go and live with them until I sorted myself out with accommodation. They didn't live that far away, but the physical distance had nothing to do with the way I felt the day I packed all my possessions and moved out. It was a huge wrench for me and for the Davieses, and it was really horrible to see my gran crying as I walked out of the front door. I promised that I would see them regularly, but it wasn't a nice experience. They had done so much for me, and basically brought me up. They had invested a massive amount of time and care in looking after Phil and me, and now we had both left. They still had Carl living with them, but he would be going through the same process in a few years. Three young lives had been looked after and nurtured by them. Three young black kids whose lives might have been very different but for Gran and Grandad. I think what they did for all of us was amazing, and what they did throughout their lives for so many other children was also incredible. They were very special people, and although what happened to Phil and me when we were children was horrendous in so many ways, we were very lucky to have had Nana Parton and then Gran and Grandad step in and be there for us at crucial stages in our lives. When I think about what they had done for us, my love for them grows stronger.

My stay with Uncle Malcolm and Auntie Christine was only supposed to last a few weeks but, in the end, I was with them for about six months. They were very laidback about me being there and I never once felt pressured to move out, but I'd had a few conversations with Phil about what I should do when I finally left, and he suggested that we rent a flat together, so about two years after he had moved out of Gran and Grandad's we found ourselves living together once again, but in pretty different circumstances. We weren't sharing a bedroom and sleeping in bunk beds, and we weren't being looked after and fussed over by Gran. We rented a one-bedroom flat conversion in a place called Smallthorne.

It was a few miles away from Kidsgrove and the factory, but it was quite near Port Vale's ground. We moved in the early part of 1981, when the weather was freezing and so was our flat. In fact, we started to call it the Ice Box because it was so cold. The curtains actually used to freeze, and although we had little gas heaters, we could never manage to get the place warm. A friend came over one evening and said we were lucky not to have killed ourselves. The heaters gave off some terrible fumes and because we were so desperate to keep warm, we never wanted to open the windows or have any other kind of ventilation.

'You're lucky you're not dead!' he shouted, laughing at the way we were huddled in a corner of the flat trying to keep warm.

The flat did have one great advantage though. It was in a converted house and we had the ground floor, but the upstairs flat was rented out by a very glamorous young woman. She was gorgeous and every Friday she would knock on our door and ask if we would pay the landlord her rent while she went out. She looked fantastic each time we saw her and she smelled great as well, because she always wore very strong perfume. We used to look forward to seeing her every week, like a couple of excited schoolboys, happily taking her money and rent book from her and saying that we would take care of everything for her.

The flat may have been cold in winter, but it was great having our own place and being independent. I was still at Staffs Hydraulics and as well as playing for Masons Arms, Port Vale and Leek, I'd also had some games for Kidsgrove

Athletic. By this time, I believed I had really improved as a player and I felt physically stronger, and Port Vale seemed to agree because during the 1981–82 season I began to play quite a few games for their reserve side. Phil would always try to be there whenever I was involved in home matches. Often there would only be a handful of people watching, but the experience I got in those games was invaluable. I might have been young, but there were often some very experienced and seasoned professionals playing for the opposition.

One cold and wet night in Bradford I came up against exactly that sort of player and he also had a priceless quality that no amount of game time can give you – class. Roy McFarland had been a brilliant centre half for both Derby County and England, he had won league titles and made more than four hundred appearances for County during his time there, and he was recognised as one of the best international defenders during the time he played for his country. At the time I came up against him in a reserve midweek fixture, his best days as a player were behind him and he had become Bradford City's player-manager. I'd been pretty pleased with the progress I had been making and my confidence as a player had grown, but by the time I trudged off the pitch that particular night I had a very different opinion of where my career might be heading. McFarland didn't give me a kick, but did give me a masterclass in how to play centre half. I couldn't do anything about it and all the self-belief I'd had seemed to evaporate during those ninety minutes. At the end of the game I just couldn't see how I was ever going to make a living from the sport. When I got back to the flat, I told Phil all about it.

'I think it's all over,' I said. 'I played against a guy tonight who is on his way out as a player and I didn't get a kick, so if I can't cause him problems, how am going to cause someone who is young problems?'

I said I was going to see John Rudge the next day and tell him that I thought I just wasn't good enough after all. I had worked so hard to give myself a chance and genuinely thought I would eventually make it, but the way McFarland had played against me showed that I was probably kidding myself. I felt totally dejected by what had happened. Confidence is a huge thing for a footballer or anyone involved in playing sport. Although I was determined and had belief in myself, I was also honest enough to realise that playing against McFarland was a reality check for me, and possibly for the first time on a football field I began to question whether I had what it takes. The confidence that had always been a part of my character drained away. I had pinned all my hopes on being a professional, put in the hours, never given up and had an inner belief that I would succeed and realise my dream, but in the space of ninety minutes Roy McFarland had destroyed the dream and replaced it with a stark reality, which I now had to come to terms with. I wasn't good enough and I had to be honest enough to tell John Rudge.

'Don't do it,' pleaded Phil. 'Don't go and see John Rudge. You can still do it. You can still make it as a player, I know you can.'

I really felt bad because my brother had been there for me from day one and had never stopped in his encouragement and support, but he hadn't been at the game in Bradford that night. He hadn't seen his kid brother look totally out of his depth against a veteran defender, whose priority at that time was more about being a manager than a player. I had a terrible night's sleep, and woke up still determined to go and see John Rudge and have an honest conversation about the way I felt, and the shortcomings in my game which I thought the previous night's game had exposed. John had been very encouraging and obviously thought I had enough potential to take a chance and get me playing with them, but I didn't want to waste my time and his by sticking around when I felt I just wasn't going to be able to take that step up and deal with a defender like Roy McFarland. When I spoke to John his response totally surprised me.

'Roy McFarland played for England, Mark,' John said. 'He's still fit and he still plays in Bradford's first team. Roy McFarland would cause anyone problems, don't you worry about that. You learn from things like last night's game. You just keep going, Mark. I'm telling you, you're doing all right.'

Hearing those words and knowing he had faith in me meant so much. I had been on the floor but both John and Phil helped pick me up. They had faith in me and said the right things. Without the two of them I honestly think my career might have been over before it had really begun. Instead, their encouragement helped to get me back on track, and I was able to put the Bradford experience behind me. I've always been a positive person, and nobody goes through life without setbacks. John Rudge was right: the Roy McFarland game taught me a lot, and after that night I managed to put the episode behind me and move on. It was such a horrible experience when it happened, but I did learn from it and soon got my enthusiasm and confidence back. As the second half of the season arrived, I was enjoying my football playing for Port Vale, Leek and Masons Arms. I just couldn't get enough of it.

7

Goal Bonus

Sharing the flat with Phil worked out well for both of us. There's no doubt we had a special bond, and still do. We had been through and shared so much together, and always got on well. Throughout our childhood, into our teens and then as young men, we had never had a cross word. We seemed to instinctively have a feel for the mood of each other and I think it helped that we not only thought of ourselves as brothers, but also as mates. We were always there for each other and that hasn't changed to this day. But, when it came to our sisters, because of the circumstances that all five of us were presented with when we were kids, it was never easy to maintain the sort of normal relationships other brothers and sisters would have. If you grow up living apart instead of living together under the same roof, things are bound to be different. Through no fault of our own, our lives and those of our sisters became splintered. Phil and I had that lovely little period when we stayed with our real gran, and for those weeks we saw a lot of our sisters, but as the years went on we began to see less of them. They lived with our mum and Tommo, we were with the Davieses and somehow or other we never really met up, and we pretty much lost touch with them along the way.

When Phil left home to live at the Baggleys' he was able to start enjoying more freedom and independence than he'd had at Gran and Grandad's. One night he was out with his mates at a club in Stoke called the Place. Without wishing to be too unkind, Stoke was not exactly spoilt for choice when it came to nightlife, and the Place was somewhere most youngsters would visit on a night out at some time in the late 1970s and early 1980s. On this occasion he felt someone tap on his shoulder and turned around to see a girl about the same age as him, whose face looked familiar.

'Excuse me,' she said. 'I think you're my brother Phil.'

It was Marie and I don't think either of them could quite believe what had happened. They stood and stared at each other, and then couldn't stop talking. Marie has since told me there might have been a gap of something like seven or eight years between seeing him as a kid and then meeting him again in the Place. That meeting meant we could all start to catch up with each other and find out what was happening in our lives. We were no longer kids, we were young adults starting out in life on our own. All of us had suffered in one way or another, but we were family. After some years of separation we were able to reconnect and that meant something to all of us.

Like Phil, my sisters soon began to understand just how determined I was to succeed as a footballer, and Marie even began to keep a scrapbook on my exploits playing for Port Vale, Leek and Masons Arms. Alan Vickers had been right when he said he would make me a better player. Being in the Leek team definitely helped my development, and as a consequence it also helped me when it came to establishing myself with Port Vale. I started to play regularly for their reserves, but because I was not contracted to them in any way, it also meant I could turn out for my other two sides.

One night in March 1982, Leek had a Cheshire League game at Chorley, and I played really well, scoring a hat-trick in a 3–2 win. I was buzzing at the end of the game and, when we went into their lounge after the match for a drink, I noticed a framed England shirt hanging on the wall. The shirt belonged to Paul Mariner and the message at the bottom of the frame thanked Chorley for everything they had done for him. Paul had started at Chorley and was having a great career, playing for Plymouth and Ipswich, as well as becoming England's centre forward. I looked at the shirt and found it inspirational because he'd started off in non-league football playing against the sort of sides I played against, but he had the talent and ability to become a full-time profes-sional, just as I wanted to do. Things got even better the next day when somebody showed me a match report that said my display was the best by a centre forward at Chorley since the days of Paul Mariner.

I knew I was improving all the time, but what mattered most was the opinion of the Port Vale manager, John McGrath. If he didn't rate me then I wasn't going to get the chance to show what I could do at league level with the first team. The team weren't doing badly and were in the top ten in the Fourth Division, but although they had a good unbeaten home record, the team had drawn a lot of matches and, in the last few games of the season, the manager had an eye on what might be needed for the new season. In the middle of April, Port Vale sent a team to play at Stoke in a testimonial match for one of their players, Alan Dodd. I was included in the squad, which was a good experience and I enjoyed it, getting a feel for what it was like to be involved with the first team. Just over a week later I was at work when I was told there had been a call for me from John McGrath, and he wanted me to go and see him. I feared the worst. I thought I had been doing well enough but maybe he'd seen something that he didn't like and wanted to let me know I wasn't in his plans. When I got to the ground, I was feeling pretty nervous. I went into his office and he asked me a question.

'How do you think you've done this season?' he said.

'I think I've done all right,' I told him.

'I think you've done better than all right,' he added. 'You're going to be on the bench for the game tomorrow.'

It took a few seconds for it to sink in. I was going to be the substitute for the home game with York and, unlike today, each team only had one. I couldn't wait to get back to the flat and tell Phil. I'm not sure who was more excited, me or him. I might have been the one who played, but he had been there alongside me every step of the way. It meant a lot to both of us. I tried to stay as calm as I could and not think about the game, but it was such a big thing at the time, and I wanted to make sure that if I was called onto the pitch at any time, I wouldn't let myself down.

In the end, I played for about the last fifteen minutes of the game, and the match ended in a goalless draw. I didn't do

Me and Phil with Nana Parton, a truly wonderful lady.

(*left to right*) Sharon, me, Phil and Marie.

Me and Phil, in matching outfits, with our friend Dumbo.

Phil and me in the sea at Rhyl. I can still remember how cold that water was.

Nana Clarke, Auntie Jean, Nana Parton, two of our neighbours, Marie, Sharon, Phil and me.

At Dove Bank Primary school, around 1972.

Taken at Nana Parton's house. It must have been a birthday party. Mustard jumpers were in, as you can see.

At Pines Holiday Camp, Rhyl, where we spent our summer holidays with Gran and Grandad Davies at our caravan. Also in the picture are Uncle Malcolm's two kids, Paul and Derek, who would often stay with us, and Carl Wright (our foster brother).

At Maryhill Comprehensive School. Our teacher, Mr Robinson, is at the back, and Captain Bright with his mustard coloured boots is in the centre.

(*left to right*) Derek, Carl, Phil, Paul and me at the caravan in Rhyl eating sherbet fountains (for those old enough to remember them…).

Nana Clarke, my maternal grandmother, a lovely women who unsuccessfully tried to get the family back together.

At a family wedding in the late 1960s. Phil and I were pageboys for our Uncle Fred and Auntie Jean.

The staff at Staffordshire Hydraulic Services, my first job after leaving school. I had some great times at this factory. (*left to right*) Mick, Steve, Steve, Pete, me, Pat, Phil, Arthur, Rob, Dave.

Phil and me with Gran Davies on her eightieth birthday.

Gran and Grandad Davies.

With all my siblings. (*left to right*) Sharon (second youngest), me (the middle child), Maureen (the youngest), Philip (second oldest) and Marie (the oldest).

Gran Davies, Trevor 'Digger' Mullet and me at Robbie and Sandra Earle's wedding. I was the best man and I always say that I'm the glue that keeps their marriage together. In actual fact, I was an awful best man on the day; luckily, they forgave me!

Port Vale U18s 8–0 win in the FA Youth Cup. Our coach, Alan Philpott, is on the far right.

During my early years at Palace. I loved this strip; it just says 'Palace' to me.

Palace versus Forest on a frozen pitch at Selhurst Park in the 1980s. Des Walker, who would later become my teammate and good friend at Sheffield Wednesday, is one of the finest defenders of his generation. *(Mark Leech/Offside)*

In full flow. Probably went out for a throw-in… *(Popperfoto/Getty Images)*

One of the finest moments of my career, beating Blackburn Rovers in the second leg play-off at Selhurst Park. We needed to score three goals without reply; we did it and got promoted into what is now the Premier League. *(Frank Tewkesbury/Evening Standard/Shutterstock)*

The FA Cup Final, 1990, doing a walk of appreciation around the old Wembley pitch with Manchester United's Paul Ince after extra time. Paul correctly predicted Man Utd would kick our arse in the replay. No one likes a smart arse. *(Ted Blackbrow/ANL/Shutterstock)*

The FA Cup Final, 1990, outside the team hotel. (*left to right*) Me, our amazing physio David West, Wrighty and Andy Gray.

anything spectacular, but I didn't make any howlers either. After the game the manager told me he wanted to include me in the squad for a midweek game we had at Colchester two days later. I knew I would have to ask for a day's holiday from work if I was going to travel with the team, but I also had something else on my mind. The day after my appearance against York, I was due to play in a cup final for Masons Arms. Russell Bromage, who had played in the team against York, knew I was desperate to play in the final having helped the side get there, but there was no way John McGrath wanted me playing ninety minutes of football twenty-four hours before I was due to be on first-team duty with Port Vale. In the end, after talking to Russell, they reached a compromise and I was allowed to play forty-five minutes of the final, which happily we won, but although I went to Colchester, I never played a part.

Five days later Port Vale were due to play their final game of the season, a home match against Torquay, and the manager once again included me in the squad. He wanted to have a good look at me for ninety minutes playing first-team football, so this time I wasn't going to be the substitute, I was going to start the game. My full debut. It was a great feeling to get picked, and I knew by now that the manager thought I had the ability to handle the situation. We won 2–0. I had a decent enough game, setting up the first goal for Paul Bowles, and I should have scored when Mark Chamberlain set me up with a good cross, but didn't react quickly enough.

'I was waiting for the ball to bounce instead of having a go straight away,' I told a local reporter.

Having got a taste of what it was like to play a full first-team game, I knew I wasn't out of my depth. I had to keep on improving, work on my fitness, my touch, my technique, but I came away from that game with Torquay knowing I could make it. I could become a professional footballer. My confidence was sky high and that is always good for a striker. I played with a freedom that allowed me to show exactly what I could do, and that I could live with and compete against the footballers playing at that level.

Torquay was the last game of the season and the players were going off for their summer break. Pre-season training would not start until July, but before then contracts would be sorted out. Some players would get new deals and others might be told they could move on. I was not contracted to the club and had played for them as an amateur. Getting into the first team near the end of the season had been fantastic, but although I felt I could play at that level, I knew one full game gave me no guarantees that the manager thought the same. He was the one who would make a decision on what would happen next for me. I had a feeling he quite liked what he saw against Torquay, and also the way I had played and scored goals for the reserves.

I was called in by him soon after the end of the season and he explained what he intended to do next. They were going to offer me a one-year part-time contract, and I was going to be paid £10 a week, but it also meant that I could only play for Port Vale, so turning out for Leek and Masons Arms had to stop. I remember some of the lads and Leek telling me not to do it, saying Port Vale would only be using me and at the end of the season they could discard me, just as they had when I was a youth team player and didn't get taken on as an apprentice. I knew what they said was true, I knew it was a risk, but at the same time I saw it as a great chance for me, and it was a chance I wanted to take. I knew it wasn't going to be easy because I was still an apprentice with Staffs Hydraulics, which meant I would have to combine training with working full-time, but it was a great opportunity for me so I would have to find a way to fit in training with them throughout the week.

Most of that summer was a happy time for me, but a phone call to the hydraulics factory one day in July left me numb and in shock. It came from my Uncle Granville, and what he said left me speechless.

'Mark, bad news, your grandad's passed away,' he told me.

Grandad had gone to his caravan in Wales without Gran, because Carl was soon going to be leaving school, and she wanted to stay with him. Granville, who lived in Wales, had called us earlier and said that his dad had been taken to hospital after suffering a brain aneurysm. He said that things weren't looking good. When my gran heard the news she and Carl headed straight to the hospital. Phil and I were going to follow as soon as we could, but Grandad went downhill rapidly, and we never even got the chance to get there before he passed away. Poor Carl was freaked out by the whole experience because he actually saw Grandad in the hospital, looking terrible, unable to open his eyes, with tubes coming out of his body and machines beeping. It must have been a horrific sight, especially for a young kid.

Naturally my gran was in bits. The man she had loved and been married to for so long was dead. They were a true partnership and had done everything together. I don't think either of them could have imagined life without the other. They were incredibly close and had shared most of their adult lives with each other. The two of them had been great parents to the three sons they had, and they had provided a loving, secure family environment for Phil, me and so many other kids who went through the care system.

Grandad had his faults, like everyone else, and he could often come across as a tough, uncompromising man with what would now be seen as very old-fashioned ways. He was of his time and environment, but he was a loving, caring man with high principles and standards. He always tried to live up to them and he expected those closest to him to do the same. I hope I have never let him down in that respect. He never made a fuss about me playing football, even when he knew I was starting to make progress, but I think he would have approved of my work ethic and determination to succeed. I wouldn't ever say that I was like him as a person, but I know for a fact that a lot of what he said and did rubbed off on me. Things like always working hard and never spending money you didn't have. They left a lasting effect on me.

When the new season started, I began a regime that left me completely knackered. I would get up at 5 a.m., get to work for 6 a.m., finish at the factory at around 3.30 p.m., then get a bus to Port Vale's ground. There was a small gym under one of the stands and when I got there, John Rudge would be waiting with a couple of young players, Robbie Earle and Andy Shankland. John would get them to work with me on all aspects of my game. My touch, heading the ball, passing, laying it off, crosses, as well as making sure my general fitness improved. He put in so much time and effort with me, and I will always be grateful that he did. Robbie and Shanks were great as well, both of them were very good players, even at that early stage. I would train Monday and Tuesday, play in the reserves on Wednesday nights, have Thursday off and then be back in to train on Friday. By the time the weekend came around I was absolutely shattered, all I wanted to do was sleep. I had a girlfriend at the time, and she must have got fed up with the number of times I was too tired to go out with her. I didn't exactly have a wild social life – pretty much everything I did revolved around me playing football.

Playing regularly for the reserves in midweek leagues was again good experience for me, but having been given that game in the first team at the end of the previous season, I was eager to get another chance to show what I could do at that level. I got a chance to do that a couple of months into the season when I was named substitute for a home match against Hereford. The manager had shaken things up a bit in the summer, selling Mark Chamberlain to Stoke City and he also brought in an experienced striker called Bob Newton, who played alongside Jimmy Greenhoff up front for the game. Jimmy was a really good striker who had played at the very top for Leeds, Stoke and Manchester United, and in the second half of the game against Hereford, I came off the bench to replace him. With a minute to go, the game was still scoreless, but then our centre back, Wayne Cegielski, headed home at the far post after Bob Newton headed on a corner, and then four minutes into stoppage time I got my moment of glory. Russell Bromage sent over a free kick and I headed in, my first goal in league football. It was the only one I scored for the first team that season as I continued to learn my trade in the reserves and the A team, scoring more than thirty goals. The first team did well that season and won promotion to the old Third Division. When the summer came around there were decisions to be made once again. I knew I'd had a good season in the reserves, scoring goals and generally improving as a player. I got asked to go and see John McGrath one day. He knew I was doing an apprenticeship and that it was about to finish.

'If you pass your apprenticeship, we'll offer you a contract,' he told me. 'If you don't pass, we won't offer the contract because you'll have nothing to fall back on.'

John knew just what a precarious business football could be. One minute everything could be going well and you're flying, the next minute everything has gone wrong and you could be out on your ear. He knew how desperate I was to make it, but he also knew that if things didn't turn out the way I hoped, then at least I would have the skills to turn to hydraulic engineering. Although my focus was on succeeding as a footballer, I was lucky to have been taken on by Staffs Hydraulics. Having to go to college for that first year of my apprenticeship might not have been exactly what I'd wanted straight after leaving school life behind, but it did me no harm at all, and set me on the path to passing an apprenticeship. The company specialised in making high pressure equipment for underwater pipes used for North Sea oil. It was owned by a man named Bill Thompson, and all the guys there were very supportive when it came to me wanting to be a footballer. I had a good time working with all of them, but once I'd passed my apprenticeship, I knew there was a decision to be made, and although I was delighted with the promise of a full-time contract from Port Vale, I wasn't looking forward to having what I thought would be a very awkward conversation with Bill Thompson. It was a small family business that employed about a dozen people, and he'd given me the chance to have an apprenticeship and a job. I owed him and the company a lot, so I wasn't looking forward to telling him that after all the time and effort he'd put into training me, I was going to leave and take a chance on being a professional footballer. It was all I'd ever wanted, but I was nervous about seeing him.

'Bill, I've always wanted to be a footballer and Port Vale have given me the chance of a one-year contract,' I told him. 'I feel bad because I know you've put me through college and given me day-release so that I could get my apprenticeship, and now I want to leave.'

'Mark, let me make this easy for you,' Bill replied. 'I was working for a big company once when I suddenly realised that there was an opportunity for me. I saw the chance to work for myself, so I re-mortgaged my house and went for it with the help of my wife, Margaret. We started off using our garage to work from and then gradually grew the business into what it is today. I know what it's like to take a chance in life. You should go for it. The one thing I have to tell you is that I can't keep your job open for you once you leave, so I hope that will help give you the incentive to be successful!'

I told him that I totally understood his position and thanked him for being so good about me leaving, and so encouraging as well. When I told the boys out on the shop floor, they all told me to go for it because they knew just how much it meant to me. What they didn't know was how much it was going to mean to me financially. When the contract was finally presented to me, I saw that it was going to be for less than I was earning at Staffs Hydraulics. I might have finally realised my dream of being a full-time professional, but when I looked at the contract the manager was giving me, I realised it was going to cost me money. I told John McGrath I was earning more in the factory than he was offering me to sign as a full-time professional. As much as I wanted the contract, I turned it down. I wasn't after a fortune, but I did feel I was worth a bit more than I was being offered. I don't think John McGrath was too impressed, but they did come back with another offer which I thought was more reasonable. The contract was for £110 a week, with £25 per game first-team appearance money. If I scored ten goals, I got a £1000 bonus and there was also a clause in the contract that said if a player was sold by the club before the end of the year, I would get an extra £10 per week! It was something John McGrath had promised when we were talking about my wages, but he was more concerned to make sure I realised what an opportunity I was being given, and I agreed with him.

'Son,' he told me, 'this isn't about money, it's about opportunity. I don't sign bad players and in three years I expect you to be playing in the First Division.'

It was nice to hear that he had that sort of faith in me, and I was confident I could repay it by being a success. Having finally got the opportunity to be a full-time professional footballer I was determined to give myself the best possible chance to succeed, and I started with the basics, like making sure that when pre-season training came around, I would be able to literally hit the ground running. During the summer Robbie Earle and I would go for long runs and do things like sprints to make sure we were ready for that first day back. It was strange because I'd been around the club for some time, but I had still been on the outside. I'd trained in the afternoons and I'd played matches for them, but I wasn't full-time, and I knew that was a big difference. On the first day of pre-season I was a bit nervous, but John Rudge welcomed me and said I was part of the first-team squad.

'Where do I get changed?' I asked him.

'In there,' said John. He pointed to the first-team changing room, so in I went. As I went to find a place to change there was some shouting and jeering from the other players.

'What do you think you're doing?' one of them asked.

'John Rudge told me to come in and get changed,' I told him.

'Not here,' he said. 'Go next door!'

I sheepishly walked out and started to make my way to the dressing room next door.

'Where do you think you're going?' It was the voice of John Rudge. I told him what had happened. He laughed and told me to go back to the first-team changing room, which I did, only to be met with more cries of 'Get out' from the other players, but I could see that quite a few of them had smiles on their faces this time. I realised it was all part of their little welcoming party. They were just joking around and it didn't take long before I felt part of the group, with quite a few of them going out of their way to try and help me with my game. They knew how desperate I was to do well.

I have to admit that one of the strangest things I had to get used to was how much time you had on your hands. I remember asking Robbie what players did in the afternoon, because I'd been used to working a full day. As a pro you trained for about two hours four times a week, had a day off and then played matches on a Saturday. I'd been used to getting up at 5 a.m. when I worked in the factory, so when I got the full-time contract I had to try and change my morning habits. Sometimes I would wake up at 8 a.m. and think I was late for work, I'd been so used to getting up early for all those years. I would try to pace myself and arrive at a reasonable time for training in the mornings, but most days I would be at the ground early, get changed, get some balls and go to the small gym, where I would kick them against the wall and practise juggling, heading and shooting, before going into the changing room to get ready for training with the rest of the team. When I first did it, the other players would ask what I'd been doing, and when I told them I could see that some of them thought I was mad. The fact was I was just so happy to finally make it as a professional. I loved the game and wanted to learn, and in many ways, I didn't really know how to act as a professional because I hadn't been an apprentice like most of the other players. Football had been all they'd known since leaving school. So many of the ways of the game were all new to me, but I was lucky to have really good experienced professionals around me. I will always be grateful to people like Ernie Moss, Colin Tartt and Bob Newton. I was selected in front of Bob once and I knew how upset he must have been, but on the day of the game all he did was give me encouragement.

'Go on, Brighty, get yourself a goal,' he told me.

I was always told to listen to people in the game and to what they had to say. Ernie really taught Robbie Earle and me how to be professionals in the way we conducted ourselves and went about training and playing in matches, while Colin would often come and sit next to me on the team coach if I hadn't had a great game and go over the match with me. He'd always be encouraging. I think most experienced or older players will take time to give a young-ster decent advice. It's what you need when you're starting out, and when I reached the stage in my career where I'd been around for quite a while, I always took the opportunity to have a word with some of the younger players at my club, people like Scotty Parker and Jermain Defoe. I'm sure some of the time they might not have liked what I was saying, but I did it with the best intentions because I wanted to try and help them when they were starting out on their careers, just as I'd been helped at Port Vale.

A couple of months into the season we played Manchester United in a League Cup tie and I managed to get off the bench. It was a real thrill to be involved and to witness first-hand how the United players went about their job. As you would expect, there were some great names in their side that night, the likes of Paul McGrath, Arnold Mühren, Bryan Robson, Norman Whiteside and Frank Stapleton. One incident that stands out was the moment I saw Ray Wilkins collect a ball and at the same time shout to their winger Arthur Graham to 'go', which he duly did and in a flash. Wilkins hit a pinpoint ball about forty yards into Graham's path. It was a brilliant piece of play and the speed with which they did it was incredibly impressive. It was the first time I'd seen such a brilliant piece of skill close-up in a game. I was also a bit in awe of the way the team looked. Their kit was pristine and the players had an aura about them. We lost the game 1–0, but gave a good account of ourselves.

The next morning, I got up early and went down to the ground and walked onto the side of the pitch. There had been almost 20,000 people in the ground the previous night and I was still buzzing about playing a small part in what was such a big game for the club. While I was standing there, I looked at the dugouts and in the away one I could see something red lying on the bench. I went over to take a look and discovered it was a red towel, but it wasn't just any old towel: it had the Manchester United crest embroidered on it. I thought that was real class, having their own crest on towels!

The season had started well for me. I got into the first team early on but was then injured. The team struggled in the league after getting promoted to the Third Division that summer. I played some reserve games and had a spell where I was first-team substitute for quite a few matches but, by December, with results not really improving, John McGrath lost his job and John Rudge became manager. Although I'd scored in a 2–1 home FA Cup defeat to Lincoln in November, I didn't get my first league goal until January when we beat Wimbledon 2–0 at home. With just four goals to my name as we entered April, any chance I had of collecting that £1000 bonus in the eleven games that were left seemed a long way off, but things can change dramatically for you in football. I made eight consecutive full appearances during that period, scored six times and ended the season with ten goals. Unfortunately, the team didn't do well enough to stay in the Third Division, and dropped back into the Fourth, but on a personal level, the season had been relatively successful. Despite not being a regular in the first team, my overall goals tally triggered the £1000 bonus in my contract, and the fact that I had reached that number in my first full season triggered another kind of bonus, as a couple of other clubs saw what I might be capable of.

8

Big Boots to Fill

No club likes to be relegated. Port Vale were no different in that respect and, like most clubs, the aim is to try and bounce back at the first attempt. In order to do that you need to keep your best players, maybe add to the squad and also make sure your team will have goals in it. Without goals you don't win matches. John Rudge knew that as well as anybody, and he also knew me. John had been brilliant with me; he was the one who had helped so much by putting on those sessions in the gym and he was also the coach who believed in me and thought I had potential. I liked him a lot and respected him, but when he asked me at the end of the season whether I would sign a new contract, I said no. I didn't want to jump in and sign, and it wasn't a spur of the moment thing. I'd been thinking about it for some time before the offer was finally made, and I'd decided that when my one-year deal ran out, I would look elsewhere.

I'd started to think about it in the last few months of the season when I'd heard from a couple of people that Leicester City might be interested in me. There were always people you met who claimed to have an 'in' with one club or another, and when this particular guy hinted that Leicester were looking at me, I began to wonder if it might be true. I told a couple of the other players and they basically said I shouldn't do anything or start building my hopes up unless there were guarantees that a club actually wanted to sign me. Having only signed for one year had been a gamble for me in many ways, but it also meant that if I did prove myself and was a success, it put me in a pretty strong position.

Some years earlier when I'd been playing youth football for Port Vale, we'd had a game against Leicester and their coach was a guy called Dave Richardson. After the match he had a word with me and said he thought I had really good potential as a centre forward, which was nice to hear, and then he gave me a bit of advice. He told me that I needed to focus more on my football game instead of running around the pitch being physical and trying to fight everybody. Once he'd said it, I knew exactly what he meant. I used to run all over the pitch, charging into defenders, but it was my technical game that would be key to me making it as a player, and if I wasn't good enough in that department, then all the charging around would not make up for it.

Towards the end of that first full season with Port Vale, Dave got in touch with me. Like a few other people in the game, he wondered what I was going to do about my contract situation. I said that I thought I would probably let it run out and not sign a new deal so that I could see what my options might be, and he told me if I decided to do that, he would speak to me. Port Vale had wanted me to commit to them before the season ended, especially when I began to hit the back of the net with that late burst of goals, but I said no. I was grateful to Port Vale for giving me the chance but even though I'd only had just one full season, I knew that being a professional footballer could be a precarious business and you had to try and look after yourself. In the season when I made my debut, but was still playing amateur football, there was a central defender called Andy Foote who played for the reserves with me. I was a couple of years older than him and one day at the end of the season there were a few of us hanging around waiting to see the manager. Andy was there to see about a possible contract.

'What do you think the Gaffer's going to give me?' he asked in his strong Brummie accent.

'A bike!' someone shouted out.

It was a bit cruel, but typical of the kind of humour you get at a football club. Andy duly went in to see the manager and came out pretty quickly, having been told he wasn't going to get a contract.

'Right that's it, lads, see yer,' he said waving to us as he walked out the door, and that was him gone. The nice thing for Andy is that he went on to have a very successful career in business, but it doesn't always work out that way, and that was why I wanted to try and make sure that I did the right thing for my future and for my development as a player.

When the season finally ended and my contract ran out, I spoke to Leicester. They seemed like a good club, with a good manager in Gordon Milne, and good players like strikers Gary Lineker and Alan Smith, goalkeeper Mark Wallington and defender John O'Neill. I felt it was somewhere I could go to continue my footballing education. I might have been twenty-two years old, but I was also aware that I had only been in the game as a full-time professional for one season, and I hadn't played a lot of first-team games during that time. John Rudge was desperate for me to sign, and tried hard to convince me that staying at Port Vale on a new two-year contract would be good for me. I think he was probably right in one way but, at the same time, the chance of joining a First Division club like Leicester was just too good an opportunity to turn down. The contract offer from Port Vale was a decent one, worth £155 per week, but despite John trying hard to make me stay, my mind was made up. I went to see Gordon Milne at his house to have a chat about a possible move and I liked him and liked what he had to say about the way I could progress at the club. He mentioned Alan Smith and the way he had come from non-league football with Alvechurch. It was all very encouraging and Gordon seemed like the sort of manager who would invest time in you, try to improve you as a player. After talking to him I decided that Leicester were the ones for me.

John Rudge knew I wanted to go there, but was still desperate to get me to sign, and even came over to the flat one evening in an effort to try and persuade me, but I told him I wasn't going to and had practically told Gordon Milne that I wanted to join Leicester. He knew I wasn't going to change my mind, but then one day told me there was another club interested in signing me.

'Howard Wilkinson wants to see you,' he said.

'I've already decided I want to go to Leicester,' I told him.

John explained that I hadn't signed any contract with Leicester and that I should go and have a meeting with Howard out of courtesy and also to see what he had to say. Howard was manager of Sheffield Wednesday, and they had just got back into the First Division after an absence of fourteen years. I knew that Wednesday were a massive club with a huge stadium and they were obviously ambitious. I agreed to go and see them and drove over to meet Howard Wilkinson. When I got to the ground I was shown up to his office and waited outside while he took a call. While I was waiting his assistant, Peter Eustace, came into the room, shook my hand and started chatting to me.

'Are you good at heading?' he asked. 'Good with both feet?'

I nodded and said I was, and then he asked what size boots I wore, which I thought was a bit of an odd question, but I told him and he got up and disappeared out of the door. A few minutes later he was back, clutching a pair of boots and some training kit. He stuck them in my hands, told me to get changed, and within minutes we were in his car and heading off to the club's training ground. When we got there, he enlisted the help of two apprentices and soon had me heading crosses, doing sprints, hitting balls with my left foot, right foot and volleying. I was thinking, This never happened when I went for talks with Leicester. I was so naive! I had a shower and got changed before going back to finally meet Howard Wilkinson. When I sat down opposite him, Howard clearly wondered what was wrong with me. I was still sweating profusely from my exertions at the training ground, and couldn't get enough water down my throat.

'Are you all right?' he asked, looking concerned at the state of me. 'You're sweating.'

'I'm just a bit hot after the session your assistant just put on at the training ground,' I replied.

'Session at the training ground?' said Howard, looking surprised and puzzled at the same time.

He excused himself and then went out of the room, shutting the door behind him. I don't know exactly what was said by him to Peter, but I got the impression he wasn't too pleased about the impromptu training session his assistant had put me through. We had a good chat about his plans for the club, and he gave me a tour of the stadium, but we didn't even talk about money. By the end of the meeting I was impressed with him and the club. He asked me if there was any other club interested in signing me and I told him there was. I didn't want to lie and he said he wasn't surprised I had other options. As we shook hands and said goodbye to each other he asked me to let him know when I had decided what I wanted to do.

'Son, can you call me at 10 a.m. and let me know?' he asked. I promised I would. Then he tried to arrange for me to get some expenses for travelling over, but I told him I didn't want them. It was a really nice gesture by him, but I'd enjoyed the whole experience, apart from the training session, and I liked him and his honesty. He struck me as the sort of manager I would have enjoyed playing for. The only trouble was, I'd made my decision and I didn't think it was fair to change my mind. As I drove back that day my big concern was having to phone Howard the next morning and break the news to him.

When I got back to the flat Phil asked me how it had gone and what I thought of Wednesday. I told him I'd been impressed, but that I'd virtually given my word to Gordon Milne that I would sign for Leicester. I didn't sleep well that night and the next morning at just before 10 a.m., and feeling very awkward about what I was going to say, I was in a phone box across the road from our flat. This was 1984 but we never had our own phone in the Ice Box. I dialled the number I'd been given and was put through to Howard's secretary who put me through to him.

'Hello, son, how are you? Did you enjoy yesterday?' he asked, making me feel even worse about what I was going to tell him.

'I really enjoyed it,' I said, 'but I want to tell you that I've spoken to Leicester. I've kind of given my word to Gordon Milne and I don't want to go back on it.'

I was relieved to finally tell him but at the same time felt bad, because he'd come across as a really nice guy and his reaction to what I had just told him could not have been nicer.

'Son, thanks for phoning and I'm really pleased you've been honest with me. You never know, football's a funny business and you might end up signing for me some time in the future. I appreciate you calling. Good luck and all the best.'

He handled the whole thing so well, and made me feel much better about the situation. I liked Howard, and I liked his honesty and openness. Once I'd told him, I felt much better about pressing ahead with the move to Leicester.

I went back to Gordon Milne and told him that I wanted to join the club, it felt right, and after going down to see him and sorting out my contract details, I was really excited about the move. The contract I signed was for three years, and I was going to be earning £300 a week, virtually tripling the amount I earned at Port Vale. I also got £150 appearance money for each game I played in or was named substitute, and a £10,000 signing-on fee, payable in three equal instalments over the three summers of the contract. I signed the contract a day after my twenty-second birthday and suddenly things were very different for me. There was a dispute over the fee Leicester wanted to pay Port Vale for me. They had offered £15,000, which Port Vale understandably rejected, and that meant that the eventual fee would have to be decided by a transfer tribunal who eventually came up with a fee of £100,000. Great for Port Vale, not so good for Leicester who were told to pay the amount in three equal stages. The first £33,333 had to be paid straight away, the second was to be made after twenty-five appearances, and the third came when I had made fifty appearances for the club.

Although I'd played in the Third Division with Port Vale, they had been relegated, so I was effectively moving from a Fourth Division club to a First Division club after one season as a professional. I could hardly believe it, and neither could Phil. I phoned him to say that I'd signed for Leicester and I could tell he was just as excited and pleased as I was. I knew that without him, none of it might have happened. He had always been there for me, encouraging me, telling me I was good enough to make it. He had been my brother, my mentor, my guardian and, if ever I was wavering in my own self-belief, he was the one who urged me on. Whenever he could he would be there to see me play. It's funny, because although he wasn't that much older than me, I think in many ways he was a father figure for me as well. It's hard to say – if you haven't had a dad around, you don't know what a dad's role is as you're growing up – but throughout my life Phil had been there and I knew what the move meant to him. I got a lot of goodwill from a lot of people once the move was formally announced, and one of the people to get in touch with me was John McGrath, who wrote a letter. He started off by saying that he didn't usually lie to people, but he'd lied to me. 'I told you when you signed that contract that I expected you to be playing in the First Division in three years, but you did it in one! Well done Mark, and I hope you do well at Leicester.'

Everything was positive, new and exciting that summer. The club arranged for me to stay in digs with a family until I got used to the area and found a place for myself. It was the sort of thing that used to happen a lot back then. The club would have a list of people who had put themselves forward as families who were prepared to have young or recently transferred players staying with them. They would provide a room and meals and be paid by the club. There were two other Leicester players, Paul Ramsey and Dave Rennie, staying in the same digs with me. The family consisted of a mum, a dad and their two daughters, one of whom was an absolute nightmare as far as I was concerned. She would come in and think nothing of taking the television remote control and switching channels, even though you might have been watching something. It was pretty clear it wasn't going to work out for me there, but I enjoyed being with Paul and Dave because we all got on and had a laugh together.

I settled in at the club pretty quickly and the rest of the players were good to me. Everything was very different to Port Vale. The facilities were better, the players were better, all the equipment you used for training was better. I loved Port Vale and will always be grateful to them, but it was simply the difference between a club in the fourth tier of the English professional game and one in the top tier. It really was a different world, but I was very much aware of the fact that I'd got my chance and gone there after only one season as a professional. I was a relative novice with a lot to learn, but I was determined to do just that. I was fortunate enough to have Gary Lineker and Alan Smith around at the club. They were not only very good at what they did, they were also willing to help me, and just watching the way they went about their business in matches was an education.

I got on well with Gary and he could see that I wanted to learn and improve all the time. He was just such a good goal scorer. His movement, awareness and instinct whenever there was a chance in and around goal was amazing. He was twenty-four years old when I arrived at the club in the summer of 1984 and had come up through the ranks, and was recognised as one of the best young strikers around. In my early days at Leicester I gave an interview to a local journalist who naturally asked me what my hopes were after joining the club from Port Vale. I told him I had been a leading scorer at Port Vale and although I knew I still had a lot to learn, I'd like to be the leading scorer at Leicester, because I believed you always had to aim high. The next day the headline was all about me wanting to be the leading scorer, and as we were getting ready for training Gary spoke to me.

'Saw the article, Brighty,' he said. 'Tell you what, you can be the second leading goal scorer!'

We both laughed, but at the same time I knew Gary was too good and too competitive to settle for anything other than being top goal scorer at the club. He had a very dry sense of humour, which I liked, and we just seemed to hit it off from the first day we met. I often used to sit next to him on the team bus and I'd ask him things about the game and about being a striker. He always had time for me and I know he wanted me to succeed in having a good career in the game.

From the start of my time with Leicester I knew I had to work hard; I always felt I was behind a lot of the other players in terms of their experience and knowhow. I would do extra sessions in the afternoon after training in order to improve my all-round game. I'd been told that hard work always gets its reward, and that wasn't a problem for me because I'd always worked hard at my game and in training.

I started the season in the first team alongside Gary as we lost 3–2 at home to Newcastle in the opening game of the season, and he got both of our goals. It was my first taste of the First Division, but I knew the months ahead were going to be about me getting used to being in and around the first team. I accepted the fact that with Alan and Gary taking the two main striker positions I was going to have to be patient and bide my time, which didn't bother me. I was part of the first-team squad and although I didn't start many games, I was often on the substitutes bench, and also scored twenty-eight goals in the reserves.

Domestically things went from bad to worse in my digs and I couldn't stand it any longer; I had to get out. One day I was getting my clothes dry-cleaned at a shop very close to the training ground and was moaning to Mary who ran the business about how I needed to find new digs until I bought myself a flat.

'It'll only be a matter of a couple of weeks,' I assured her, and then ended up spending months at her house. She was a really nice Irish lady with a husband, Len, and two sons, Paul and Dave, who were a similar age to me. They really made me feel comfortable and I loved living there, which probably accounted for the reason why I didn't exactly rush to move out. She used to cook lovely meals, and Fridays it was always something like steak, Mary saying it would help me play well the next day. She would always say grace before the meal, and the two boys would also chip in with their own comment, which used to wind her up every time.

'Yes, thank you, St Michael,' they would chorus, knowing Mary always bought the food from Marks & Spencer.

I did eventually move out and get my very own flat. Owning a property was a big thing for me, and it was also the first time in my entire life that I had lived entirely on my own. It was part of how things had changed for me in a relatively short period of time. Moving to Leicester had given me the opportunity to be part of a First Division club and to play at that level, and the summer of 1985 presented me with another opportunity when Gary moved to Everton for £800,000. He had ended the season as the First Division's joint top scorer with twenty-four goals, so it was no surprise that the league champions would want to add such a great goal scorer to their team. It was also no surprise that whoever replaced him in the Leicester team would have big boots to fill, and I was the player who was going to be asked to do just that.

Everyone associated with the club knew Gary's departure was going to be a big loss for the club in terms of what it meant to the team – losing someone who regularly contributed more than twenty goals in a season was a blow – but at the same time, it was a great opportunity for me. When he left, I suppose it was my chance to show what I could do. Gary also told me when he left that my big chance had arrived. We weren't the same type of player, but what the team would need was goals, and I hoped I would be able to provide them. So did Gordon Milne.

'It's your time,' he told me, and I knew he was right.

It was down to me to show I was up to the job. The first day of the season is always something you look forward to, and everyone associated with a club wants to know who they will be playing. When the fixtures came out, we saw that Leicester's first game of the 1985–86 season would be at home against the champions, Everton. Gary may have left the club but he was still going to be starting the season at Filbert Street, the ground he had called home for so many years. Like so many things that happen in football, you just couldn't make it up. The return of Leicester's favourite son. As if trying to replace Gary in the team wasn't hard enough, I now faced the prospect of people being able to draw direct comparisons during the ninety minutes we were going to be playing against each other. So, no pressure!

Pre-season went well for me and everything leading up to the first game of the season could not have been better. As you might expect, there was a lot of excitement and interest in Gary coming back to face his old club, and I think a lot of people were wondering how I would shape up to the task of replacing him in the team. There had been speculation when Gary went that Leicester would immediately go into the transfer market to try and replace him with a more experienced and proven striker, but Gordon had held off on doing that and wanted to see if I could step up. If I did, it would obviously save the club some money.

Filbert Street was packed on the day of the match, and it could not have gone better for Leicester, or for me. We won 3–1 and I scored two of the goals. The first was possibly one of the best of my career as I bent the ball around their keeper, Neville Southall, from the edge of the box with the outside of my right foot. It was a really sweet strike and at the end of the game I was absolutely delighted with how things had gone, and so was everyone at the club. The only disappointing thing about the game from my point of view was that it was never on *Match of the Day* because of some sort of industrial dispute that was going on, so there's no footage of it anywhere.

At that point the board were probably thinking they'd pulled off a major coup. They had sold Gary for £800,000 and at that point had only paid £33,333 for me. If I maintained the sort of form I displayed against Everton, they were laughing, even if they ended up having to pay the full £100,000 to Port Vale for me. The other effect the game had that day was to send expectations through the roof. Nobody should ever get carried away by one game, but it had been against the league champions, and I had scored two really good goals. You couldn't blame the supporters for being optimistic about what might happen in the coming season. Until the game against Everton they had only seen me start a few games, or come off the bench, but once there was the chance that I might be the player to replace Gary, they expected me to deliver something. I could understand that they were looking for me to provide goals and help the side do well, but just two wins in the first fourteen league games soon provided everyone with a dose of reality, including me.

The two goals I scored in the opening game didn't exactly prove to be a springboard for my goal scoring that season, or for my Leicester career. Things seemed to go from bad to worse. I did chip in with the odd goal, but I was never quite able to hit the heights of that first game and, as the season went on, my form began to suffer. I've always had inner belief and drive, but it's difficult to maintain that when you are not playing well. I became anxious in matches and every time I did something wrong on the pitch, I could hear the groans from the crowd. Some of the more experienced players in the team would tell me to keep working hard, and that was never a problem because I always did. They'd tell me to keep grafting, to tackle, to challenge, to win free kicks, to do everything I could to try and turn it around, because they knew how much I wanted to do well, but they also sensed the whole thing was beginning to turn against me.

Dave Richardson would put on extra sessions for me in the afternoons and always gave me encouragement, telling me that hard work would not go unrewarded. The trouble was, the harder I worked, the worse things seemed to get. I did score in an away game at the end of October against Tottenham when we won 3–1, but by then I'd already missed some opportunities in other games, and I think there was a general feeling among a lot of the fans that I wasn't going to be able to fill those big boots left by Gary.

9

Christmas Jeer

I was desperate to turn things around because I knew that the only way to get the fans back on my side was to start scoring goals. I'd had no problem scoring when I was at Port Vale, but that meant nothing to the Leicester supporters. I began to over-think what I was doing on the pitch. When you're playing well and scoring, everything seems to come naturally. You don't think, you just react and do things instinctively. I had started to hesitate whenever the ball came near me, I wanted to take an extra touch and, in that split second, an opposition player would tackle me or get in a block when I had a chance to score. I was desperate for a goal because I knew that as a striker you can play badly, poke one in right at the end of a game and all is forgiven, the fans are on your side and you end the match as a hero instead of the villain. Gordon Milne was still very good to me and very supportive. He spoke to me in his office a couple of times and told me to keep working, and that he still believed in me. He told me he was the one who had brought me to the club, and he'd done that for a reason, which was nice to hear, but I knew he needed to have a striker in the team who was going to contribute not only effort but, more importantly, goals.

When you are playing in a game your focus is on the match and what is happening on the pitch. Obviously, you're aware of the crowd and of the noise they generate. You can also pick up on the general tone of how they feel, the cheers, the groans, that sort of thing. I had become aware of the groans that sometimes came my way if I did something wrong with the ball during a game, but one day I also became aware of something else from a section of the crowd. It wasn't moans or groans, it was the sound of comments aimed in my direction, and they had little to do with the way I was playing, but a lot to do with the fact that I was black.

The comments were unmistakably racial, and it wasn't just me who heard them: some of the other lads in the team did as well. It didn't just happen once either, and news of it must have filtered through to the press because I was approached by a national tabloid who asked if I wanted to do an interview about what was going on. In fairness, it was a minority of the fans in a couple of sections of the ground but it was there nevertheless. I could hear it and the manager could hear it, and he also became aware that the press had asked me to talk about it. I went to see him and had a chat. Without actually talking about it directly he said he knew what a difficult time it was for me, but that unfortunately the sort of thing I was experiencing from the terrace happened in football. I wasn't the first and I wouldn't be the last. He advised me to keep working hard on the training ground and that everything would eventually come good for me.

'You'll get the goals, you'll get the performance, the crowd will turn and everyone will be fine with you,' he told me.

He also advised me not to talk about it to the press, and I didn't. I honestly don't think Gordon wanted to necessarily cover anything up, and he certainly didn't ask me to bury it. I think he was trying to protect me in a way. He knew I was under enough pressure already to try and provide goals, and I suspect he believed that putting myself in the national spotlight by going ahead and doing the article would have put even more pressure on me at a time when I just wanted to concentrate on my football and getting my game going again. Going public would add fuel to the fire.

Times were very different back then. Things that were accepted by players, black and white, would not be accepted by players in the Premier League today. If you were a white player having a bad time in the mid-1980s you might get stick from fans. If you were a black player having a bad time, you would get stick with some racial abuse thrown in for good measure. It was the way of the footballing world that I was playing in back then. I did think about doing the interview, but the other thing that concerned me was the lack of control over the headlines they might use and the way in which the article might be written. A tabloid is going to want the piece to be sensational and I didn't want to lose the effect of what I wanted to say. I was working really hard to turn things around, and I knew if that happened it would shut everyone up, but it wasn't exactly a pleasant time for me.

Apart from the racist element that emerged there was also another pretty unpleasant aspect to my not playing well and scoring goals, when some of the crowd decided to boo my name when it was announced on the PA system in home matches before a game. Now this sort of thing is bad enough if it happens in a packed stadium, but I was also playing some reserve games in midweek that season, and it happened in them. Just a few hundred people in Filbert Street to watch the reserves, my name is read out and some of the supporters start to boo. I could hear it as it echoed around the ground, and so could Phil when he came down to see me play in some of those games. I'd be lying if I said I just shrugged it off and ignored it.

Something like that has an effect no matter how far you try to put it to the back of your mind and get on with playing a football match. It wasn't funny, but in football there is very little that is not fair game when it comes to dressing-room humour. Robbie Kelly and Robbie Jones were two young players at Leicester during this time and, like everyone else at the club, they knew I was struggling to find my form. One day the two of them decided to give me a new nickname. Very soon I was no longer 'Brighty' when they spoke to me, but 'Serginho'. For those who don't know, Serginho was a Brazilian centre forward who played at the 1982 World Cup in Spain. He was big and lumbering, not at all the sort of forward normally associated with Brazil, and a lot of fans thought he was the reason they didn't win the World Cup that year. The two Robbies thought it was hilarious and, I have to admit, I did laugh when they started using the nickname for me. Humour like that can help you get through some difficult times at a football club, although it did get on my nerves a bit once and I asked them to stop using it.

'But Serge, why?' they laughed, and I ended up laughing with them.

The nickname wasn't just used by them. Very soon after they started using it, so did all the other lads, and it stuck. Gary McAllister had joined the club from Motherwell in the summer and we soon became good friends. I could see very quickly that he was an excellent midfield player and after Leicester he went on to prove just how good he was, in a long and distinguished career that included playing for Liverpool and Scotland. He was very supportive when I was going through my bad spell with Leicester and our friendship has carried on over the years. We speak to each other every now and then, and he will often start the conversation by asking, 'How you doing, Serge?'

I can't pretend that it was a particularly happy period for me professionally and, towards the end of the year, I got some news that, although not entirely unexpected, was still incredibly upsetting for Phil and me, when we were told that Nana Parton had died. She had been unwell for some time and was in a nursing home in Kidsgrove. Her daughters had told us about it and we visited her several times in the home, sitting with her, holding her hand and just talking. She was such a lovely lady, and we both knew how heartbroken she was when she was no longer well enough to look after us. She had desperately wanted to stay in touch with us when we went to the Davieses, but the authorities had decided that wasn't a good idea. I can only imagine how upsetting that might have been for her. You don't foster kids and then just forget about them when they no longer live with you.

I'm sure we remained part of her life, and she certainly remained part of ours. We saw her in later years and it was clear that having to let us go was really upsetting. One minute we were very much part of her home and her life, and then we were gone. The fostering system can often be a gut-wrenching experience for the kids involved, but it shouldn't be forgotten how tough it can be for the foster parents. They invest so much into the whole thing, not just physically, but also emotionally. She appeared when our lives were in disarray, when we were vulnerable and probably quite confused by what was going on around us. She gave us stability. She loved us and we loved her. When she passed away, it was very sad for Phil and me.

It obviously wasn't a great time for me as a player either but as bad as things were for me on the pitch, I think that whole period helped to spur me on in an effort to get my career back on track, and the one thing I couldn't be accused of was a lack of effort. If I hadn't played or been on the bench for the first team on a Saturday, I would go down to the ground on the Sunday morning to play head tennis with Paul Ramsey, and often it was against the two Robbies. It was fun but at the same time I always saw it as having a serious side, because it helped to improve my ball skills. Using your right foot, left foot and head in a small space and having to move and be agile at the same time definitely improved me.

Like Gary, Paul was another good friend and was one of the first players I got to know at the club, when we shared those digs. We'd have a laugh and a joke and he was always good company. Around Christmas that year we decided to go into town and do some late-night shopping. Leicester city centre was packed with people looking to buy stuff in the shops and there was a really nice feel to the place. As we were walking along the pavement, I heard a man's voice shout from the other side of the road.

'Bright!'

I looked across but couldn't see who was shouting, then I heard the same voice once again.

'You're never a First Division striker, you're shit!'

Paul started laughing, not because what the guy had shouted was funny, it was more a case of him trying to take the sting out of the situation, but it did bring home just what a lot of the fans might have been thinking about me, getting jeered at in the street when you're out Christmas shopping. Even Paul could see I might have a problem that was just not going to go away.

'You know sometimes, Brighty, no matter how hard you try, it just doesn't work out,' Paul told me. 'I think you're doing everything you can, but sometimes you need to move on.'

He wasn't the only player to think that. I also had a conversation with Bobby Smith, one of the older and more experienced players, and one of the older statesmen at the club, and he was very honest with me.

'I don't think it's going to happen for you here,' he said. 'The crowd are all over you, and I think you might need to get away. I think you've got it, but you might need a fresh start, somewhere you can relax and play your football.'

Being able to relax had certainly become a problem for me during one period in the season. I found myself unable to sleep at night. I'd wake up in the early hours of the morning and sit in a hanging basket chair I had which looked out onto the road below and the park on the other side of it. I would sit for hours sometimes, desperately hoping that I would begin to feel tired and want to go back to bed and sleep, but it would never happen. I knew my body needed rest and I was feeling exhausted when I had to go in for training each morning, but no matter how hard I trained, I could never seem to get the full night's sleep I wanted, despite feeling tired. I would doze off to sleep for a few minutes at a time in the afternoons, but not sleep at night. It began to concern me and I told the physio about it, and he told the club doctor who asked me to go in and see him. I explained the whole thing to the doctor, talked about my situation at the club and generally told him how I was feeling, and how a lack of sleep was making me exhausted. He opened a drawer in his desk and took out a mini flipchart. He handed it to me and asked me to read the question on the first page, if my answer to it was a 'yes' I should then flip the page over and answer the next question, and keep going until I came to a question where my answer would be 'no'. I read the first question, which asked if I was having trouble sleeping, and the answer to that was obviously 'yes', which meant I then moved on to the next question. There were about six questions in all, and then I found myself staring at the final page. This time there wasn't a question. Instead it was a clear statement:

'You are suffering from depression.' I couldn't believe what I'd just read.

'Come on, Doc,' I said. 'There's no way I've got depression, I just can't sleep at night.'

'No, Mark,' he told me. 'It's not just about the fact that you are finding it hard to sleep at night. All the things you've told me and all the answers you've given to the questions on that chart point to you having all the symptoms of someone with depression.'

What he said really knocked me back, but my immediate reaction was to deny it and claim there must be some other explanation. I just couldn't believe that was the cause of my sleepless nights, it had to be something else. He didn't sit across the desk from me and prescribe a cure, which was probably what I was hoping he would be able to do. The initial plan was for me to try relaxing a little more and to just sleep when I could. He was ready to spend more time with me in the future, but I thanked him and never did go back to see him, which wasn't his fault. I simply didn't want to make an issue of it. Of course, that was stupid really, but in order to understand my thinking, you have to realise how different things were in football back then. Having a physical injury was one thing, but something like depression was a mental thing, and to so many people in the game, admitting to something like that would have been seen as a weakness in a player. Managers, coaches, even other players would have looked on you as being a bit soft. Someone who wasn't tough enough and couldn't handle the pressure of being a professional footballer. As amazing as it might seem now, depression would not have been taken seriously by so many in the game back then. They would have told you to pull yourself together, get on with your life, stop moping around, dig in, keep playing football, because that was what you were paid for. There was no real awareness of depression and what it could do to you. It's really only in recent years that things have changed, and there is so much support and help out there now for players. Attitudes have changed, thank goodness, and the old 'pull your socks up, and get on with it' mentality has gone from the game.

I thought there would be some kind of stigma attached if others found out about what I had been told, and I thought that I needed to be careful. I was already struggling with my game and I didn't want any other issues making things worse for me. I trained hard and tried to get into a routine of relaxing more and not worrying about when I slept. If I came home from training and fancied a sleep for a few hours, but then didn't sleep too well at night, I tried not to get too stressed. Gradually I began to get a more normal sleep pattern, and I put the whole thing behind me. I never really admitted to myself that I had been depressed, but I suspect a qualified doctor had a much better idea of what he was talking about than I did. Had I been in that same position as a player now, I think things would have been very different for me with regards to the way I would have approached the situation I found myself in.

I think that perhaps one of the things that helped to resolve my sleeping problem was deciding that I had to draw a line under my time at Leicester. There was no point in kidding myself. I had to get away for the good of my career. The season had started so well for me with those two goals against Everton, but things just went downhill from there. Having stolen the show from Gary in that first game the contrast in our fortunes was pretty stark, and we still have a laugh about it now. He went on to score thirty-eight goals in fifty-two games for Everton, got a move to Barcelona, and also collected the Golden Boot at that year's World Cup in Mexico. I went on to struggle with my form and scored just six goals. The contrast in our playing fortunes could not have been greater, but I still thought I could be a success if I got away and kickstarted my career with a new club.

I had already begun to think seriously about doing just that, when we heard there was going to be a change of manager. Gordon Milne was moving upstairs at the club to become general manager, and they were going to bring in Bryan Hamilton, who had been at Wigan, as the new first-team manager. When I heard the news, I knew my days at Leicester were probably numbered. He and I had 'previous', as they say. I had played against Hamilton when he was player-manager at Tranmere and I was in the Port Vale team, a few years earlier. He'd made some comments during the game and I just had the feeling he didn't fancy me as a player.

I had a lot of respect for Gordon Milne and he'd had enough faith to sign me. During his time in charge of the team I suspect he felt that one day I would become the number nine he always thought I could be, but it never really happened. A manager can give you the chance, but then it's down to the player. I'd desperately wanted to repay his faith by scoring goals and helping the team do well, but sadly that never quite happened, and with Bryan Hamilton's arrival I just felt my days at the football club would be numbered.

I can't honestly say I liked his style of coaching or management, and I think it's probably fair to say that he wasn't too keen on me either. I got a real insight into the way he operated and what sort of manager he was on a pre-season tour of Sweden. I phoned home one day and picked up a message telling me that a very good friend of mine, who was also a footballer, had been badly injured in a car accident. His name was Trevor Brissett, and he'd started his career at Stoke but then had some time at Port Vale. At the time I received the message in the summer of 1986, he was playing for Macclesfield Town, who were then a non-league team. The message said that he was in a car with some of his teammates travelling to a pre-season game, when they were in a collision with another car. Trevor had broken his legs and arms and was in a terrible way. I went to see Bryan Hamilton and told him what had happened, explaining that Trevor was a good friend of mine, and I asked him if it would be OK for me to return home a bit early so that I could go and see him. I think we only had a couple of days left in Sweden anyway, but he just told me I couldn't go. I tried to explain just how bad the accident had been, but he still said no and that I'd be travelling back with everyone else when the tour was over. I was a bit taken aback by the way he refused to entertain the idea of me leaving early, and so were a few of the other boys when I told them, but if I'm honest, perhaps it was a bit naive of me to think he would have acted in any other way.

When I got back to England, I went to see Trevor in his hospital room, and it was a bit of a shock. He was lying on top of the bed in a spread-eagled position, both of his arms and legs were in plaster and the rest of his body was bandaged. He was in a terrible state and told me how he had to be cut free from the wreckage and had passed out because of the pain. Not surprisingly he was later told by doctors that there was no way he was going to play football again as a professional, but although he accepted that would be the case, he also became determined to get fit and well enough to step on a football field again and participate in a match. After a long period of recovery, he got his wish when he came on in an end-of-season game for the final few minutes of the match. He showed such bravery and determination to make it happen, and once he'd achieved what he set out to accomplish, he ended his career and went into coaching, which he did for about twenty years. Sadly, Trevor's story did not have a happy ending, and in 2010 he died having been diagnosed with cancer. It was a tragic way for his life to end and was devastating for his wife Sharon and their two daughters, Lauren and Morgan, and for everyone who had known him. We were young fit guys together and he'd come through something which could quite easily have killed him. To then hear that cancer had ended his life was not only a shock, but made me realise what a terrible illness it is, striking as it can anyone at any time in their lives.

Once we were back from Sweden everyone was looking forward to the start of the new season and our first game, which was a home match against Luton Town. Despite the fact that I didn't think the manager rated me, I did get picked for the opener, but as things turned out my season for Leicester began and ended in August. The next game I played in was at the end of that month in an away fixture with Wimbledon. I found myself out of the team but played in the reserves. Whether Bryan Hamilton fancied me or not as a player didn't matter. I was determined to train as well as I could and if there was no future for me at Leicester, then I had to make sure other clubs liked what they saw, even if it was in a reserve game.

When I was trying to establish myself at Port Vale and played in reserve games, the club had an experienced goal-keeper named Barry Siddall, who sometimes came and watched the matches and he had given me some very good advice.

'It doesn't matter who you're playing,' he told me once, 'there will always be someone in the stand watching who can influence your career, so always give your best.'

It was something which stuck with me, especially in the dark days when I was turning out in midweek games for the reserves in front of a few hundred people and getting booed, but I never gave anything less than 100 per cent, and that was also the case in training. One day we were doing some sprints and I slipped, which meant I had to struggle to get my momentum and pace back as I finished the run. As soon as I had, Bryan Hamilton was in my face asking what was wrong with me and implying that I was shirking. It was just about the worst thing he could have done, because there was no way that was the case. I was absolutely incensed and booted a cone towards him.

'Go fuck yourself,' I told him and walked back into the changing rooms.

Our physio, John McVey, was there and had seen what had happened. He came running over and told me to calm down.

'Mark, don't do this,' he said.

I was in no mood to listen to his advice, and as far as I was concerned what the manager had implied was out of order. I felt as though he had been chipping away at me for some time. I went and showered before walking out towards the car park. It was only then that I realised I didn't have my car at the training ground. It was in for a service and one of the other players had given me a lift in. There was no way I could lose face by turning around and walking back to wait for a lift home, so I just carried on walking, eyes focused on the road that led out of the ground, with cheers, laughter and a load of comments from the rest of the lads.

'Brighty, see you later!' they were shouting.

It was one of those classic moments where you are so angry and keen to make a stand that you just end up looking a bit ridiculous. Even I had to smile at how I must have looked. I ended up having to get a cab to my flat, and not long after I got home there was a call from the club. It was Gordon Milne's secretary and she said he wanted to see me. I told her that I had nothing to say, but eventually agreed to go in and see Gordon. When I arrived, he asked me to explain what had happened. We ended up having a good chat and he insisted he still believed in me as a player, and understood what a difficult period it was for me. He settled me down and I appreciated what he did, and the way he still thought I would go on and be successful. He was right, but it was a shame for him that he never saw that happen at Leicester. He'd had faith in me and had always tried to help, but that incident on the training pitch was really the beginning of the end of my time at Filbert Street.

10

Headline Writer's Dream

Barry Siddall was right, there were people watching in the stands when I was playing, and one of them was Brian Horton, who was the Hull City manager. He asked Leicester if he could talk to me about a possible move and I went along to see him. I liked him a lot and he certainly wanted to sign me, which was great because it showed he thought I could do a job for him and his club. He also said he believed he could help me improve as a player, which was something else that was nice to hear. The trouble was I just didn't fancy moving there. I didn't really want to move north. Some of the other lads had told me that if I got the chance to move, I should go south, and that was really what I wanted to do. Brian could see that I wasn't keen on a move to Hull and he was very good about it. Then he gave me some information about the position I was in at Leicester.

Agents were few and far between in those days, so players didn't have the sort of information about what was happening with their careers in the way that they do now. Brian was very honest with me and basically said that if I didn't want to sign for Hull, then I should still make sure that I got away from Leicester. He told me that the club didn't want to have to pay the last part of the money that would be due to Port Vale if I were to make fifty appearances for Leicester. The club had paid out that initial £33,333 fee set by the tribunal when they signed me, and after I had made more than twenty-five appearances, they'd had to pay another £33,333 to Port Vale, but Brian explained that they were not going to leave themselves liable to fork out another £33,333 payment. That, in effect, meant I wasn't going to be playing first-team football for them. It sounded as though they didn't think I was going to be able to cut it at the top level, and because of that a decision had been made about my future, or lack of it, at Leicester.

I thought it was really good of Brian to put me in the picture, and after speaking to him I knew exactly where I stood. I had to get away, but I wanted to make sure it would be the right club and the right manager for me. As much as I wanted to leave, I didn't want to make the mistake of moving for moving's sake. I was twenty-four years old. I wasn't a youngster, but in footballing terms I didn't have that many games under my belt as a professional. I didn't see my time at Leicester as a waste, because I'd continued my foot-balling education there and played in the top division, but it had become frustrating for me. I never lost my belief that I could do well and be a success, but my confidence had taken a knock and my form had suffered. Hull were not the only team interested in me. I was told that Walsall also wanted to talk to me, but they were in the Third Division, and having played in the First Division, I didn't want to slip that far down the leagues, so I decided to bide my time in the hope that something else would come along. Luckily for me, that's exactly what happened.

In November 1986 Steve Coppell was thirty-one years old and had been the manager of Crystal Palace for a little more than two years. As a player he had been a superb winger for Manchester United and England, before a knee injury led to him having to retire at the age of twenty-eight. The Palace chairman, Ron Noades, surprised many people in the game when he decided to give the untried Coppell the chance to manage the club. They were in the Second Division and had finished fifth the previous season. Both Coppell and the club were ambitious, and they apparently wanted to sign me. I have to admit that when I was told by Leicester that Steve Coppell wanted to meet me, I was excited. I had a lot of respect for him as a player and he had been a real star name in the game. He was still so young it seemed a bit strange that he was now a manager, and this was his third season in charge of Palace. He'd already done a good job with them and there were quite a few people that season who had tipped them as possible promotion candidates. I didn't know anything about them as a club, or even who played for them, but the idea that they were interested certainly lifted my spirits, even before I had met Steve Coppell.

I was told by the club that Palace had been given permission to talk to me, and that Steve Coppell wanted to meet me at Watford Gap services on the M1. He was coming up from the south and I was told to cross the bridge that ran across the motorway at 2 p.m. the next day, and he would be waiting for me. Sure enough, the next day I did as I had been instructed and as I came down the stairs and into the car park, there was Steve Coppell waiting for me.

'Do you want a cup of tea?' he asked.

I said yes and a few minutes later we were sitting at a table by the window having a chat. I have to admit it did feel a little strange sitting opposite someone I had only ever seen on the television playing in big games for United and England, and I was a bit star struck, but he was very easy to talk to and it soon became clear that he had decided I was the player he wanted as his centre forward at Crystal Palace. It was music to my ears in so many ways, but I didn't want to get carried away by it all. I was positive in my own mind that I had to make the right decision for my career. Steve laid out his plans for the team really clearly for me and said that he thought Palace would be the right club for me. He was very honest and said that he was new to the job of being a manager and was still learning, but I could tell he had definite ideas about what he wanted to do as a manager and how he wanted his team to play. He told me that he knew it would be a big move in terms of my lifestyle, but assured me that as a northerner himself, he really liked the area and London. He also told me that he had watched me play in a reserve game and been amazed that I had been booed by my own supporters before I'd kicked a ball.

'Takes some doing, that!' he joked in his gruff voice.

He said he just couldn't understand why they did it, and I knew he realised just how bad things were for me at Leicester.

It felt so good to be talking to someone with his reputation and standing in the game, hearing him say he believed I was right for Palace. Then he said something that really surprised me. He told me he had a young striker at the club who had been signed from non-league football.

'He's the most exciting player I've worked with,' he told me. 'I think you could really help him on the pitch and I think the two of you could work well together. The other thing is, if you hit it off and are successful, the two of you will be a headline writer's dream. His name is Ian Wright. They'll have a field day with the Wright and Bright thing.'

I suddenly thought, Steve Coppell is a guy who has played with great players at Manchester United and with England. If he thinks this young striker is that good, then he must be something pretty special. At the end of our meeting he asked if I was interested in joining Palace, and I told him I was. We shook hands and he told me they were playing a League Cup game at Nottingham Forest the next week and suggested I go to the match and have a look at the team for myself. When I got in my car to travel back to Leicester, I felt excited. I even stopped and phoned Phil to tell him what had happened and how I felt about the whole idea of moving down to London to play for Palace.

I went to the game the next week and watched from the stands as Forest won the game 1–0 with a goal from Nigel Clough. Steve called me on the phone the next day and asked me what I thought. I told him I liked the look of the team, but also asked him where he thought I was going to fit in, because I didn't want to sign and then have to be content with sitting on the subs bench. Ian Wright had played up front with Andy Gray, the two of them looked good as a partnership: they terrorised the Forest defence and Andy had looked really sharp.

'You'll play up front with Ian,' he assured me. 'He doesn't know it yet, but I'm going to play Andy in central midfield. He's got a good range of passes, he's tough, he can tackle, he's really strong and he's got a great engine. I want a big number nine, who is mobile and who can help Wrighty. You can help him, you can guide him on the pitch.'

I went to Leicester with less than thirty first-team games to my name as a professional footballer, and when I spoke to Steve, I had still only played seventy-odd matches in total, but I did feel I had learned a lot about what I should do on the pitch and how I should conduct myself as a professional. It was nice to hear Steve talking the way he did and having enough faith in my ability to be the right person for the job he had in mind. I'd already thought about the move and what it might mean for me. Having spoken to him again I was convinced it would be the right club for me.

It was all very exciting stuff and things moved quickly once I had told him that I wanted to sign for Palace. I had to travel down to London for my medical before signing, and went along to it with the Palace physio, Dave West. I couldn't have been happier as I went in to be examined by the doctor who was carrying out the medical, but a little while later all the elation I had felt suddenly disappeared when he came out to speak to us.

'I can't pass you medically fit,' he said.

I couldn't believe what I was hearing. All my hopes of a fresh start were suddenly being shattered by what he was telling us. He said I had osteitis pubis, which means that the pubis bone in the pelvis had begun to erode and it could mean that I might not be able to play at some stage in the future. I couldn't believe there was a problem. I hardly ever missed training and I knew I was one of the fittest players at Leicester, but the specialist insisted that the X-rays had shown there was a problem. As I travelled back in a cab to the Palace ground I was in a bit of a daze, but then I began to get angry. My dream move could be in tatters. Being told I hadn't passed the medical was serious but, as is the case so often in football, some of the darkest moments can be defused by humour.

'I hear we've signed a crock,' were the first words Steve said to me as I walked through the door. He was sitting in his office with Ron Noades, and both of them were laughing.

'I'm not having it,' I told them. 'You phone the physio at Leicester and he'll tell you, I don't miss training, I train every day, there's never been anything wrong with me. I don't have a medical problem.'

Steve said they were going to put me in a hotel overnight and they were going to discuss what could be done about the situation I found myself in. I was annoyed and frustrated by what had happened, and that night I couldn't help thinking that when I saw Steve the next morning, he was going to tell me the move was off because they couldn't risk signing me. I phoned John McVey, the Leicester physio, to tell him what had happened and he said he'd already spoken to

Palace about me. He'd told them that he would back me against their fittest player any day of the week. He'd said that I was in the top two or three at Leicester when it came to long runs and sprints, and that there had never been a medical issue with me.

I went to Palace's ground, Selhurst Park, the following morning to see what Steve and Ron had decided. The good news was that they said the deal wasn't off; the bad news was that they wanted to sign me on a temporary three-month deal so that they could have a look at me and make sure there was nothing wrong with my fitness. My first thought was that I didn't want to do it. I didn't want to put myself in a position where I signed for three months and then the deal was called off, leaving me to head back to Leicester with my tail between my legs, but when they explained things further, I began to see it from their point of view. They had to be cautious and couldn't just go ahead with the transfer after the medical I'd had flagged up a potential problem. Steve said that if I was as fit as I claimed, I had nothing to lose, and I agreed with him. Having made the decision, I began to feel much better about the whole situation. I knew I was fit and I had no doubts about my ability to train or play games.

I went back up to Leicester to get some clothes and other stuff, Palace put me in a hotel in the Croydon area and, on 13 November 1986, I signed a temporary three-month contract. Two days later I made my Palace debut in a 3–3 home draw with Ipswich. I scored our first goal and Ian got a dramatic late equaliser to earn us a point. I was off and running in the best possible way, and it felt good.

In fact, everything about being at Crystal Palace felt good to me. I believed I was at the right club at the right time in my career. The only possible cloud on the horizon was the decision that had to be made about offering me a permanent contract. I very quickly felt part of everything that was going on at the club and there was a good group of players there. It was very mixed, young players, older players, black and white players, and there were a lot of laughs. I got some stick right from the start because Dave West had devised a specific programme for me that meant that I couldn't put any stress on the core area of my body because of what the specialist had said at my medical. It meant I was excused from doing sit-ups and press-ups, which was something Steve Coppell always got the players to do in training. It was fifty press-ups and a hundred sit-ups at the end of every session. He always used to say, if you've got a strong gut, you've got a strong body, but while the other players were on the grass doing sit-ups at our training ground in Mitcham at the end of the morning, I would be heading for the changing rooms.

'Brighty, where're you going?' they shouted the first time I did it.

'Sorry, lads, Dave West and the manager say I can't join in,' I said, laughing as I waved at them and kept walking. They would have a go at me every time, and every time I would wind them up by saying the same thing.

Despite what had been said at the medical I never had any problems and a matter of weeks after I put pen to paper on the temporary contract Steve had a word and assured me that there were no problems and they were going to sign me, which was obviously a relief. Three months and five goals after first pulling on a Palace shirt I officially signed a permanent contract that was to run until the summer of 1989, and the club handed over £75,000 to Leicester as my transfer fee. It was a lot for Ron Noades and the club to invest in me at the time, but what I didn't know was the full story of how I had come to the attention of Palace. I knew Steve had seen me play in the reserves for Leicester, but it was Ron who had watched me a couple of years earlier when I was at Port Vale. He had gone to watch a match at Southend on a Monday night in March 1984. I was a substitute, but came on and scored a goal, hit a post and generally did well as we won the match 2–1. Ron was impressed with my performance and particularly with the way I held the ball up. He made a note in his programme against my name and remembered me when Palace began to look for a forward who could play alongside Ian. Once again, Barry Siddall's theory proved to be spot on.

My money went from the £300 a week I was earning at Leicester to £400 at Palace, and for the final year of the contract I signed, the figure increased to £450 a week, but I was now living in London, and believe me, there was a world of difference, in terms of living costs, compared to Leicester. In fact, there was a world of difference full stop, and I loved it. I wasn't exactly the wide-eyed northerner, but I enjoyed being in London. I had visited before, but hadn't spent a lot of time in the capital, so being right in the middle of it all was exciting for me.

I very quickly became friendly with Ian Wright, Andy Gray and Tony Finnigan. We were all young black guys of a similar age, and we would often go out as a group. They used to laugh at my northern accent because the three of them were very much south Londoners. They also loved the fact that I was so blown away by being in London, and it was very different for me. Often it was little things that surprised me and the three of them found it hilarious. One night we'd all been out to a club in London and were just about to go across Westminster Bridge. Andy was driving and I suddenly shouted from the back seat.

'Stop the car!' I screamed.

'What's wrong?' said Andy, looking puzzled.

'Big Ben,' I said. 'I want to get out and have a look.'

'Shut up, you northerner,' said Andy, and the three of them were laughing their heads off at me, and I had to laugh as well because I could see how funny my little outburst must have seemed.

They couldn't believe I was that impressed by seeing Big Ben, but I honestly was. They'd grown up in London and seeing all of the capital's sights meant nothing to them, but for me it was special. These were places I had only ever seen on TV or in photographs. London was so big compared to anywhere else I had ever lived, and there was just so much to see and do, including getting myself sorted out with a place to live. After putting me in a hotel, I moved into a flat the club had in Purley, but I wanted to buy my own place. I put my flat in Leicester up for sale and it went on the market for around £19,000. Tony offered to show me around some areas of London where he thought I could buy property that would also provide a sound investment. He tried to convince me to buy different places in Clapham and Battersea, saying they were guaranteed to increase in value. He proved to be spot on with his advice, but at the time they all seemed too expensive and I didn't feel comfortable in stretching myself financially. In the end I paid £65,000 for a flat in Battersea, south London, which I thought was an enormous amount, and so did my brother Phil when I told him. In fact, I think he thought I had gone mad, but I quickly realised how different London was, and how much my life was going to change.

I don't think I'm overstating things by saying that the move to Crystal Palace changed the direction of my life forever. I might not have been aware of it at the time, but I can now see that's exactly what happened. It changed me in so many positive ways. It broadened my education, I mixed with more black people than I had ever done before, London was so much more multicultural than anything I had ever experienced, and I immediately loved it and felt very much at home. There was always a lot going on and, perhaps most important of all, I grew in confidence as a player and as a person. It was great being somewhere that I was liked. The fans were really good to me and very soon after moving down, I began to feel much more like the person I was at Port Vale. When I was there, I was on the up, I was driven, I had the bit between my teeth and I was very determined. When I went to Leicester I was still on the up and driven, I learned a lot in that first season with them and I enjoyed it, but the second season was different. That was when the pressure was on and I knew I needed to keep scoring to stay in the team. It didn't work for me and it wasn't the greatest of times, so getting the move to Palace came at just the right moment. I felt better about myself, my confidence returned, I was liked by the fans instead of getting booed by my own supporters, and it did wonders for my self-belief. Even in the dark times at Leicester, I still believed I had the ability to be a good striker who could score goals, and when I made the move to Palace, I began to show that was true. It was a relief; everything in my career began to look positive once again.

11

Angry and Hungry

S teve Coppell had a very clear idea about the type of team he wanted to create at Palace. When I joined the club that team was still a work-in-progress, but it was clear he wanted to change things to suit his plan. It wasn't going to happen overnight, but he was determined that it was going to happen. He knew he couldn't make wholesale changes all at once, and that things would have to be done gradually. That was why signing the right kind of players was going to be the key factor in making sure his plan worked, and that Palace got what they wanted. Promotion.

I've already mentioned the fact that there was a real mixture of players in the squad I joined in November 1986. There were quite a few players who were around my age, like Andy, Ian, Tony and Gary O'Reilly, who joined the club not long after me; then there were some younger players like John Salako coming through; but there were also some older players, such as goalkeeper George Wood, who was thirty-four, and Palace's legendary defender, Jim Cannon, who was thirty-three. Steve had started the process of moving some players on and getting in others to take the club forward, and there was a common theme to the sort of players he wanted. He wanted them to be angry and hungry. By that I mean that he wanted players who had a point to prove, who had maybe been slapped in the face in football-ing terms, but who had ability, who were athletic, and who were young enough to stay around as the club moved forward. I think I fitted that profile, so did Gary O'Reilly and so did Alan Pardew when he came from Yeovil Town, who were a non-league club at the time. Ian Wright also fitted the category and his story was perhaps the most remarkable of anyone who was in the first team at the time.

He had come straight from playing for Ten-Em-Bee, who were a Sunday league team in south London, and he was desperate to succeed as a professional footballer, just as I had been. Palace had given him a trial in the summer of 1985 and Steve Coppell was so impressed by his raw talent that he and Ron Noades decided to offer him a contract. Ian's story is amazing really: he walked in the gates at Palace with a pair of boots in his hands, went on to have an amazing career and ended up as an international player, and I have nothing but admiration for him and what he went on to achieve. A lot of young people today will know Ian Wright, and if they didn't actually see him play, they will still know how highly he was rated, but they probably won't know how hard he worked to make sure he had the career he did. I'm just pleased I had the opportunity to not only play alongside him, but also to help him develop as a player.

The more I saw of him in training and the more I played with him in matches, the more I could see why Steve felt he had a special player. I could also see why he'd wanted someone like me to play up front with him. We immediately got on as people, but it wasn't a case of us instantly forming a great playing partnership as strikers. Things like that don't just happen overnight: you have to put a lot of hard work in and hope that it eventually pays off. The great thing was that both of us wanted to work hard. Ian was the sort of player who always wanted to learn and improve his game, and so did I. We did a lot of work on the training ground on playing as a striking partnership, and we also talked a lot about how we should approach matches, and about each other's game. I'm sure some of what we did was instinctive, but there was no doubt that things like taking up a certain position when your partner has the ball, and knowing which runs to make and when to make them, were all about the work you put in during training each week. Ian was twenty-three at the time, about seventeen months younger than me. He trusted me and believed in me. He would often look across the pitch at me, seeking approval when he'd done something good, and I constantly tried to nurture and encourage him. If things went right, I would heap praise on him, but if he got something wrong, I would tell him. Once he had grasped a lot of the stuff we worked on, it was just a case of refining our play together, and we got better as a result.

I enjoyed the rest of my first season, not just because I was playing regularly and felt part of the whole set-up, but because the team played pretty well and were in with a chance of the play-offs right up to the last game of the season. Any chance we had of doing that came to an end in our last game of the season when we were beaten 3–0 at Hull.

Ian finished top scorer for us in the league that season, but between us we hadn't managed to reach the twenty mark. I sat next to Ian on the bus as we travelled back from Hull and we both decided that we would have to do better the next season. We had to improve our goal tally, as individuals and as a pair. Nearly all teams played with two men up front at that time, and the pairing was often crucial to how their team performed and the level of success they achieved. We would both look at some of the really good partnerships, like Ian Rush and Kenny Dalglish, Graeme Sharp and Andy Gray, Tony Cascarino and Teddy Sheringham, see how they worked and what they did right and wrong. The two of us constantly wanted to learn and get better. If we did that, we knew we would start to score more goals, and I was determined to hit the ground running at the start of my first full season.

That summer was my first experience of a pre-season with Crystal Palace, and I really enjoyed it. It was also apparent that the changes Steve Coppell wanted to make to the squad were beginning to take shape with the arrival of midfielders Geoff Thomas from Crewe and Neil Redfearn from Doncaster. One of Steve's big things as part of our pre-season preparations was a ten-day trip to Sweden where we played about five games, and worked really hard on our fitness in the training sessions when we weren't playing. Going away as a group for a trip like that also helped build the kind of squad unity and togetherness that you need when you're going into a new season. Steve Coppell wasn't the sort of manager who treated his players like kids: you were adults as far as he was concerned and I found it very refreshing. He trusted us and if you, as a player, repaid that trust, then everything was fine. He had no problem with us going out to have a couple of beers after a game, but insisted that it only happen if we all went out. It was a group thing, we all either went out or we all stayed in. He would tell us what time he wanted us back, and we all respected that. None of us tried to take advantage and stay out longer than he'd said. We all worked hard and then enjoyed our time off, and we did it together. The atmosphere and the respect the players had for the manager struck me as being very different to the last time I had been in Sweden. That had been with Leicester a year earlier, when Bryan Hamilton wouldn't let me travel back to see Trevor Brissett in hospital after his horrendous car accident.

I had only been at Palace for about eight months but knew I liked Steve Coppell's management style. He wasn't that much older than the players he was in charge of, but everyone respected him and he was tactically very aware. He treated me and the other players the way we liked being treated, and when he spoke to you about football, or any other subject, he made sense. When you are a manager, no matter how many coaching courses you go on, there is nothing that can prepare you for what happens in the job every day. A manager has to deal with so many things, but Steve always seemed in control, even though he admitted when I had my first chat with him that he was still learning about the job, learning how to be a manager. He was honest and open with his players, and over the years that I played for him at Palace that never changed.

He was always the boss, but at the same time I had never seen players laugh and joke with a manager the way some of the Palace lads did, and Steve loved it. I just wasn't used to it, but it was often very funny. Players never really misbehaved, so there was never any need for big fines to be handed out, but Steve would fine you for something like being late when the coach was about to leave from the training ground for an away match. It was nothing too serious, he would simply say you were fined and then it was up to the player to decide just how much he ought to pay, depending on what had happened. It was usually no more than £5, or maybe £10. One day I got stuck in traffic on the way to the training ground and after I parked my car and ran to the waiting bus, there was Steve sitting in the front seat waiting to welcome me on board.

'Brighty, you're late,' he said with a deadpan expression.

'Sorry, boss,' I said.

'You'll have to pay a fine,' he added.

I took a £5 note out of my pocket and went to hand it over. Steve didn't look too impressed, so I put it back and produced £10 instead. He took the money with a smile on his face and nodded, but I wasn't the only player late that day and pretty soon after I arrived, Alan Pardew's car came screeching to a halt. Pards came running over to the coach and saw Steve waiting for him.

'Sorry, boss, traffic,' he said, getting a stony-faced look from Steve.

'Brighty was late as well, and he's just paid me his fine,' Steve informed him.

Pards could see he needed to hand over some cash and took £10 out, but Steve just looked at him as if he was really disappointed. Pards reached into his pocket and produced a £20 note, which he duly handed over, and then headed to the back of the coach to speak to me.

'You got a fine for being late as well,' he said. 'How much?'

'Ten pounds,' I told him.

'What! I don't believe it, he's just done me with that look of his and I handed over twenty pounds,' he said, shaking his head and laughing at the same time.

Steve had a good rapport with all the players who were at the club during the time I was with Palace, but I honestly think he loved the banter he had with Andy Gray. Andy was a real character, and along with Ian Wright and Tony Finnigan was one of the players I became friendly with as soon as I came down from Leicester. He was a very good player and a real streetwise south Londoner, who always had little enterprises going on. He would buy and sell stuff all the time.

'Got a nice pair of shoes for you in the car, boss,' he'd say, and then try to sell them to Steve.

Andy was a natural athlete with a great build. One day after training Steve did his usual thing of telling everyone they had to do push-ups and sit-ups, but Andy just walked back to the changing rooms.

'Andy, come on, sit-ups,' shouted Steve.

Andy turned around, lifted up his top and showed everyone his perfect six-pack.

'I don't think I need to, do you?' he shouted back.

We all laughed and Steve was laughing along with us, but I suspect only Andy could have got away with something like that. He was a one-off and seemed to be able to get away with things that other players would never dream of doing. He called me once on the morning of a home match and said there was something wrong with his car and asked if I could give him a lift to the ground. Andy was a pretty laid-back sort of character and I knew that punctuality was not the sort of thing that really bothered him too much. He also knew I was completely the opposite in that respect, I hated being late, so I warned him that if he wasn't ready when I got there, I would just drive off without him. As soon as I got to his house Andy appeared at the door. I was impressed and surprised, but then I saw what he had in his hands: he was holding a McDonald's bag in one and a milkshake in the other. I couldn't believe my eyes.

'Andy, what are you doing?' I asked him.

'I'm starving, I didn't have anything to eat this morning,' he told me, as if having a McDonald's, fries and a shake was perfectly normal a few hours before he was due to go out and play a league game for Palace.

'Are you mad?' I said. 'You're a professional footballer and you're eating junk food. You should be ashamed of yourself. I don't know how you're going to be able to run around and play after that lot.'

Andy just smiled and told me to relax as he tucked into his burger, pulled out some fries with his other hand and then washed the whole lot down with his milkshake. I just shook my head and that made him enjoy the whole situation even more, because he was getting a reaction from me and he loved it. We got to the ground, changed, did our stretches and went out for our warm-up before the game. Halfway through the first half, Andy hit a magnificent shot and scored for us. As he ran back to the halfway line after getting everyone's congratulations, he looked across at me, tapped his stomach with his right hand and mouthed 'Macky D!' to me, with a big wide grin on his face. I just had to laugh along with him. What else was I supposed to do? It was typical Andy Gray.

The boss loved him as a player and he loved his personality, which was why it was a bit of a shock when he was sold to Aston Villa a few months into the season for £150,000. It was a great move for Andy because although Villa had been relegated and were in the Second Division like Palace, they were a very big club, with the resources to push for promotion and an immediate return to the First Division. We were still building towards making a challenge for promotion and he obviously felt the time was right for him to move.

The club used the money to bring in Glenn Pennyfather from Southend and in the New Year goalkeeper Perry Suckling joined from Manchester City, a clear sign that Steve Coppell was continuing to change the squad, with George Wood moving on to Cardiff. We were doing well in the league and we were up there battling for a possible promotion place. On a personal level, I was having a great season, with both Ian and myself getting goals. It was really satisfying, because we'd both worked very hard on the partnership and had been determined to do better than we had done in the previous season, but I don't think either of us could have imagined we would do quite as well as we did. I ended the season as top scorer with twenty-five league goals and another in the League Cup, while Ian got twenty in the league and three in the League Cup.

One of our local south London rivals, Millwall, were also doing well that season and they had a pretty lethal strike partnership in Teddy Sheringham and Tony Cascarino. By the time the final game of the season arrived, Millwall had already ensured that they were going to be promoted as champions, but we had a chance of claiming a play-off place. We needed to win our home game with Manchester City and hope that Millwall would do us a favour by winning their home game against Blackburn Rovers, who were also in with a shout of claiming a play-off spot. We beat City 2–0, but unfortunately Millwall must have been celebrating all that week after making sure of promotion and they ended up getting beaten 4–1 at home by Rovers, which meant Blackburn gained the final play-off place. It was a big disappointment, but we knew just how close we were and there was a determination from the manager and the squad to make sure we didn't miss out like that again.

The summer of 1988 signalled the end of an era in many ways when Jim Cannon left Palace, having earned legendary status at the club after fifteen years as a player. I know that Ian had a tough time with Jim, the atmosphere between them wasn't good, and there had been a training ground bust-up. It wasn't good, you can't dress it up any other way, but I never had a problem with him as he treated me differently. The manager had told me at one stage to be patient because he was going to change things, and from the moment I arrived that had been happening. I think that Jim going was the last part of him moving on the old guard. He replaced him with Jeff Hopkins from Fulham, and another departure was Tony Finnigan. He wanted the chance of regular first-team football, Blackburn offered it, and he was off. It was sad to see him leave the club, but he had to think about his career. Tony was such a Londoner, it was hard to think of him living in the north, but that's exactly the nature of football. As a player you sometimes get to a point in your career where you need to leave, need to get a fresh start, just as I had when I moved from Leicester to Palace.

I think it was clear that Steve wanted to try and make sure we gave promotion a real go. He brought in midfielder Dave Madden at the start of the season and by the turn of the year Alex Dyer had joined from Hull, replacing Neil Redfearn, who went to Watford, and winger Eddie McGoldrick came to the club from Northampton. Steve also got a new assistant manager when Ian Evans left to take over at Swansea and Stan Ternent replaced him.

We stayed in and around the play-off places as the crucial final weeks approached and in April put together a really good run of results, winning six matches to help us move up to fourth in the table, and there was a genuine feeling that we might be able to get automatic promotion. Going into the final match we were third in the league. If we were going to gain an automatic spot, we needed to beat Birmingham at home by a margin of five goals, and Manchester City had to lose at Bradford. We beat Birmingham 4–1 and City drew their game at Bradford. We finished third, out of the automatic promotion places, but with a chance of going up through the play-offs. It had been a massive effort from everyone, but there was a lot of disappointment as well, because we'd gone so close to going straight up. The format of the play-offs had changed, and instead of the fourth from bottom team in the First Division being involved, it was a straight fight between four teams from the Second to see who would go up with champions Chelsea and Manchester City. It meant that having finished third we would play Swindon, who had finished sixth, while in the other semi-final, fourth-placed Watford met fifth-placed Blackburn.

We'd played forty-six games in the league and it had been a long, hard season. If we were going to get promotion by winning the play-offs it meant we would have to play four more matches, and the final game would not be until the beginning of June. The manager called us all together for a meeting and said that if we were the third best team in the league we had to go out and prove it in the play-offs, then he surprised us all by telling us we would be doing some running sessions up and down hills in preparation for the games we faced. None of us could really believe it. Then he gave us his reason.

'We're going to be fitter, stronger and mentally tougher than any of the other teams,' he said.

The running certainly helped us and we did feel we were in better shape than any of the other three teams, and we also had a good group mentality. We were hungry for success and the chance to play against the best teams in England by getting promoted. We had a strong bond, there was no hierarchy, we all felt equal and we all wanted to help each other. Steve had always said to us that any team was only as strong as its weakest link. The great thing about the team was that when you looked around the dressing room, you didn't really feel as though there were any weak links, and when you stepped out onto the pitch there was a definite feeling that we were all in it together, that you could rely on your teammates.

The first leg of the semi-final was at Swindon on a Sunday afternoon. As you might imagine, the game was a pretty tense affair, and even though we knew we were a better team than them, we never really produced the kind of form we were capable of, and we ended up losing 1–0 after Jeff Hopkins scored an own goal. Losing was really disappointing and we were more determined than ever to make sure we put things right when we got them back to Selhurst Park, and what happened after the first game gave us even more motivation.

As we walked down the tunnel one of their players shouted at Wrighty. It was nasty and it was racist, everybody heard it and, quite naturally, Ian reacted to it. If it hadn't been for some of us holding him back, I think he would have ripped the guy's head off. Steve Coppell and some of the other players managed to get him back to the dressing room, but Ian was raging and just couldn't calm down. He still wanted to go across to their changing room and drag the player out, but when he realised that wasn't going to happen, he picked up a fire extinguisher and threw it at the door. He was steaming and the rest of us were in no mood to calm down either. What had been said was not only completely out of order, the words had been delivered with real nastiness. It wasn't something that had been shouted in the heat of the moment, or to wind Wrighty up, it was a nasty racist comment spoken from the heart.

We were all disappointed with the result, but knew we were more than capable of winning the second leg and getting enough goals to go through. We also had the added motivation of what had happened in the tunnel, and without letting the incident get in the way of putting on the performance we needed, all of us knew if the chance came during the match, we would exact a bit of retribution on the player who'd had a go at Ian. The second leg took place three days after the first game, Selhurst Park was jumping and our fans were amazing. We won 2–0 to go through to the play-off final. I scored one of the goals and happily Ian got the other. Job done, and the player who made those comments didn't exactly have a great time. We didn't go out of our way to target him, but let's just say that we took any opportunity we got to make his life a misery that night. Every time he was tackled he really felt it, and any chance we had to physically get to him, we did, whether he had the ball or not. Winning was the most important thing, but making sure he had a nightmare of a game was a bonus for all of us.

Blackburn came through the other semi-final against Watford and a week after beating Swindon, we travelled north to play them in the first leg. When we'd played them away in the league that season, we had scored four goals. The trouble was, they scored five and we lost the match. It wasn't the greatest defensive performance, but we were confident of being able to make sure the same thing didn't happen again. How wrong we were. We didn't play at all well and Howard Gayle scored twice to put us 2–0 down at half-time; we were lucky it wasn't worse. We just couldn't seem to get our game together and Blackburn had the upper hand, but in the second half Eddie McGoldrick knocked the ball in from close range and we were right back in it. From feeling flat and dejected we suddenly got a lift and renewed hope. All we had to do was hold on, because we were confident a one-goal deficit could be overcome back at Selhurst, but the mood changed dramatically when their veteran striker, Simon Garner, got a third goal for them. It was a sickening blow. We hadn't played well and deserved to get beaten, but that didn't stop us all from feeling frustrated and angry in the dressing room after the game. We all knew we were within touching distance of the First Division, the top flight, the promised land of football in England, and we'd just gone and made a complete mess of things. There was a lot of shouting and finger-pointing in our dressing room after the match, there were arguments breaking out all over the place and it took a while before Steve Coppell could calm things down. The good thing was that we had the chance to put things right very quickly, because the second leg was going to be played three days later.

As bad as the atmosphere had been immediately after the game, we all slowly began to calm down a bit on the coach journey home. The anger that we'd all felt started to subside and when we began to think about the return leg, there was a feeling that it wasn't over and that we could come back from the bad result we'd got at Blackburn. Instead of the arguments and disappointment, we were soon geeing each other up, saying that we could do it in the second leg, that we were a better team than them and how we needed to go out and prove it.

Once again, the atmosphere at Selhurst Park for the return leg was incredible. It was even better than it had been against Swindon, the place was packed and the noise was deafening. Ian sent the fans wild with a goal in the first half that reduced the deficit and then a couple of minutes into the second half we were awarded a penalty. It was a big moment for us and an even bigger one for Dave Madden as he stepped up to take it. You could feel the tension around the ground, but Dave didn't let it affect him and calmly slotted it home with his right foot. With most of the second half still to play we were on level terms, and it started to look as though we would be able to go on and win it, but after ninety minutes we were still level and we went into extra-time. It was nail-biting stuff. Obviously both teams wanted to win it but, at the same time, the longer a game like that goes on the more conscious you are of not wanting to make a silly mistake. There were just a few minutes left in the second period of extra-time when Eddie McGoldrick somehow managed to cross the ball from the right and Ian got between two of their defenders to head it into the far corner of the goal. The crowd went mad and some of them ran onto the pitch. The match wasn't over, there were still a couple of minutes left to play, but both teams knew the goal had won it and there was no coming back for Blackburn.

When the final whistle blew the fans streamed onto the pitch once more and we were mobbed by them. They were amazing scenes and it was a fantastic feeling to be part of it all. After coming so close the season before and then missing out on automatic promotion we had battled our way through the play-offs and come from behind to make it into the First Division. All the players had dreamed of playing against the top teams, of going to places like Old Trafford, Anfield and Highbury. I'd had a taste of it at Leicester and even though it hadn't worked out for me, I still knew I could do it at the top level. I was better equipped to play in the First Division than I had been before, and I knew that Ian and I could do well as a partnership playing at a higher level. I also knew that getting promotion was a dream come true for him. In four years, he'd gone from playing Sunday football in a local south London league to being a First Division footballer. It really was amazing.

The celebrations after the game were crazy. There were fans everywhere and I found myself in the directors' box with Wrighty doing a live radio interview with Jonathan Pearce for Capital Gold, trying to make ourselves heard above the noise from the fans. Everything about the night was fantastic, and to this day I will always say that it was one of the best things that ever happened to me in football. I know Ian thinks the same, and any of the players who were involved will tell you they agree. It was so satisfying to do what we'd set out to do. Having come so close the previous year, we'd all agreed at the start of the season that when the final whistle of the final game blew, we wanted to be in the First Division, and we had achieved that.

None of us had ever really experienced anything like it before. The bunch of hungry and angry footballers that Steve Coppell had put together now knew what it was like to taste success, and all of us knew we wanted more of it.

12

The Night a Team Was Born

The way we ended the season left everyone associated with the club on a high. The scenes at Selhurst Park were unforgettable and the thought of being in the First Division was incredibly exciting for all the players. Ian and I had often talked about playing there and pitting ourselves against some of the best defenders in the country. None of us could wait to get started, and it really wasn't that long between getting promotion and playing our first game of the new season. We didn't have the usual time frame because we'd been competing in the play-offs. We'd beaten Blackburn to get promotion in early June, and a couple of weeks after that fantastic night, the fixtures for the new season were released. We were going to be playing away in a London derby against Queens Park Rangers at Loftus Road on the opening day in August, which meant we would probably be up against a familiar face in the opposition.

Andy Gray had moved on from Aston Villa after about fourteen months with them and joined QPR. It seemed like a good move for Rangers and for Andy. They'd signed a great midfielder, and he was playing in the First Division and was back in London. I'm sure that when the fixtures came out there were a lot of our supporters who thought about the prospect of Andy running out at Loftus Road to play in front of them, but I doubt there were any who thought he would be wearing a Palace shirt when he did. Andy had been a big part of the Palace team when he decided he wanted to move on to Villa. From a career point of view, nobody could begrudge him the chance to move to a huge club who eventually got promotion to the First Division in the season he joined them, but he was hard to replace in the Palace team and in the dressing room. He was a very good player, a big character and, as I mentioned, he had a great relationship with Steve Coppell. I'd obviously spoken to Andy since he'd left the club, but wasn't prepared for the call I got from him that summer.

'Bright eyes, tell the boss I want to come back, I want to come home!'

In many ways it was typical Andy. I'm pretty sure he might not have wanted to come home if we hadn't got promotion and still been in the Second Division, but having said that, I knew he had a genuine affection for the club. He knew the place inside out and knew pretty much everyone there behind the scenes, as well as most of the players. In many ways, it made a lot of sense for him, but also for Palace. We had just been promoted and it was obvious that any team moving into the First Division would have to strengthen its squad. There was no doubt Steve wanted to do that, and if he was looking for someone in midfield then Andy, who had been playing in the top flight for the past season, might well fit the bill. I told Steve about the phone call and what Andy had said, but I'm not sure whether my conversation with him had any influence on his decision to eventually make Andy's wish come true when he signed him just before we were due to play Rangers in the opening game of the season, and he also signed Andy's experienced teammate, left back Mark Dennis, at the same time. Andy played in the game a day after officially signing for us, but it wasn't a particularly happy return for him as we were beaten 2–0.

Our first home game was a big one. It was against Manchester United and we managed to do a lot better, coming from a goal down at half-time to earn a draw with an equaliser from Wrighty.

It was great for him to score his first ever goal in the top flight in front of his own fans and against a club as big as Manchester United. The two of us had talked a lot in the past about what it would be like playing against the best defenders around and whether we would be as successful against them as we had been in the Second Division. Apart from scoring goals and working hard, we always wanted to make sure any defenders we played against knew they had been in a game. We weren't exactly the nicest characters on the pitch, but it was all part and parcel of looking after yourselves and gaining the upper hand, because if you didn't lay down a marker early on, you were handing the advantage over to them. Sometimes a defender would try to get talking to Ian, and usually got the same response.

'Fuck off! If you want to talk to me, see me in the bar after the game,' he would tell them.

'What's the matter with him?' they'd ask me.

'Fuck off,' I'd tell them, as they stared at us.

When that happened, we knew we had them, we were in control, and apart from the verbal aggression we also made sure that we took any early opportunity to clatter them, which also helped to put them on the back foot. It often worked for us in the Second Division and although we were no less aggressive as a pair after we were promoted, there was a definite difference in the quality of defender we came up against. Sometimes that quality was a bit unexpected as well. After that United game we had another one at home, against Coventry City, and I came up against their centre half, Brian Kilcline. We were about the same age and a lot of people thought he was no more than a big, brooding defender who liked to get stuck in. That was all true, but there was also a lot more to his game than that. His positional sense was excellent and he was very good at cutting out danger. When I played against him that day, I hardly got a kick, and just to make matters worse, he managed to get the only goal of the game.

By the end of August, we'd played three games and only got one point. We badly needed a win and happily we got one. After a draw and then a defeat, we played Wimbledon in a third consecutive home game, and this time we tasted victory for the first time since being promoted. Geoff Thomas and Ian got the goals and we were off and running. It gave everyone a big confidence boost and we needed a win, because the longer you go without one, the more likely it is that doubts can begin to creep in. It was also timely for another reason, because our next game was only three days away: a midweek fixture against Liverpool at Anfield. It was one of those fixtures we had all dreamed about when we got promoted but, unfortunately, the dream turned into a nightmare.

We were all looking forward to playing at Anfield, even though we knew we were going to face one of the best teams around at the time. Liverpool were the FA Cup holders and had just missed out on becoming league champions the previous season. We knew it would be really tough up there, but there was excitement rather than fear in our dressing room before the kick-off. It only took seven minutes of the game to find out exactly what we were up against, when Steve Nicol gave them the lead. By half-time it was 3–0, but perhaps the writing was on the wall and when the full-time whistle blew, that writing said 9–0. It was total humiliation. We even missed a penalty at 6–0 when Pards was brought down, but Geoff Thomas hit his left-foot shot way over the bar. After one of their goals I was waiting to restart the game and asked Ian what the score was. I wasn't sure whether it was seven or eight goals we'd conceded at that point. Neither was he.

The Liverpool players didn't really have a go at us, although Ronnie Whelan did ask jokingly whether we trained with a ball, and one of their other lads asked the referee to have a count-up because he thought they might have more players on the pitch than we did. Even some of the Palace fans tried to use humour to deflect the pain they must have been feeling, because apparently they sang, 'We're going to win the league' when we were 8–0 down. It was a horrible experience and Steve Coppell knew just how humiliated we all felt. He spoke to us in the dressing room after we trooped in.

'That'll never happen again in your professional careers,' he told us. 'We came here as a team and we're going to leave as a team. Now, get washed and changed, I'll do all the talking to the press. Let's get back on the bus and get away from here as quickly as we can.'

As we were having a bath after the match our right back, John Pemberton, at least managed to defuse the situation and bring a bit of a smile to our faces.

'I think they'll be all right this season, don't you?' he said.

The journey back to London was a bit of a blur because we were all still numbed from what had happened. The next day I didn't even want to go out and get a newspaper. I knew they would all be saying how terrible we were, and having a laugh at our expense. That year some friends of mine bought me the VHS tape of the game as a Christmas present for a laugh, but even then I couldn't bring myself to watch it. When I eventually did, a few months later, the scary thing was that we were really trying, and we never stopped throughout the game. The other thing that came across when I watched the tape was how naive and cavalier we were. We were all so desperate to play in the big games, but that night was an extreme example of what could go wrong against really good sides. We had to learn, and learn fast. We began to do that, and sometime later Gary O'Reilly looked back on the whole shocking episode and the way it affected us as a group of players.

'That was the night a team was born,' he said, and he was right.

As terrible as the result and experience had been, we all knew that we couldn't afford to let it affect us. We had to recover quickly from the battering we got at Liverpool because four days later we played an away game at Southampton. Quite naturally there was a lot of attention on how we would react after the result at Anfield, and we showed our character as a team to come back from being a goal down to draw the game 1–1. We then won home games against Nottingham Forest and Everton to finish September in a much better way than we had started it. Those wins gave us a lot more belief and certainly helped the team to put the Liverpool result behind us, but there was one player who really suffered because of the nine goals we conceded at Anfield, and that was goalkeeper Perry Suckling. He played no better or worse than any of us that night and it certainly wasn't his fault that we conceded so many goals. Perry had been an important part of our team when we got promoted and he was a good keeper, but Steve Coppell had to make the sort of tough call managers often face, and a couple of months after that night in Liverpool he decided to pay £1 million for Nigel Martyn from Bristol Rovers, who went on to not only have a great career with Palace, Leeds and Everton, but also to become England's goalkeeper as well. It was an awful lot of money for Palace to spend and although that sort of fee had been paid in transfers before, it was the first time £1 million had been spent on a goalkeeper. Steve also strengthened the defence by buying Andy Thorn from Newcastle. He was a centre back with great awareness on the pitch and had been a part of the Wimbledon side that pulled off the FA Cup final upset by beating Liverpool in 1988.

Andy made his league debut for Palace in our away game at Old Trafford against Manchester United, the sort of game any player looks forward to. At that time, they were not the dominant force they would later become in the English game, but United were still a huge club with a magnificent history, and Old Trafford was certainly not an easy place to go to and get a good result. It was the club the boss had played so brilliantly for, and it was obviously a big moment for him to go back there as a First Division manager. It was a big stage for us, just as Anfield had been earlier in the season. United were not as good a team as Liverpool at that point, but we clearly didn't want to let ourselves down again at one of the top sides, and happily we didn't. In fact, we won the match 2–1 and I got both of the goals. It was great for the team to go there and win, to show that we were capable of beating one of the biggest names in the game. On a personal level it was fantastic to get the two goals that gave us the win. Steve Coppell told me after the game that I should feel pleased with myself, because not that many strikers went to Old Trafford with their team and scored two goals.

The win came in the early part of December and, like any other club, we were well aware of how important the Christmas period can be for a team, with matches coming thick and fast. Before that began, all the players got the chance to relax at a party thrown by Richard Branson's Virgin Atlantic company. They were sponsoring us and we had their logo on the front of our shirts, and were always very generous with things like hospitality. The players loved it and on this particular occasion, Mitchell Thomas, who was playing for Tottenham at the time and was a big friend of Ian Wright's, came along as well. We all had a great time at the party and Mitchell volunteered to be the driver on the night with Ian, Geoff Thomas and me as the passengers.

It was late when we left and drove back through some pretty deserted streets on our way back to my flat. Along the way we stopped at some traffic lights and pulled up alongside a car with a man and a woman in it. We could see that they were having some kind of argument as we waited for the traffic lights to change, and the guy in the other car suddenly looked across and saw that we were looking at him, and wound his window down.

'What are you looking at?' he shouted at us. This was a bit like a red rag to a bull for Wrighty.

'What you looking at then?' Ian screamed back at him, and just for good measure as we began to pull away, he stuck a finger up at the guy.

We were still all in high spirits and began laughing as Mitchell cruised down the road, but the laughter soon disappeared when I spotted what the guy in the other car was doing. Instead of turning left at the lights he had swerved around and was now very obviously behind us.

'The guy's following us,' I told everyone. 'He's put his foot down and he's roaring up behind us.'

Wrighty wasn't impressed.

'Mitch, pull over,' he said. 'What's he going to do? There's four of us, he'll soon change his mind when we get out of the car.'

Mitchell dutifully pulled over so that the three passengers could get out to confront the guy, who had already stopped and opened his door, ready to continue the argument.

'What's your problem?' he snarled at us.

'What's yours?' Ian snapped back, confident the guy would see he was outnumbered and come to his senses, and not want to escalate what was already a pretty silly late-night argument. That might have been what we all thought, but it very quickly became obvious that seeing us all standing by our car didn't seem to worry him at all.

'I asked what your problem was,' he said, and this time his words seemed to have a bit more menace in them.

'Why, what are you going to do about it?' Wrighty smirked, but the guy didn't blink and instead gave Ian a lop-sided grin of his own.

'I'll tell you what I'm going to do about it,' he said, looking very calm and confident, and it wasn't long before we discovered why. Without bothering to look at us and what we might be doing, he bent down slightly behind the door of his car, pulled out a gun, and then pointed the thing straight at us. For a split second I wondered if it was a fake one, but the reality soon hit us. Yes, it was real. My next thought was whether it was worth me trying to run, but that option quickly disappeared when I realised I couldn't move my legs. I was gripped by fear. I wasn't the only one, and Ian quickly understood we'd picked a fight with the wrong guy, a fight we weren't going to win.

'I'll tell you what you're going to do now, shall I?' said our friend with the gun. 'I'm going to count to five, and if you lot don't get in your car and fuck off, I'm going to start shooting. One . . . two . . .'

They were the last words we heard because we all bundled into our car and screamed at Mitchell to put his foot down and get the hell out of the place as soon as possible. We were all in shock as poor old Mitch drove as fast as he could to my flat. We certainly didn't say anything to each other, we were too stunned. The bloke must have been a maniac to do what he did, and we all knew maniacs did not operate in the same way most normal people do. For all we knew, he could have decided to follow us, ready to blast away at the car for the hell of it.

When we got to my flat, we virtually fell out of the car because we were desperate to get inside. We ran up the stairs as if it was some weird training drill we'd been asked to do at Palace, and at the same time I fumbled for my keys. When I opened the door, we all piled in, virtually falling over each other, before quickly slamming the door behind us and locking it. We were all professional athletes but, believe me, we were out of breath and sweating. Our minds were still racing at the thought of what had just happened. I closed the curtains and cautiously peeked through a gap to see if the bloke with the gun had followed us. One by one we all checked the street outside. There was no sign of him and we breathed a collective sigh of relief. It was only then that our confidence began to return.

'I could have taken him, you know,' said Ian. 'I was ready.'

'Yeah,' we all chimed in. 'We could have done it, no problem!'

The reality was, we shit our pants. The relief of getting away from the situation unscathed seemed to overwhelm all of us, and as a result we began to joke around even more as we boasted about the way we would have handled things. We were very soon talking as if there had never been anything to worry about. Of course, nothing could have been further from the truth. The reality was that we were a bunch of footballers who had been having a great night out before it all went very badly wrong. We had literally found ourselves staring down the barrel of a gun. Crazy. The only experience any of us had of shooting involved a ball and a goal. Stopping to confront the guy almost turned out to be the worst decision any of us had ever made, and we might easily have ended up paying for it with our lives. We'd all been used to making headlines on the back pages of newspapers, but that night we came very close to being front-page news for all the wrong reasons.

We had a disastrous spell of results to start the New Year, losing all of our league games. The one bit of success came in the FA Cup with a 2–1 home win in the third round over Portsmouth at the beginning of January and a 4–0 home win against Huddersfield at the end of the month. The draw was kind to us and we got another home tie in the fifth round, beating Fourth Division Rochdale 1–0. Suddenly we were in the quarter-finals of the FA Cup, and although we were going to have to travel for the first time in the competition that season, it was going to be against another Fourth Division team, Cambridge United. The week before the game we got a great result in the league against Tottenham at White Hart Lane, when an Alan Pardew goal gave us all the points.

There was a feeling around the club that we had a great chance of getting into the FA Cup semi-finals. Cambridge were not going to be easy to beat, but we were the First Division side and we knew we had better players. We just had to make sure we were professional on the day and got the result we needed. Once the game at Tottenham was out of the way the focus was on Cambridge and what could prove to be a special day for the club. The only problem was, I wasn't going to be there. I was suspended, but also had a hamstring injury that was causing me problems, and had an injection to try and move the healing process along. Knowing I wouldn't be available, Steve Coppell agreed to let me go away to Florida for a few days to relax and hopefully help with my recovery from the hamstring injury. I was really disappointed at not being involved in all the build-up to the game at Cambridge and I would have loved to have played in the match, but once it was obvious that wasn't going to happen, then getting away to Fort Lauderdale didn't seem such a bad idea. Virgin sorted out a ticket for me and I stayed in an apartment by the beach. I was friends with the boxer Nigel Benn and knew he was in Miami preparing to challenge Doug DeWitt for the WBO middleweight title the following month in Atlantic City, so I went down to see him for a day and he showed me around the area. It was nice to have someone I knew to hang out with while I was there and I think he appreciated seeing a familiar face to help break things up for him during all the hours of training he was putting in.

Like any footballer, I hated missing out on matches because of injury or suspension. It was bad enough when you had to sit in the stands and watch your team play a crucial game on the pitch but, believe me, when you're more than 4000 miles away, and there's a five-hour time difference, it makes matters a whole lot worse. Ian Wright's mum loved Crystal Palace, she was a genuine supporter. I knew she used to listen to the commentaries on Capital Gold whenever the team were playing, and I was certain she would have been glued to her radio listening to the match at Cambridge. Things were pretty different in 1990: there was no instant news the way there is these days when you can find out about the result of a football match within seconds of it ending, wherever it is in the world. The English football results were printed in a very small section of the local paper in Fort Lauderdale, and you only got them the day after the match had taken place. I worked out that the game with Cambridge would end at about 11.45 my time, so I made sure I was in the apartment ready to phone Ian's mum, Nesta, as soon as the match was over. I loved Wrighty's mum and had got to know her well since coming down from Leicester. I would often go to her house with Ian. She was a lovely lady, and I used to call her Mummy; I still do to this day. She was also someone who wouldn't put up with nonsense from anybody. I sat on my bed and dialled her number. Had we made it into the semi-finals, or had we come unstuck against Cambridge and become the victims of a Cup giant killing?

'Mummy,' I said as soon as she answered, 'how did we get on?'

'Who is this?' she said, clearly not recognising my voice.

'How did we get on?' I asked again, desperate to get the result from her.

'Who is this?' she said once more, and I got the impression she thought I must be someone having a laugh at her expense.

'It's me, Mark. How did we get on against Cambridge?' I said.

'Where are you?' she said, clearly wondering why I wasn't at the game myself.

'I'm in America,' I told her.

'What are you doing in America?' she said with a puzzled voice.

'I'm suspended and I've got an injury, so I'm in Florida for a week,' I explained.

'Oh, Geoff Thomas scored, we won 1–0.'

I dropped the phone and started to bounce up and down on the bed like a kid. I couldn't believe it, we were in the FA Cup semi-finals. Then I heard Ian's mum, who was still on the phone, asking if I was all right.

'I'm fine,' I told her. 'That's brilliant news, we're in the semi-final of the Cup!'

'Yes,' she agreed. 'It wasn't a very good game.'

I had to laugh. I knew she was probably right, but I didn't care how good or bad the game was. We had won and that was the main thing. I went down to the beach, but I couldn't focus on anything. It was an unbelievable feeling, pure excitement, knowing we were going to be playing in an FA Cup semi-final. I started to think about what it would be like at that moment in our dressing room at Cambridge. I knew the boys would be buzzing, and I would catch up with them later on the phone, but I was gutted at not being there to join in the celebrations with them.

When I got back to London there was obviously a lot of excitement surrounding the semi-final, even though most people weren't giving us a chance to reach the final at Wembley. The reason for that was the team we had been drawn against. Liverpool. Obviously, a lot had been made of the fact that they had beaten us 9–0 at Anfield, but they had also come out on top in the return fixture at Selhurst, beating us 2–0 during the bad run of results we'd had at the start of the year. That game was significant for another reason, because Ian had to come off with an injury which was later found to be a broken leg. He had somehow managed to come back in time to play in the Cup against Cambridge, but then in a home league game with Derby less than two weeks later, he broke his leg again. It was a real blow for Wrighty and for the team with the semi-final against Liverpool looming, and despite the warm weather trip to Florida, my hamstring had not really improved. It was depressing and it looked as though the injury could keep me out for longer than everyone had thought, but with a week-end home game against Aston Villa coming up, Steve Coppell came to me with a surprising suggestion.

'Brighty, would you go to see a faith healer?' he asked me.

'Boss, the problem's not in my head,' I told him. 'Why would I go to see a faith healer?'

Steve told me that this particular woman lived in Hampshire and came very highly recommended, and she'd been used by quite a few players. He asked me what I had to lose. If it worked that would be great, and if it didn't, I would be no worse off, and so the day before the game with Villa I met the boss at the training ground and he drove the two of us down to see a woman called Olga Stringfellow. When we got to her house we were met at the door by Olga's assistant and shown to a room that had some strange stuff decorating the walls. Things like spears, masks and drums seemed to be everywhere. I exchanged glances with Steve, and he could see from the look on my face that I was wondering what the hell I was doing in a place like this.

Olga finally came downstairs to meet us. She was a quite a small woman in her mid-sixties, and she asked me to show her exactly where the problem was. I pointed to my hamstring and told her how tight it felt. I explained that usually I would have no trouble bending forward and touching my toes, but said that with the injury that sort of thing just wasn't possible. She put her hand on the sofa with her palm facing upwards, and I had to sit with my hamstring touching her hand as she told me that her energies were moving into me. I looked at the boss, but he looked away. I'm sure if he hadn't, I would have burst out laughing because the whole thing just seemed ridiculous.

After about a half an hour of doing this, she asked me how I felt, and I told her there was no difference. I still couldn't touch my toes. Olga left the room for a short time and then came back to start the same process over again, before going out again. Steve asked me how I felt and I told him that it felt like my leg was sweating, but when I looked it was totally dry. She returned once more, this time clutching a book which she gave to Steve for him to look at. It had all sorts of news clippings about her and how she had helped all sorts of people around the world including Middle Eastern princes and American millionaires. She told us that her healing powers were a gift, which she was unaware of for some time, but when she became aware of having them, she had to put them to good use. I later found out that she was born in New Zealand and had been a journalist before writing some romantic novels, and then turning to healing.

The last part of my visit seemed more bizarre than anything that had happened before, because as she put her hand on my hamstring and started moving it up and down, she also began to make some very strange noises that sounded like a horse. Once again, I had to stop myself looking at Steve, because by this time I think we were both wondering what we were doing there. Just to add to the strangeness of the trip, Olga then started talking, but it didn't sound like any language I'd ever heard and I asked her what she was doing.

'I'm just asking Papa above if you are going to be all right, and he says you're going to be fine,' she told me.

'You couldn't ask him what the score's going to be tomorrow, could you?' said Steve, quick as a flash in that deadpan voice of his.

He may have said it in a flippant way, but Olga took him seriously and told the boss that it was going to be a good day for him. We both thanked her for her time and what she had tried to do for me but, as we left, I couldn't help telling her that I felt no different, I still had an injured hamstring.

'You won't until tomorrow,' she claimed. 'Then you'll feel fine.'

In the car on the way home, we both had a bit of a laugh about the whole experience and what had gone on. It had been strange and it might not have worked for me, but I could see why the boss thought it was worth a try. The good thing was that we kept the visit to ourselves and none of the boys knew anything about it. I went to bed that night annoyed that I was only going to be a frustrated spectator at the Villa game. I phoned our physio, Dave West, and told him what had happened and how I felt no different. He knew how desperate I was to play again, but could only sympathise with me and say that although it was frustrating, the injury would eventually heal.

The next morning, I got out of bed to go to the bathroom and immediately realised something was different, I couldn't feel the pain of my hamstring injury. I stood in the bathroom and gingerly tried to touch my toes, expecting to suddenly feel the pain once more, but nothing happened. My hamstring didn't hurt and I had no problem touching my toes. I put the heel of my foot on the side of the bath and stretched my straightened leg. Still no pain. The leg felt good. I put a tracksuit on and ran from my apartment in Knightsbridge down to Hyde Park and began to put myself through a series of exercises. Running, jumping, sprints, stops, starts, moving from side to side, and I did them all without any pain. I ran back home and immediately phoned Dave to tell him what had happened.

'And there was no pain at all?' he asked.

'None, Dave, honestly,' I told him.

'OK, come in and I'll give you a full fitness test,' he said.

I got to the ground and did the fitness test with Dave, all the sorts of thing I'd done on my own that morning and a bit more. By the end of it he was convinced I was fit enough to play against Villa, and then phoned Steve to tell him what had happened. I couldn't quite believe it myself, but I felt fine, and there was no sign of the hamstring injury. Olga had said I would be all right, and I was. Everyone arrived for the game and the boss made an announcement.

'There's one change to the team,' he told the rest of the lads. 'Brighty's fit enough to play, so he comes straight in up front.'

There was a moment's silence and then I heard Eddie McGoldrick shout at the top of his voice.

'It's a miracle! It's a miracle!'

Pretty soon all the players were all joining in and laughing. What I thought had been a well-kept secret concerning my visit to see Olga was obviously out of the bag. Someone had let something slip and the boys knew all about it. Naturally they weren't going to let me off easily, and they couldn't stop making jokes about it.

'Brighty, Brighty, touch me, I've got a pain in my shoulder!' one of them would shout, but the fact was, the hamstring problem was gone. I played against Villa and we won 1–0. I didn't have any injury worries as the semi-final with Liverpool got closer. Unfortunately, the same couldn't be said for Ian.

13

Ecstasy to Agony

The FA Cup has a magic all of its own, and that was never more evident to me than in 1990. To hear about a result and then to start jumping up and down on a bed, in the way I had done in Fort Lauderdale, showed just how magical I thought the competition was. The idea of playing in a FA Cup semi-final really was a dream come true. It meant the world to me and all the Palace players. That's why it was so heart-breaking for Ian when he realised he was not going to be able to play in the game with Liverpool at Villa Park. The broken leg hadn't healed in time for him to take part in the game, so he knew he would have to sit it out and watch us trying to pull off the impossible dream by beating the Cup holders, and the team who also happened to have been top of the First Division table for months.

Not surprisingly, most pundits made Liverpool heavy favourites. Not only were they flying in the league, they had also had those two wins against us, and a lot of people thought we were probably still deeply scarred by the 9–0 defeat early in the season. The truth was, we had got over that result, and although we were by no means safe from the prospect of relegation, by the time we came to play Liverpool we were fifteenth in the league, with confidence in our own ability to make sure we stayed up. There were still six matches left to play in the league after losing 2–0 at Norwich in a midweek match, four days before our Villa Park semi-final. Enough points up for grabs to ensure safety, but all of that had to be put to one side as we attempted to create a bit of Crystal Palace club history by reaching the FA Cup final for the first time.

Our semi-final and the other one between Manchester United and Oldham at Maine Road were going to be played on the same Sunday, and they were going to be shown live on television, the first time it had ever happened. Our game was going to be the first on, with the other semi-final kicking off after we'd finished. It added even more excitement and interest to the matches, and Steve Coppell was determined to make sure his planning and tactics for the match were as good as they could be. His planning for any game was always good and he tried to leave nothing to chance. None of us were stupid enough to think we were a better team than Liverpool. They were a magnificent side with a magnificent pedigree, but this was the FA Cup, a competition that, over the years, was littered with upsets. Only two years earlier nobody had given Wimbledon a chance in the final against Liverpool, and yet they had caused one of the competition's biggest ever upsets by winning 1–0. We were realistic enough to know that if we were going to have any chance of winning, we would all have to be on our game. We couldn't afford to have a couple of players who had off-days. Everyone had to be at it from the first whistle, and we had to stick to the instructions we were given.

It was a special game and a special occasion for the club and for all of us. We travelled up on the Friday and stayed at the New Hall Hotel in Sutton Coldfield. It was a historic country house hotel, with a moat, which was set in twenty-six acres of grounds. All very nice and a bit of a contrast to the ground we used the next day to go through our set-pieces. It was a school pitch and we had to crawl under some fencing to get onto it. Andy Gray wasn't too happy, not because of the pitch, but because he wanted more tickets for the game and couldn't get them. We all had family and friends watching. Phil had always tried to watch me whenever he could and my sisters would come down and see matches as well. Andy had the hump, but when I asked him why he was moping around, he just told me not to worry.

'It'll be all right on the night, Brighty,' he told me.

Steve had decided that, in the absence of Ian, I would play up front on my own. It might not seem like such a big deal these days because, for so many teams, having a lone striker is quite normal. It was different then: strikers came as a pair, a double act, with teams usually playing a 4–4–2 system. Steve wanted me up front, he wanted to go man-for-man at the back and he wanted five across the middle. He knew Liverpool often dominated possession in a game, and he was content for them to have the ball, but we all had to work hard at making sure we defended as a team, and then try to make sure we used set-pieces. We wanted to get free kicks and corners because our set plays were a big part of our game. Delivering the ball accurately and then having people like me, Gary O'Reilly, Thorny and Pards to attack it in the box was going to be a key factor for us. The boss told us to think positively; he didn't want any negative thoughts and told us to believe in each other. We all had to be strong and we couldn't afford to have any weak links. He said that everyone was already convinced that the final would be between Liverpool and Manchester United, but that we were capable of making sure it would be us in the final instead.

I've always believed that being a professional footballer is not just about having ability, it also involves mental strength and belief, which are things I've always possessed, even in the bad times I had at Leicester. It was something Wrighty had, and it was something we always talked about. We went into every game thinking that if we played well, we would win, and that if we got a chance in a match we would score. Of course, it never happened every time, but that was our mind-set, that was how we approached matches, and on the eve of the game with Liverpool I felt exactly the same. If we all played as we could do, and if chances were created, then the team was capable of taking them and winning the match, but I also knew we would have to play out of our skins to make it happen.

The match at Villa Park kicked off at noon, and the atmosphere was incredible. Ian Rush gave them the lead in the first half and when I came in at the break, I doubt that I'd had more than a few touches, but Steve was calm about the whole situation. We'd stuck to our game plan, passed the ball when we could and stuck to the man marking.

'Nothing changes,' Steve said in the dressing room. 'We still need to score a goal, but we need to get up and support Brighty more.'

I told Steve I felt as though I hadn't really had a kick, but he said it didn't matter. I was occupying the back lads in the Liverpool team and that was what he wanted me to do. I just needed to keep on tackling and chasing, and sooner or later we'd get something. It turned out to be a lot sooner than even he could have hoped for, because within moments of the restart, we were level, and I scored the goal. John Pemberton broke down the right, crossed to the far post, John Salako had a shot that was stopped by Liverpool keeper, Bruce Grobbelaar, the ball fell to me, and I just swung my left foot at it. We were back in the game.

Andy Gray might have had the hump twenty-four hours earlier because of a lack of tickets, but he'd told me he'd be 'all right on the night', meaning that although he was a bit fed up with his ticket allocation, he wouldn't let it affect his game, and he was true to his word. We knew the quality of his deliveries from free kicks and corners would be a key factor for us, and it was his free kick which led to us taking the lead through Gary O'Reilly. Unbelievably we found ourselves 2–1 up, but great teams never panic when they go behind in a game, they just keep playing because of the self-belief they have in their own ability to win matches, come what may. A well-worked free kick eventually gave Steve McMahon the chance to equalise, which he gratefully took, and then a push by Pembo on Barry Venison in the box gave them a penalty. It was heart-breaking. We had come back from a goal down to lead the game and now with very little time left in the match they had the chance to make it 3–2, which John Barnes did from the spot.

There would not have been too many people in Villa Park that afternoon who thought we had a chance of coming back from a blow like that, but there seemed to be a collective belief within our team that we were not going to be denied. Our heads didn't drop. Instead we showed the sort of resilience that had been absent seven months earlier on that dreadful night at Anfield. The ball was launched into their penalty box, I challenged for it and then Geoff Thomas somehow managed to win the ball with his head twice before Andy came running in, leapt into the air and nodded it into the net: 3–3. Extra-time. It had been an amazing ninety minutes, but Steve Coppell made sure it was the next thirty minutes that we focused on as we sat on the grass.

'This is your moment, this is your time,' he told us. 'You're younger, you're fitter and you want it more. They've been to FA Cup finals, they've won medals. You haven't, but this is your chance, your opportunity. If you really want it, this is your time, you can do it.'

I'm pretty sure we were all knackered. It had been such an incredible game of football to play in, and both teams had put an awful lot into the match. We were probably close to running on empty, but we somehow managed to find the energy from somewhere. We left it late, but we had another goal in us. It came from the sort of set-piece we had used many times before, but never with such devastating consequences. Andy took a corner on the left, hit the ball to the near post, Andy Thorn nodded it on, and Pards rose at the far post to glance it in. Perfection: 4–3. We had done it.

Against all the odds we had beaten a team most people believed were the best in the land, and we were going to be playing in the FA Cup final. Even now, with my playing career behind me, it still gives me a thrill thinking about how happy I felt after that game. The sheer ecstasy of the moment when you realise you have won and that you're going to play in the final, something you have dreamed about doing as a kid, something that so many great players never experience. It was such a wonderful feeling for everyone associated with the club. The fans, the board, the management and the players, we were all in it together. It was a victory for all of us, and all of us found it hard to take in just exactly what had happened.

Andy Gray certainly played a major role in helping us get the win: his set-pieces during the game had been tremendous, he'd scored a goal and made two others. When the whistle blew and the match was over, he came running over to me.

'Brighty, we're going to be playing in the FA Cup final!' he shouted at me.

He had a massive grin on his face and we both burst out laughing, because we knew how much it meant to us. It meant a lot to Ian as well, even though he knew he faced a race against time to get fit enough to play at Wembley. He came hobbling on from the side of the pitch, with his leg in plaster, and jumped all over us. Just like the rest of the team, he was going mad with excitement.

In the dressing room Steve Coppell was shaking every-one's hand and hugging them. Telling each player how well they'd done. It meant a lot to me and to the rest of the lads because the boss was not given to handing out praise lightly. In fact, I could probably count on one hand the number of times he said I'd played well during the entire time I was at Palace. He expected us to do our jobs and get on with play-ing without having to say 'well done' all the time, but when he did, it felt special and you knew he truly meant it. As you might imagine, the celebrations went on for some time. Ron Noades came into the dressing room and got soaked with champagne, and everyone was on a high. We did interviews with the media after the game and a lot of us were asked who we wanted to play against in the final, Oldham or Manchester United. We said United. We wanted one of the biggest clubs in the world, and after the way we had come through against Liverpool we began to think that it really could be our year.

The one thing I do have a slight regret about on the day was the fact that I didn't travel back with the rest of the team on the coach. Mitchell Thomas had come up for the match with a good friend of ours, and I travelled back with them in their car along with Ian. It was chaos on the motorway, with traffic at a standstill in places, as thousands of Palace fans made their way home. It wasn't long before we were spotted by some of them, and because we were all going nowhere, people were getting out of their cars and coming over to hug us. We signed bottles of champagne for some guy, and at one stage Wrighty propped himself up with his head poking through the opened sun roof of our car. The fans loved it, and so did we. It was a magical day.

I couldn't help thinking back to all those times as a kid when we were fostered, when I always believed that someday I would be a professional footballer, and when Phil was always there to offer support and encouragement. Now I was going to play at Wembley in an FA Cup final. It really was unbelievable.

There was a gap of just under five weeks between our game with Liverpool and the Cup final. United and Oldham had drawn their semi-final 3–3, a few hours after we'd beaten Liverpool, and in the replay three days later it was United who edged it 2–1. So we knew who we would be playing at Wembley, and Ian knew he had a fight on his hands in order to get fit enough to take part. Breaking your leg is horrible for any player, and to do it twice in such a short period of time was really tough. We had come through against Liverpool without him, but everyone at the club knew just how important he was to the team, and what a huge boost it would be if he could play against United, but before then we had the little matter of making sure we stayed in the First Division. Getting to the Cup final had been a tremendous achievement, but none of us wanted to walk out at Wembley knowing that the following season we would be playing in the Second Division. We won two and drew one of our last five games to make sure of staying up, and were safe by the time we drew 2–2 at Selhurst against Manchester City in our last game of the season, finishing fifteenth in the table.

One of the great traditions of the FA Cup for the two teams reaching the final was the players' pool. This was basically something which was set up by each squad to try and cash in on the fact that they were the finalists. It meant that things like newspaper articles, TV and radio interviews were all done for different fees and the money was pooled to be shared out among the squad once the final had taken place. It was a way of producing a financial bonus for the squad, and the idea had started when players' wages were nothing like they are today. Things like producing a Cup final record were all part of the sort of activities players got involved in during the lead-up to the big day at Wembley. Having someone to organise the pool was essential, and in our case that someone was a larger-than-life character named Eric Hall.

Eric was an agent in an era when there really weren't too many around. His background was in the music business, and he'd moved into football without really knowing too much about the game. That didn't matter to Eric. What did matter was the way he could make a deal and come up with ideas that would make his clients money. He was a short guy who smoked cigars that seemed bigger than he was, spoke in a loud voice, called everyone 'Bubbalah', and his catchphrase was 'monster'. Everything was 'monster' for Eric.

'Lads, lads, I've got a monster deal for you all!' he'd tell us, puffing on his huge cigar and strutting around outside our training ground at Mitcham. He was non-stop and just seeing him in action made you feel exhausted. Naturally the Cup final record was part of what he had us doing. We sang 'Glad All Over', the Dave Clark Five song from the 1960s, which they played at Selhurst whenever we ran onto the pitch at the start of a game, but when we got into the recording studio, everyone was hopeless. We were like fish out of water, we had no experience of doing that sort of thing, so they sent out for a crate of beer to help loosen us up a bit. At least we lost our inhibitions, and we belted the song out. Then it was a question of Eric plugging it and trying to get us as much radio and TV airtime as he could.

'We're going to have a monster number one hit on our hands, Bubbalahs,' he insisted, but we never did, although we did feature on a few shows, awkwardly singing in front of the television cameras. Eric also did a deal with the *Today* newspaper and on the morning of the final he wanted us walking around with copies of it. The same thing happened with Ray-Ban sunglasses. The classic one was when he wanted us to walk about with opened umbrellas that had advertising on them. He wasn't worried about the fact that it was May and the weather was fine.

'Just open them up and be seen with them,' he insisted.

We had a lot of fun in the build-up to the game, but at the same time knew just what a huge match we were going to be involved in. The final meant so much to all of us, everyone was desperate to play in it, nobody wanted to miss out, but inevitably that happens whenever a team is picked, no matter what the game is. The big question in the final few days before the game was whether Ian would be fit enough to start. He'd made a remarkable recovery from the injury, had played a reserve game and been training with us. Of course, Ian was desperate to play. He'd worked so hard since our win in the semi-final when many people thought he didn't have a chance of being anywhere near fit enough to be considered for the final. Steve Coppell knew he had a decision to make and there was a lot of press speculation in the last few days leading up to the game. In the end he decided to go with the eleven players who had started against Liverpool, and Ian was going to be on the bench with Dave Madden. I don't think Steve thought Wrighty was match fit enough to last the whole ninety minutes because he'd missed so many games, but it was clear he was happy to have him come off the bench if needed and make an impact at some stage in proceedings.

There are so many things to take in on the day of an FA Cup final. Like so many fans and players, all of my experiences of the event had come from watching previous matches on television, thinking how fantastic it must be to take part in it. You couldn't help being excited by the whole occasion. The coach inching its way through the crowds, seeing the colours both sets of supporters were wearing, hearing the chants, and seeing the iconic twin towers as we approached Wembley Stadium. Arriving at the ground was like nothing else I'd experienced before a match. We drove in through the famous wooden gates and into the huge tunnel with a changing room on each side. As we got off the team bus, I could see from the look in the eyes of a lot of the lads that they were probably thinking exactly the same as me:

This is it. We really are about to play one of the biggest games in the world, against one of the biggest teams in the world.

We were shown to our dressing room, and the size of it was so different to our normal home-team changing room at Selhurst. We also had a guy who seemed to be there to look after us, getting us drinks and generally making sure we had everything we needed. He was the one who handed out the telegrams, with that lovely message from Mr Arkle. Walking out onto the pitch before the game was amazing as well. We all tried to stroll around looking nonchalant, but you couldn't help being caught up in the emotion of the occasion. Quite simply, it was special. We had another visitor in the dressing room before we started to get changed for the match. It was someone who spoke to us about the etiquette of meeting a member of the royal family and the other dignitaries who were there. I don't think too many of the boys took it seriously, and I can't remember anyone paying much attention to what was being said. All we wanted to do was complete our pre-match routines and make that nerve-wracking walk from the tunnel, through the arc of sand that was behind each goal and on to the halfway line for the introductions.

The set-up at the old Wembley was different to the modern one, and having the dressing rooms at one end of the stadium, instead of in the middle as they are today, made the entrance of the teams much more dramatic. The walk was something else that we had all seen on television, watching past finals, and it was another special moment we were all looking forward to, including Ian. So, you can imagine his reaction when he was told before the match that only the manager and the eleven players who were going to start the game were allowed to make the full walk to the halfway line.

The substitutes had to peel off before the teams walked across the sand and make their way to the benches at the side of the pitch.

'No chance, there's no way I'm doing that,' he said. 'This is the FA Cup final, the biggest game I've ever been involved in. I've watched teams coming onto the pitch and dreamed of doing that walk. I might not be playing, but I'm doing that walk. I want to experience that walk.'

And that was exactly what he did. We all lined up in the tunnel behind Steve Coppell and made the walk together. The noise when both teams walked out numbed our ears, and then there were the hundreds of red and blue balloons that the Palace fans released as soon as they saw us emerge. We all tried to take in the sights and sounds, but it all started to become a bit of a blur in many ways, and the thing we wanted most of all was to line up and hear the referee blow his whistle to start the match.

Nineteen minutes after he did that, we found ourselves in front. Phil Barber sent over a free kick from the right and Gary O'Reilly glanced a header into the net. Our fans went wild and so did we, but with less than a quarter of the game gone there was a lot of work to be done. It would have been nice to have gone in at the break with the lead, but ten minutes before half-time United equalised with a Bryan Robson header, and in the second half they took the lead with a Mark Hughes goal. It was time for Steve Coppell to make a substitution.

After sixty-nine minutes he brought Ian on for Phil Barber, and three minutes later Wrighty had equalised for us. With his first touch of the game he latched on to my assist, cut inside on the left of their penalty box, beat two men and slid the ball into the far corner of the net. It was incredible. We were back in it and suddenly seemed to have the upper hand, but we just couldn't grab a third before the end of the ninety minutes.

Once again we were into extra-time in a massive FA Cup match. Ian's introduction and the way he'd scored just after coming on had given everyone a lift, and there was a belief in the team that we could go on and win it. When Ian grabbed a second just a couple of minutes into the first period of extra-time, that belief went through the roof. With perfect timing he arrived at the far post to knock in a left-wing cross from John Salako. We had come back to turn the game around, and Ian's introduction and goals had been the main factor in making that happen. It was hard not to get carried away by what had happened, and the fact that we were so close to winning the Cup.

I know I shouldn't have done it, but I found my mind racing forward, thinking about lifting the trophy and parading it in front of our fans. I might have been a professional footballer, but I was also a human being, and I just couldn't stop myself thinking ahead to what might happen. It was stupid, I know, particularly as those thoughts were shattered when Mark Hughes scored with about seven minutes of the game remaining.

Instead of the celebrations I'd hoped for, we were faced with the prospect of having to play a second game five days later. We'd had what would have been a historic win snatched away from us, and it was hard to take. The team had worked so hard and Ian's contribution was incredible. He deserved more after coming on and turning the game around for us. As for my own performance, I wondered what had happened, because the game simply seemed to pass me by. I didn't feel as though I had contributed enough, I just never really got going. It all felt very flat after the match. We hadn't lost but I couldn't shake off the feeling of disappointment, and it probably had more to do with the way I had played than the fact that United had grabbed a draw with that Mark Hughes equaliser.

We were due to have a reception at the Royal Garden Hotel in Kensington. When we arrived and stepped off the team bus, we could see all of our families and friends waiting for us in the reception. I could see my girlfriend standing there and waved at her to come over to me as I stood in the entrance to the hotel. I had my bag in one hand and told her that I just wanted to get outside and have a walk in Kensington Gardens, which backed on to the hotel. After walking with her for a couple of minutes, we sat on a bench, not really saying very much. She could see how upset I was and then I suddenly started crying.

'It was the biggest game of my life and I hardly had a kick of the ball,' I told her. 'It passed me by, and I couldn't seem to do anything about it.'

It was a horrible feeling and I told her I just couldn't face going back to the hotel, so we got a cab back to my flat instead. I think I was also conscious of the fact that Ian had scored those two goals and had a great game. I was so pleased and proud of him, but I didn't want to be negative around him, and the truth was that I couldn't seem to shake off the feeling of disappointment in my own performance. If we had won it would have been fantastic, but I know I would still have been unhappy with my own performance and the contribution I made. Not long after we got back my phone rang. It was Steve Coppell.

'Where are you?' he asked.

I tried to tell him how I felt and that I just couldn't face being around a load of people.

'Get back here now,' Steve said. 'Your family and friends are here waiting for you.'

I knew he was right. My brother and sisters were there along with Gran and some of my friends. I knew they cared a lot about me and realised it was a massive day in my life, and I was pleased I was able to make sure they were there to share it with me. They had come to support me and, whether I was disappointed or not, I realised I should be there with them. It was a big occasion and they deserved to be part of it and enjoy everything that went on. Not being with them was selfish, so we got a cab back to the hotel and went to the reception that had been organised. It was the right thing to do and it actually helped to lift my spirits. It was a pleasure to be with all the players and their families. There were lots of laughs and jokes. It did everyone good to relax before the serious business of preparing for the replay a few days later.

With hindsight I would have to say that our best chance of winning the FA Cup in 1990 came in that first game. We still believed we could win going into the replay, but we never quite got our game going. United seemed to be more confident and assured in the second game, as if they believed that we wouldn't be able to turn it on again. It was as if they thought we'd had our chance and blown it by letting them come back to draw the match. What I do know is the replay was nothing like as good as the first game. After the game we were accused by some people of being overly physical in our approach, but I can honestly say that was not what we set out to do. I think it was just the way the game went. There were a few tackles flying in, but it wasn't just us. Steve started with the same team that began the first match, and once again Ian came on as a substitute for Phil Barber, but he couldn't produce his goal-scoring magic from the weekend. We created chances but didn't take them; they created chances and took one of them. It came in the second half when Neil Webb hit a long pass out to the left and Lee Martin ran from deep to get on the end of it and score. The game will be remembered not as a classic, but as the match that gave Sir Alex Ferguson his first trophy as Manchester United manager. The rest, as they say, is history.

Losing the match was horrible. The team had worked so hard and we'd ended up with nothing. There were a lot of tears in our dressing room after the game from players who had given everything on the pitch and got nothing for their efforts. I wasn't just upset, I was angry as well, and the first thing I did as I slumped in my seat was throw my loser's medal against the wall of the changing room. It was petulant, but I couldn't help myself. Someone picked it up, put it back in the box and handed it to me, but it was almost as if having the medal just confirmed what we all knew. We were losers, and it wasn't a nice feeling. Somebody asked Andy why he didn't go with his runner, Lee Martin, for their goal.

'I just didn't think Neil Webb could hit the pass,' he said apologetically.

'Andy,' I said, 'Neil Webb can't tackle, can't run, can't head the ball, but the one thing he can do is pass it!'

Poor Andy said that he'd make it up to us.

'What the fuck are you going to do to make up for losing the Cup final?' asked Ian.

Andy said how sorry he was and we knew that was true. It was just one of those things. Mistakes happen – we all make them in a match. Sometimes they don't make a difference, but sometimes they do. The manager told us to get showered and changed because we were all going up to see our family and friends. He knew how devastated we all were, but he was determined to be positive.

'We've lost to one of the biggest clubs in the world,' he told us. 'There's no shame in that, so go and meet your families and hold your heads up.'

That was exactly what we did and, as disappointed as we all were, it did us good. Gran Davies had watched the match with Ian's mum. The two of them had sat next to each other and they were sitting together again when I walked up to the lounge after the game. I knew Gran was proud of me and of what I'd managed to do. She and Grandad Davies had been there for me for so long, they were my foster parents but also so much more. I'd spent ten years in their home and been part of their family when I dreamed of being a professional footballer. I wondered what Grandad would have made of me playing in an FA Cup final. He never did watch me play in a game. When I was still wrapped up in those dreams of being a footballer and asked him to come and watch me play in a local cup final, he told me that if I was any good, he'd hear about me. It was typical of the sort of comment he'd make. If he had still been alive, he would probably have heard about me, but I'm not sure he would have been too complimentary about my performance that night. When I went over to see Gran she noticed I was holding a box.

'What's that, Mark?' she asked.

'It's my medal, Gran,' I told her.

'Oh, that's nice,' Gran said.

'It's not really, Gran, it's a loser's medal,' I explained.

'Never mind,' said Gran with a consoling smile. 'It's only a game. You can't win them all.'

As bad as I felt that night, I couldn't help laughing when she said that. It was the biggest game of my life and I'd finished on the losing side, but Gran was just trying to make me feel better. And she was right, you can't win them all, although it would have been nice to have won that particular one.

The season had ended in disappointment, but when you put it into perspective, we had come an awful long way in a short period of time. A year earlier we had just won promotion from the Second Division. We had managed to stay in the First Division when many people thought we were favourites for relegation at the start of the season, and we had reached an FA Cup final, defeating in the semi-final the team who would eventually become league champions. Not bad really, and we were growing as a team and as individuals within that team. On a personal note, the season had been a good one for me. I scored twelve goals in the league and five in the various cup competitions to finish as the club's top scorer. I also got the Palace Player of the Year award. Losing to Manchester United had been hard to take, but that summer I unexpectedly got an honest assessment of our efforts at Wembley from one of English football's all-time greats. I was back in Stoke attending a function and Sir Stanley Matthews, who was seventy-five at the time, was there as well.

'I saw the game on the Saturday and thought your team played well and deserved to win,' he told me. 'In the second game you just wanted to kick people. You didn't deserve to win.'

Thanks, Sir Stanley.

14

All Good Things

A part from time being a great healer, we also found that a post-season trip to the Caribbean helped us get over our Cup final disappointment, a tour that took in Trinidad, the Cayman Islands and Jamaica. We even managed to catch up with some of Wrighty's relatives in Jamaica, and it was certainly good to get away and unwind after what had been a pretty tough season. Steve freshened things up in the squad for the 1990–91 season by bringing in players like right back John Humphrey from Charlton and big centre half Eric Young from Wimbledon. Players who were experienced and knew their way around the First Division.

Having survived in the league and then gone all the way to the Cup final in our first season after promotion, I think there was a growing confidence in the squad, and we certainly felt as though we belonged in the top flight, a fact that was underlined by the start we had to our second season when we remained undefeated after our first ten league games. Our first defeat came at the beginning of November against Manchester United at Old Trafford. By then we were fourth in the league and, after losing that game, we put together another run that saw us lose once in nine games. As we reached the end of the year, we had been beaten twice in twenty games and were third in the league. It felt as though we had truly arrived. We feared no one, but there were plenty of teams who feared us, and I think a lot of them started to look at us in a different light.

We also started really well in the League Cup, or Rumbelows Cup, as it was known then. The competition seemed to mean a lot more to all the top flight teams back then, and they would always field their strongest line-ups. We beat Southend 8–0 at home in the first leg of our second-round tie, with Ian and me each getting a hat-trick. We won the second leg 2–1 and then beat Leyton Orient over two legs, before coming unstuck 2–0 at Southampton in the first knockout stage of the competition. Any hope we had of putting together another great FA Cup run disappeared in the third round, although it took three games against Nottingham Forest before we finally went out, drawing 0–0 at our place, then 2–2 in the replay, before they beat us 3–0 in a third game that was also played at the City Ground. However, there was another cup competition we played in that season, and we did rather well in it.

It was the Full Members Cup, which was sponsored by Zenith Data Systems, and was known as the ZDS Cup. The competition had been created in 1985 with all the teams from the top two divisions in English football taking part. It might not have had the same sort of status as the League or FA Cups, but it did have a final that was played at Wembley, and having beaten Bristol Rovers, Brighton and Norwich, we found ourselves there in April facing Everton. Of course, it wasn't the same as those two games with United eleven months earlier, but it was a Wembley final and that, in itself, is special. Once again, we went to extra-time. It had finished 1–1 after ninety minutes when Everton's Robert Warzycha equalised after skipper Geoff Thomas had given us the lead, and then Ian scored twice in extra-time along with John Salako to give us a 4–1 win. It might not have made up for losing against United, but the climb up the steps to the royal box seemed a lot sweeter, and it was great for our fans to be able to cheer a win as Geoff lifted the trophy and turned towards the Palace supporters.

We finished the season in third place, behind Liverpool and champions Arsenal. I think the team had maximised its potential. I don't think we could have finished any higher than we did. It was a brilliant season and we only had to look at all the teams who finished below us to realise that. It was the club's highest ever league placing, and we hadn't been out of the top four all season, which was a tremendous achievement, but despite all of that it was another disappointing end because we were denied the chance to play in Europe. English clubs had been banned from playing in Europe following the Heysel Stadium disaster which saw thirty-nine people die when there was a riot and a wall collapsed before the start of the 1985 European Cup final between Liverpool and Juventus. As a result, English sides were banned from European competition, but in 1990 it was confirmed that English clubs, with the exception of Liverpool, would be allowed back into Europe for the 1990–91 season. Then, in April 1991, Liverpool were allowed back into European competition for the 1991–92 season. Had that not happened, our third-place finish would have seen us competing in the UEFA Cup. It would have been nice to have got some reward for all our work throughout the season. I think our consistency and level of performance deserved that, and our fans deserved the chance to cheer on their team in Europe.

Having had such a good league campaign, I was naturally looking forward to the 1991–92 season, and before long we started training in preparation for it. I was twenty-nine years old and desperate to make sure I kept myself in good condition so that I could prolong my career and play at the top for as long as possible. I enjoyed my life in London but had always kept in touch with my family and tried to pay visits to see them as regularly as I could. Before pre-season training started I decided to spend some time visiting friends and family in Stoke because I knew it might be some time before I could do it once the matches started to come along.

Some years earlier I had received a letter addressed to me and sent to Selhurst Park. When I opened it, I saw that it was from my dad. I was fuming. He'd walked out on us all those years ago, hadn't been a part of my life, left his kids and his family, been a big part of the reason Phil and I had been put in care, and now he'd suddenly decided to contact me. He'd obviously seen my name in the newspapers and decided to write. I was in the Palace dressing room at the time and Tony Finnigan was there with me. He could see how angry I was when I'd opened the envelope and read what was inside.

'Who's the letter from?' he asked me.

'My dad,' I said. 'He's never been in my life once, never been there for me, and now because he's read about me in the newspapers and seen me playing football on the television, he gets in touch.'

'It's your dad, Mark,' Tony said. 'You should write back.'

I never did, but it was only because of Tony that I didn't tear the letter up on the spot. Instead I photocopied it and sent it to my sisters, who were equally annoyed when they read it.

On my way back to London for the start of pre-season training I stayed at my sister Marie's house in Lichfield for a couple of days, and we decided to go out in the evening for a meal. As we were eating our meal the subject of our dad came up, and we spoke about the time he'd written to me. The letter had his address on it, and he was living somewhere in Burnley.

'Shall we go and see him?' she asked me.

'What, now?' I said.

'Yes, now,' she insisted.

So that's what we did. We drove from Lichfield to Burnley, I stopped at a local police station to ask directions and we finally arrived at his house. He had married again and his wife answered the door and let us in. We sat down in their front room and we noticed a picture, which was apparently of their son. Eddie didn't stop talking, saying how he'd seen me climbing off the Palace team bus for a game at Manchester City, and how he was so proud of me. I just sat there and let him talk and ramble on. After about ten or fifteen minutes of this he looked at Marie, and then spoke to me.

'Mark, who is this beautiful girl you have with you? Is she your wife?' he asked.

'You might not believe this, Eddie,' said Marie, looking directly at the man who was our father. 'I'm your oldest daughter, Marie.'

Quick as a flash, Eddie threw his arms open wide and spoke to both of us.

'My prayers have been answered, my prayers have been answered!' he said in a loud voice, smiling and looking as though he was going to burst into tears at any moment. It didn't fool either of us. Marie began to question him on a few things that had happened when we were kids, and it was obvious he wasn't very comfortable with the direction the conversation was taking. His wife tried to interrupt to say that Eddie hadn't been well and now we had turned up with lots of questions.

'Excuse me,' I said, 'I'm now in my late twenties, and he's never really been in my life. I think we've got every right to ask whatever questions we want.'

'I don't think you should be talking to your father like that,' she insisted. Then Eddie intervened.

'Shut up!' he shouted at her. 'I'm talking to my kids.'

I looked at Marie and she looked at me. It was a horrible moment, and you could tell his wife had been put firmly in her place. There was an awkward silence and then she left the room to go upstairs. As she walked through the door, he told her to bring the biscuit tin down with her, which she did and then handed it to him. Eddie opened the lid and rummaged through its contents before producing a small red plastic

In an iconic Palace shirt and with a fashionable high-top haircut. I have some great memories wearing that shirt. *(Colorsport)*

Manchester United defenders Gary Pallister, Steve Bruce and me battle for the ball in the 1990 FA Cup Final replay at Wembley. I might have accidentally caught Pally with a loose elbow here…
(Mark Leech / Offside)

The only time I played for England was for an over-35 team in Johannesburg.

Playing in the 1993 League Cup Final for Sheffield Wednesday against Arsenal.
(Bob Thomas Sports Photography via Getty Images)

Chris Waddle and me after our 2–1 win in the FA Cup semi-final against Sheffield United in 1993. He scored the first; I scored the winner. *(Mark Leech/Getty Images)*

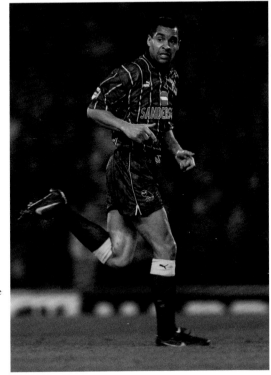

I joined Sheffield Wednesday as the finished article, a complete player. I had some great times in south Yorkshire which I'm very proud of and I'm still the club's leading scorer in the Premier League. *(Michael Mayhew/Sportsphoto)*

With an eight-month-old Isaiah in Dubai.

With Isaiah at Selhurst Park. *(Hy Money)*

Mrs Bright the first, aka Michelle Gayle,
attending A Touch of Pink party in 2006.
(Gareth Cattermole/Getty Images)

Visiting my father's homeland, the Gambia.
This is me in Banjul, the capital, with some kids
outside my uncle's offices.

Christmas party time. If you want to get ahead, get a hat. Me, DJ Spoony, Wrighty and Dion Dublin on route to a PLP Christmas party.

With my former Leicester City teammate and close friend Gary Lineker and his eldest son George. *(Shutterstock)*

Wrighty and Brighty.
(Nick Harvey / WireImage / Getty images)

With the chairman of Crystal Palace FC, Steve Parish, a very special person. Over the years we've had plenty to smile about and I don't think Steve gets the credit he deserves at times. *(Colorsport/Andrew Cowie)*

Steve Parish with his daughters, Jess and Izzy.

With my brother Phil, on holiday in Barbados, 2017.

(above) Caribbean adventure in Barbados: *(left to right)* my son Isaiah, me, sister-in-law Jane, Phil, and their children, Georgia and Taylor.

(right) At the Best of Africa Awards in 2018.

The last full family photo before my mum died in 2011.

Meeting the Duke of Edinburgh at a Duke of Edinburgh awards day at St James's Palace in 2016. He asked me which team I played for. When I told him, he said, 'anyone who plays for a team with Palace in their name will do for me'.

Who would have thought that a kid from Kidsgrove would be allowed inside No 10 Downing Street?

Two photos taken twenty-nine years apart. The top picture is me with Dave and Chris Wight in London 2019; the bottom picture was taken during the Crystal Palace post-season tour of the Cayman Islands in 1990.

With my partner Dee on a mini-break to Rome in 2019.

object, which he held up to the light. He smiled and handed it to us. It contained a small colour slide picture, with a magnifying viewer at the front that you looked through. The picture was of a little girl in a red coat, wearing a hat and scarf. It was Marie. It was all quite sad. He'd kept the picture, but had never once tried to keep in touch with any of us.

That night was the first time I had seen my dad since I was a tiny child. It was also the last time I saw him before he died in 1997. I drove back to London the next day thinking about how strange the visit had been, but I was glad we did it. Seeing him and his wife was odd. He'd left us and just carried on with his life regardless of the pain and suffering he had caused. He'd just moved on, started again and forgotten about us. That was the truth, and there was no way it could be dressed up as anything else. It wasn't a great feeling. I'd never known my dad as a boy, and as we left that night, I realised I would not know him as an adult either. He'd chosen to take himself out of our lives. For whatever reason that was the way he was made. It was hard to understand, but it was a fact.

Some years later, after I'd retired from playing, I made a journey to the Gambia in an effort to try and find out more about my dad's family. I went to Banjul, because I had found out that it was where his family were when he left to travel to England. I wasn't really sure how to start, but one day I got talking to a couple of guys who owned a beaten-up Land Rover and did local safari trips. I told them why I was in the country and they asked me what my dad's name was.

'Eddie Bright,' I told them.

'We know an Oakes-Bright family,' they said, and that was that. They went off to see the guy who turned out to be my dad's brother. He was a local solicitor, and I went to see him and had a long talk. Apparently my dad just decided to take himself off and eventually ended up in England. None of the family knew why he did it, but it sounded very much as though he wasn't quite like the rest of the family. He was also a very good all-round sportsman and a very good cricketer. It was good to get an idea of what he was like and it was also nice for me to connect with a part of the family I'd had no contact with. I stay in touch with them all, and have been to the Gambia on several occasions since that first trip.

After that visit to see my dad I was also glad to get back to London and concentrate once again on my football with the start of pre-season training. It was a period I always liked as a player, when everything was fresh and you had high hopes for what was to come. It was always a time for hard physical work, but I didn't really mind that. You could feel yourself getting fitter with each day that passed, and although there were friendly matches, it wasn't the same pressurised grind of games that come along when the season actually starts. We'd had three great seasons with a core of players who had grown together. Like any other squad, there are always new players coming in and others going: that is the nature of football. One day you are at a club, the next you're on the move. As a player that should never surprise you, but I have to admit that a phone call I got while lounging on my sofa at home one afternoon in September 1991 did just that, and more. It came from Ian Wright.

'Big un,' he said as soon as I answered.

'Yeah, how's it going?' I asked him. It was the same start to a telephone conversation we'd had hundreds of times before, but what he said next had me sitting bolt upright.

'I've just signed for Arsenal,' he said.

I was in shock. I heard what he was saying but couldn't properly take it in.

'I've signed for them and they're about to announce it,' he went on. 'I just wanted to tell you and thank you for everything.'

We both got a bit emotional. It was the end of a footballing partnership. One that we had both enjoyed so much and which had been very successful, but I wanted to let him know how pleased I was for him and also how proud. I told him he deserved it. For him to have arrived six years earlier straight from Sunday league football and to be going to a club like Arsenal was incredible. He had worked so hard throughout his time at Palace and earlier that year had also got himself into the England side. He never stopped wanting to improve, to learn and I knew he would be exactly the same at Arsenal, and that he would do well there. Although we weren't going to be playing together any more, we both knew that our friendship would carry on. We were mates, and that wasn't going to change.

When I put the phone down, I was still stunned. I thought about the game we had played at Oldham the previous Saturday. We'd played well and won 3–2. Ian, John Salako and I had scored the goals. We'd played in our away strip which was just like the Brazilian kit, and we'd all been so happy on the way back to London because it was our first win in four games. That was going to be Ian's last appearance and last goal for Crystal Palace. It was still hard to get my head around what had gone on and how quickly it had happened. I knew I would be going into training the next day and Ian wouldn't be there, he'd be at Arsenal. We had jokingly been called 'a team within a team' by the boss once. He'd been a bit concerned about the way we would often slaughter some teammates verbally if they didn't provide the service we wanted. We promised to stop doing it, but it didn't last long and we were back to moaning and groaning if we didn't get the passes we wanted. The fact was, we never saw ourselves as being outside the team, quite the opposite. We loved being part of the team, but at the same time the other lads knew that, if we got what we needed, the two of us would back ourselves to score against any side, and that meant we all did well.

We had worked hard at developing our partnership on the field, and it wasn't just by chance that we'd had success as a pair up front for Palace. Of course, the fact that we got on well off the pitch certainly helped. We were never in each other's pockets, but we did socialise together and there was a definite rapport between us. We had a lot of laughs and when it came to playing games we knew we could rely on each other. That didn't mean we would hold back if we weren't happy with something the other had done in a game. We would sometimes have a go at each other, but it was never malicious or personal; it was always about the game and making sure we played well in matches.

Steve had spoken to Ian and me once about the possibility of a top side coming in for one or both of us. He'd been very straight and honest about the prospect and basically told us that we had both been playing well for the team and doing our jobs. He said that he didn't want either of us to go, but added that if a top side came in for one of us, he wouldn't stand in our way because he thought we deserved the chance to test ourselves. It gave both of us a bit of a boost to hear the manager talk like that. He was being honest with us, as he always was, and we both took his little chat as a compliment.

All the players knew about Ian's move when I went into training the day after he'd called me, and it felt very strange. It was as if somebody had died. We were all looking at each other without really finding the right words to say. We all knew we were losing a great player, but he was more than that at the club. He was a massive presence in the dressing room. He was charismatic, confident, tough, passionate and wore his heart on his sleeve. What you saw was what you got, and we all knew it was going to be a huge loss. Steve called everyone together.

'Ian's gone to Arsenal and I think he deserves the chance,' he told us. 'This football club will last longer than any of us here and what we've got to show now is that we're not a one-man team. Everyone has got to lift their game and show we can survive without Ian Wright and, as great as he was for us, that is what we've got to do.'

Steve also pulled me to one side later that week and had a word.

'Obviously everyone's going to be looking at you, Brighty, and I think it's a great opportunity for you to show just how good a player you are without Ian being around,' he said. 'It's a big test for you as well as for the football club, but you don't want people pointing the finger at you saying you can't do it without Ian Wright. I think this is going to be good for you.'

Until he spoke to me, I hadn't really thought about things like that, but knew he was right. People would be looking at me, and they would also be looking at any player Steve brought in to play alongside me up front. They didn't have to wait for long, because about a week after Ian went to Arsenal for £2,500,000, Palace spent £1,800,000 on signing Marco Gabbiadini from Sunderland. When I heard about it, I thought it could work. He was twenty-three years old, quick, strong and had looked good whenever I'd seen him play, but it just never happened for him at Palace, and three or four months later he was on his way to Derby County for £1,200,000. When Ian left, he was more or less the finished article; Marco was younger, had been used to playing a different style of football, and found it difficult to adapt. I told him once that when I jumped for the ball and flicked it on, he had to go, anticipating where the ball was going.

'I can't keep doing that, Brighty,' he said. 'I need a breather.'

'That's the way we play, mate,' I told him. 'It's hard, but if you do it, you'll get used to it.'

I tried to protect him a bit if ever I did an interview by explaining to reporters that it wasn't easy for him to come into a club and try to adapt to a different style of play, but there was no protecting him from Andy Gray at half-time during one of the games.

'When Brighty lays the ball off you've got to go,' he told Marco. 'I'll find you and put you in.'

Marco looked at Andy and made some kind of comment, and Andy just exploded with rage. Before anyone could do anything about it, he'd jumped over the treatment table and had his hands around Marco's throat. It had all happened so quickly, but once we realised what was happening the rest of us pulled Andy off as Steve Coppell told everyone to calm down. There was an uneasy quiet in the dressing room before Andy broke the silence as he looked directly at Marco.

'You couldn't tie Ian Wright's laces,' he said. It was ruthless. No one was going to replace Ian. It was impossible. He was the fans' favourite, he was the staff's favourite, and he was the players' favourite. I'd never known a manager bring someone in, realise it wasn't working and then sell him so quickly. To his credit Steve could see it wasn't going to work and he did something about it by selling Marco to Derby.

When Marco was transferred, I had several different people playing alongside me up front. Steve was clearly in the process of changing things and we'd had people like Stan Collymore and Chris Coleman join the club, and although Chris was a defender, both he and Stan played as my partner on occasions. That season also saw the emergence of one of the club's youngsters, Gareth Southgate. He'd played at the back end of the previous season and was clearly one of the kids who looked like he'd have a bright future. He could play in midfield or defence and quickly became part of the first-team set-up. About a month after Marco departed another familiar Palace face moved on, when Andy got a surprise move to Tottenham. It was a temporary transfer to begin with, but then became permanent at the end of the season when Spurs paid £700,000 for him. Like Ian, there was no doubt that Andy was a big personality within the team and the club, and he had been a major part of Steve Coppell teams on two separate occasions, but once again, getting the chance to join a big club like Tottenham was difficult to turn down.

When Ian and Andy left the club, I stayed in touch with them, just as I had with Tony Finnigan. Of course, there was a bit of a gap when they left the club. It is a fact of life when you're a footballer that things can change for you overnight, and I think any player will tell you that you have to be pretty resilient to cope during the course of a career, but also that change is very much part of everyday life. The three of them had made my move to Palace a lot easier when I first arrived from Leicester; they were the first real friends I made, and we got on so well and socialised together.

Andy was probably one of the funniest characters I ever came across during my time as a player, and he could do things that nobody else would get away with. As I've said, he loved the idea of making a bit of money away from the game, and it didn't stop when he left Palace. I got a call from him one day and he said he had something for me. When I met him, he produced something wrapped in cellophane.

'What's this?' I asked him.

'It's a tracksuit, but I've only got it in a small size. Just give me a score for it,' he said.

'Then it's no good to me, is it?' I told him.

'It's not for you, give it to the missus,' he suggested, meaning it would be a nice present for my girlfriend.

I took the tracksuit and handed over the £20 Andy wanted for it. I knew he didn't need the money, but also knew he loved doing little deals. When I next saw my girlfriend, I gave her the tracksuit. The next day she phoned to say she'd tried it on and it fitted, but there was something she wanted to tell me.

'It's got some letters on it,' she said. I assumed it was some sort of designer label, but then she told me what the letters were. 'They're on the sleeve and on one of the legs. THFC.'

I couldn't believe it, except that really, I could, because it was typical Andy. I phoned and told him what had happened.

'Just tell her to pick the letters off,' he told me, and he wasn't joking!

Despite all the changes during that season we managed to finish tenth, which wasn't bad considering all that had gone on, and I scored twenty-two goals. I scored on the opening day of the 1992–93 season as well when we drew 3–3 at Selhurst against Blackburn Rovers, and it was to be my last goal as a Crystal Palace player.

Three weeks later I played my last ever game for the club in a 3–0 defeat at Aston Villa, and six days after that, I became a Sheffield Wednesday player. After almost six years my departure was as quick and sudden as that. There's a cliché that things move fast in football, and that could certainly be said of my transfer to Wednesday.

A few days after the Villa game Steve Coppell pulled me to one side and said he wanted to talk. He said that the Sheffield Wednesday manager, Trevor Francis, had been on the phone and made an offer for me. He also told me it was the third time Francis had tried to buy me. When Ian left, I had started to think of what it would be like if a club came in for me. It wasn't something I thought a lot about, but it did pop into my thoughts from time to time. Things had worked out really well for Wrighty since his move and, whenever we spoke, he would tell me just how much he was enjoying himself there. I began to ask myself whether I would move if a good opportunity came along.

When Ian went, I suppose I was a little bit apprehensive about what might happen. I always knew I would score goals with him in the side, because he made so many for me over the years. He would cut balls back just at the right time for me to run on to them and he managed to put me in on goal a lot during matches. Ian was a different type of player, he had the skill and pace to create and score goals in any team, and he was a big part of my goal-scoring success at Palace. I'd had nearly a season playing without him and still managed to score goals on a pretty regular basis. Palace scored fifty-three goals in the league that season and I got seventeen of them, and I also got four goals in the League Cup. It not only proved to other people that I could do it without him as a partner, it proved that point to me as well. Steve appreciated what I'd done after Wrighty left, but the team and squad were having to change and evolve.

'At the moment, Brighty, I'm rebuilding, and it's going to be a frustrating year for you,' he told me with his usual honesty. 'I'm not pushing you out the door, and if you want to stay, I'll give you another contract, but you might want to go and speak to Trevor. They've got a good team and it looks pretty much like the finished article, so go and see what he's got to say.'

I drove up to Nottingham to meet my agent, and then the two of us travelled up to Sheffield together to see Trevor. Having an agent back then was a bit of a novelty. It was the first time I'd used one, but with the deals in football becoming bigger and more complicated, more players had started to use an agent to negotiate on their behalf. Until then you either did it all yourself or got a good solicitor and accountant to help take care of things. These days there probably isn't even a youth team player who doesn't have an agent, and they are now very much part of the modern game.

I knew Wednesday had some very good players in their squad and one of them was Chris Waddle, who had joined them from Marseille that summer. Trevor had asked him to come in and talk to me about the club, and Chris told me that Trevor had done a good job of selling the club to him. He told me all about the players and said he thought I'd enjoy playing for Wednesday, and I knew the side had a good blend with some very experienced players in it. I liked what I heard from him and what Trevor had to say about the team, and how he saw me as the type of player who could do well at the club. By the time I'd finished talking to him, I'd made my mind up that a move to Wednesday would be good for me. It was a place where I thought I could do well. They had a massive stadium and a huge following. The team seemed to be poised to win things and I wanted to be a part of it.

When I said yes, it wasn't for the money, because the deal they offered me wasn't much more than what I was getting at Palace. I didn't even want to leave London. It was more about me as a player and as a person. There were good footballing reasons for me making the move to Wednesday and I wondered what it said about me if I turned the opportunity down. I thought that if I didn't move it would have meant I was prepared to stay in my comfort zone. I could have stayed at Palace where I knew everybody and everybody knew me, it would have been the easy thing to do, but I wanted to test myself. I was thirty years old and I knew I wasn't going to get many more chances to go to a big club. I phoned Steve and told him I was signing for Wednesday.

The next day I went into the Palace training ground early to collect a few things, including my boots. None of the players were there, but the boss was. I went into his office to tell him about the deal and what had happened the previous day, then he gave me some advice.

'Brighty, play the same way for them that you play for us. Don't go there and change your style of play,' he told me. He also said that I'd get everything that I was owed by the club, which were bits and pieces spread over the length of my contract I'd had with Palace. He said I deserved it, and he thanked me for the way I'd represented the club and what I'd done during my time there. Then he left me with a typical Steve Coppell comment as I walked out of his office.

'Out into the big bad world on your own now, Brighty!' he said.

We both laughed, but I knew it was his way of jokingly wishing me well. He'd been a brilliant manager and I had so much to thank him for, but I think he appreciated the way I had gone about my business as a player, and how I'd played my part in some fantastic years for Crystal Palace Football Club.

I shook hands with the few members of staff who were at the training ground, and then I had to go because I had to get up to Sheffield. I didn't even have time to wait for the players. It was horrible really. Everything happened so quickly, and you find yourself in a strange situation, because your life changes overnight. I'd spent almost six years at Palace, the best part of my career, and I fell in love with the place. Palace was part of me and I felt part of Palace, it was as simple as that. As I drove out of the training ground for the last time, I remember thinking, What have I done? I'm not ashamed to say that when the time came to leave, I doubted myself. During my time at the club, London had very much become home for me. I'd loved it right from the beginning and the place just grew on me, and as much as a big move excited me, it was also tinged with sadness at having to move north, but the reality was that I could be back in London pretty quickly on the motorway. It wasn't as if I was moving to the other side of the world, but it did feel strange.

I went home to pack some things and then drove up the motorway. On the way I decided to phone Ian's mum. I knew she had probably heard about me going and I wanted to talk to her about it. She was a bit upset, saying that Ian had gone and now me, and then she started crying and said that now I was moving to Sheffield I wouldn't go to see her any more.

'Don't be silly, of course I will,' I told her, and then I found myself crying along with her. I drove along with tears streaming down my face. It should have been one of the happiest days of my life and yet, at that moment, I was hit by a real sadness. I loved popping in to see her, and I knew that whenever I was back in London, I would pay a visit, but I also understood what she meant. Palace was her team, Ian and I had played for them, and she loved the fact that we would just drop in and see her together. It was one of the things that would change in my life, but that was part of what happened when you moved clubs. At least Wrighty was still in London and near her, but I was going to be up in Sheffield, and popping in after training was no longer a realistic option for me.

The move was a big gamble. It wasn't like it is these days when going to a bigger club virtually guarantees that you are financially set up for life. Yes, the money was good, but it was nothing like it is today for a Premier League striker. It doesn't take much working out that a four-year contract on £100,000 per week these days should pretty much set you up for life, unless you do something wrong with your money. After I stopped playing, I went through all of my old contracts and decided to add them up to see just how much I had earned as a player. The amount came to just under £1.2 million. At the time I did this little calculation it was rumoured that Wayne Rooney earned that much in a month. It was a sobering thought and an illustration of how times had changed financially.

For me back then, it was all about taking an opportunity with a big club that had the potential to win trophies. I backed myself to succeed there, but at the same time I admit there was a bit of doubt and I did feel slightly vulnerable. It was the first time in almost six years since I'd had to start again at a new club. Part of me was thinking, Do I want to put myself through this, when there is never a guarantee that things will work out? I only had to look back at Marco's brief spell with Palace to realise that, but everything Trevor Francis had said led me to believe I was going to play on a regular basis.

He wanted me as one of his strikers and the guy I would be playing alongside was David Hirst.

15

Familiar Faces

My transfer to Wednesday in September 1992 was valued at £1,375,000 and involved cash plus another striker, Paul Williams, moving in the other direction to join Palace, with Steve Coppell hoping he would help pose a new goal threat for the club alongside Chris Armstrong, who had joined from Millwall about ten days before I left.

Things happened really fast that week. I officially signed on the Friday and then found myself playing in the first team the next day at Nottingham Forest in a game we won 2–1. There was no time to get to know the rest of the team. It was just a case of going in at the deep end and getting on with playing the match, but it didn't take me long to realise that I had joined a club with some very good players already in the squad. I could see exactly what Steve Coppell had meant when he talked about them looking pretty much like the finished article as a team. There was a lot of skill and knowhow throughout the side. They were an experienced team and I very quickly got the feeling that I had joined them at the right time: they seemed like a group who were capable of challenging for trophies. Trevor had told me that he thought he had a team who could win things, and that he wanted me to be part of that. All managers will try to sell a club to you when you're considering a move, but I got the impression from Trevor that he knew what he was doing, and he knew the level of ability he had in the side. He was a great striker himself, and understood better than anyone the value of having people in a team who could score goals.

He already had David Hirst at the club, and I think he hoped I could form the same kind of partnership with him that I'd had with Wrighty. I knew that if we came anywhere near doing that, there was a team around us who had enough about them to push for honours. It was probably the right time for a lot of players in the squad, because so many of them had been around in the game for a while, had ability and were confident of what they were capable of doing on a football pitch. David was injured and out of the team when I arrived at Wednesday, but once he was fit and firing on all cylinders, it was very clear to me just what a good player he was, and the more we played together during my time at the club, the better we got as a partnership. We had a very good understanding and, in a lot of ways, he reminded me of Ian. He was driven, determined, aggressive and very strong. He didn't stand for any nonsense, and was happy to have a stand-up row with someone if he thought it was called for, but once it had happened, he was ready to shake hands and move on. To be honest, I realised once I began training and playing with him that he was much more skilful than I had previously given him credit for. He'd played three times for England and had enough quality to have been a regular international, but was unfortunate to have a certain Alan

Shearer coming through at the same time. When I arrived, Manchester United had him on their radar; they'd tried several times to get him, including a bid in the summer, and when another was knocked back a couple of months after I joined the club, they ended up buying Eric Cantona. There is no question in my mind that Hirsty could not only have played for United, but that he would have scored a lot of goals for them had he gone to Old Trafford. As things turned out, United's loss was mine and Wednesday's gain.

The overall make-up of the squad was different to Palace. When I went to Selhurst Park most of us were young, with the whole 'angry and hungry' philosophy running through the team. When Steve added players, they were of a similar type. Everyone was looking to prove a point, and over a three- or four-year period, I think we all grew as players, and did just that. Winning promotion, getting to a FA Cup final, finishing third in the league and even winning the ZDS Cup, it was all part of the process Steve wanted in an effort to grow the club.

At Wednesday, the majority of the team were not young and had been around the block. Viv Anderson was thirty-six, Danny Wilson was thirty-two, Nigel Pearson was twenty-nine, Peter Shirtliff thirty-one, Chris Woods thirty-two, Nigel Worthington thirty-one, Chris Waddle thirty-one and John Sheridan twenty-eight. Trevor Francis might have been considered a young manager at thirty-eight, but he was also still registered as a player, and was in the team when I played my second match for the club, losing 1–0 at Norwich. There were some youngsters like Chris Bart-Williams and Gordon

Watson in the squad, but the team itself was usually made up of mature professionals. There were a lot of talented players throughout the team and there were a few who were exceptional. When I first joined the club, the assistant manager, Richie Barker, had a word with me.

'I'm not sure you've played with anyone like Sheridan and Waddle,' he told me, and then he offered me a bit of advice. 'Just make a run and they'll find you,' he said. He was right.

The two of them were unbelievable footballers and Chris Waddle was the best player I ever played with throughout my career. He was exceptional as a player and as a person he was incredible, someone who was such great company. During my time with Wednesday he made a lot of goals for me, and his delivery was so accurate. He could bend a ball into you with the outside of his foot that was perfection, and it was just up to me to arrive at the right time and knock it in. Richie was correct when he told me to run and Chris or John would find me. They did, so many times. John was very talented and could pass the ball so well. Chris would also tell me that I had to try and win free kicks in a certain area and then leave it to him to curl a shot in.

'I'll play the ball into you, Brighty, you hold it up and make the defender foul you,' he would tell me.

His preferred area was about twenty-five or thirty yards out on the right as we were playing, but to the left-hand side for a goalkeeper. I saw him hit so many good shots from that area. Goalkeepers always struggled to get near to them and, quite often, they would end up having to pick the ball out of the back of the net without really knowing what had happened. He really was the most gifted player I've been in a team with, and the only thing he couldn't do was head the ball, although he once nodded one in from about a foot out and never stopped going on about it!

There was a clear feeling at the club that with the players we had we could be successful and win things. That first season in 1992–93 did not go as well as we would have hoped in the league. David Hirst had some injury problems, which didn't help, but we struggled to get any winning consistency until a ten-game unbeaten run around the turn of the year propelled us up the table into fourth place by the end of February, and in the same month we made sure of a place in the League Cup final, or the Coca-Cola Cup as it was known then. We'd beaten Hartlepool, Leicester, QPR and Ipswich on our way to the two-legged semi-final against Blackburn, which we won with a 6–3 aggregate score. The other semi-final was between Palace and Arsenal, so I knew that if we got through, I faced the prospect of facing either my old club or my old striking partner. In typical fashion Ian scored a goal in each leg as Arsenal got through 5–1 on aggregate, and so it was Wrighty who lined up against us on 18 April at Wembley.

It wasn't the only cup competition we did well in that year, because by the time we faced Arsenal in that Wembley final we already knew we would be meeting them again at the same venue in May to contest the FA Cup. Both Arsenal and ourselves had got there by beating our local rivals in the semi-finals. We got the better of Sheffield United, and they beat Tottenham. The semi-finals were no longer on neutral club grounds as they had been when I had last played in one with Palace. Both were played at Wembley. Ours was on the Saturday and the second semi-final followed a day later. Derby games are always intense affairs and our match with United was no different. The game divided the city. On paper I knew we were the better team, but at the same time I knew all about what could happen in an FA Cup semi-final, when the unfancied team upset the odds. The one thing we knew we had to do was match them for work rate, and if we did that we were all confident that we would come out on top because we had better players. My old Palace teammate, John Pemberton, was in their side and I remembered how he galloped down the right that day at Villa Park and crossed for me to score against Liverpool.

I had quite a few chances to score against Sheffield United, but at the end of the ninety minutes the two sides were level at 1–1. Chris Waddle had scored for us with one of his magical free kicks, hitting a screamer from about thirty yards, in just the place he'd wanted me to win free kicks. He told John Sheridan to leave the ball to him because he was going to have a shot. John looked at him in amazement and asked if he thought he was Roy of the Rovers! As things turned out, Chris scored the sort of goal that would have been considered too outrageous even by Roy's standards. Unfortunately, we couldn't hang on to our lead, with Alan Cork equalising for them, and that's the way it stayed during the rest of normal time. As we got ready for the extra thirty minutes, John Sheridan came over to me.

'If you'd have scored from one of those ten chances you had, we'd be in the final now,' he told me.

There were a few words exchanged between me and him. I didn't like his comment, but at the same time, I knew he was right, which probably made me even more annoyed. I felt like everyone was looking at me to be the one to score, and just before we walked back onto the pitch John came over to me once again. I thought he was about to have another go, but he didn't.

'Brighty, you'll score the winner here,' he said.

He was right, because despite having a poor game in front of goal that afternoon, everything was forgotten when I headed in a corner from the left for what proved to be the winning goal. All the frustration and tension of the afternoon disappeared when the referee blew the final whistle, and for me it was more a sense of relief. If we'd lost the game, I knew a lot of it would have been down to me for not converting some of the chances I had. I didn't want the club and the fans to miss out on a FA Cup final because of me. It's a worry every striker has because, at the end of the day, you're supposed to be the guy who is paid to put the ball in the back of the net and win games. It's the sort of pressure you have to learn to live with, and when you score and are the hero, no matter how you've played, it's a fantastic feeling. By the same token, you can play well and not score, leaving you totally frustrated and your team beaten. The semi-final was such a special game for everyone connected with the club and the city, although not all the population would have been happy at the final whistle. The feeling at the end, when it sank in, was just as it had been back in 1990. Absolute elation. I went to find poor Pembo to console him. Nobody wants to lose a semi-final. He had played well, and so had United, but the game wasn't just about winning a semi-final, it was about local pride and what it meant to the people of Sheffield. I always used the phrase, 'older, bigger, better', when I compared us to United. We were an older club, we were a bigger club, and we were a better club than United.

Two weeks later we were back at the famous stadium for the League Cup final against Arsenal. We knew it was going to be a tough game, because matches against Arsenal always were. Their manager, George Graham, had them very well organised and as a forward you knew that they possibly had the best-drilled defence in the country, and then there was Wrighty. I knew he was capable of causing havoc against any team and I also knew just how desperate he would be to win his first trophy with the Gunners.

When we were at Palace, we would always room together for away trips, and we'd literally spend hours talking about what it would be like to win trophies. Leagues, cups, playing games at Wembley, all the sorts of things we hoped we could achieve, and as we lined up in the tunnel waiting to go out on the pitch, I knew exactly how he would be feeling and what he would be thinking. I knew he was desperate to win, and he knew the same was true of me. We both looked straight ahead, which some people these days may think is strange, considering all the handshakes and hugs that go on with current players who are waiting to go onto the field. It was just a different era then, and neither of us even made eye contact. You didn't get players talking to the opposition in the tunnel before a match, even if you were the best of mates off the pitch. It was all about being focused on the game and not losing concentration. Having a laugh and joke before the game just wouldn't have felt right. Ian and I used to speak to each other on the phone regularly, but in the week leading up to the final, there was no contact between us. There was no point. The game was there to be won. One of us would end the day as a winner, the other would be a loser. It was a fact we were both aware of, so there was nothing more to be said.

The last time I'd played in a major Wembley final I'd come away feeling terrible, not just because we'd lost that replay to Manchester United, but because I felt I really hadn't done myself justice, so when I walked out to face Arsenal, I was determined that wouldn't happen again. Win or lose, I wanted to make sure I played well, and I didn't want the game to pass me by as the match had almost three years earlier. I think I achieved that. I had a good game, but we didn't play as well as we could collectively and paid the price. We took the lead with a goal from our American midfielder, John Harkes, but Paul Merson equalised for them before the break and in the second half Steve Morrow got the winner for Arsenal. Everyone was naturally disappointed. Two years earlier Wednesday had beaten Manchester United 1–0 to win the League Cup, and the club were desperate to win it again. Carlton Palmer could see how dejected I was to end up on the losing side again.

'You didn't deserve to be on the losing side today, Brighty,' he said. It was good of him to say it, but we all knew we had enough about us as a team to have won, even against a very good side like Arsenal. Then he started to look forward to the next time we would meet them at Wembley. 'This game's gone, but we'll take the big one.'

Two weeks before the FA Cup final we played Arsenal in a league match at Hillsborough, and I scored the only goal of the game. By the time the season came to a close we had finished seventh, I'd scored eleven league goals and so had David Hirst, while Paul Warhurst had netted six. He was a defender, but had been used as a striker when Hirsty had been injured and proved to be very effective. In a twelve-game run he scored twelve league and cup goals, and he'd played along-side me at Wembley in the Coca-Cola Cup final. His form even earned him a call-up to the England squad.

We played our last league game of the season away at QPR just four days before we were due to play Arsenal in the FA Cup final, and a couple of days after that we all went off to Bisham Abbey to prepare for the match at Wembley. On the day before the game we were due to train as normal. David Hirst was fit and raring to go, but defenders Nigel Pearson and Peter Shirtliff both had injury problems. It was a blow not to have them available, but with Paul Warhurst around it at least meant we had a defender with the sort of pace needed to combat someone like Ian, who could leave people for dead with his speed. Paul had a word with Trevor Francis and basi-cally told him that he didn't want to play centre back, he wanted to play centre forward. Trevor told me and said that he was going to have to tell Warhurst that David and me were going to be his forwards against Arsenal, and that Paul was going to be playing at the back. I was amazed that Paul had even thought that he should be playing up front. He might have done well in an emergency capacity, but his natural position was in the middle of defence. We weren't going to be playing a pre-season friendly the next day, where the manager might want to experiment and try out different formations, we were facing one of the best teams in the country in the FA Cup final at Wembley.

Trevor called everyone together and announced that David and I would be playing up front and that Paul was going to play centre back, but he said no, he wasn't going to play there. Paul's nickname was 'Albert', after the *Coronation Street* character Albert Tatlock who always seemed to be miserable. A few of the lads tried to persuade Paul to reconsider.

'Come on, Albert,' they said, 'this is the FA Cup final,' but he still refused to entertain the idea of playing at the back, and said that if he wasn't going to play up front he didn't want to be in the team. I don't think any of us could quite believe what was happening. The eve of the FA Cup final and here was a player basically saying if he didn't get his own way and play where he wanted to play in the team, he wasn't going to play at all. Paul walked off and a few of the players walked after him to have a word, then they came over to me and asked a question that I could not believe.

'Brighty, do you think you could play centre back against Wrighty?' they said. I couldn't believe what I was hearing.

'Are you kidding me?' I asked them. Their thinking was that because I knew Ian so well, I would know his game and be able to use that if I marked him.

'Hold on,' I told them. 'You want me to play in an FA Cup final in a position I've never played in before, against a player who I know will absolutely kill me, just because a guy who is a centre back wants to play centre forward. Is that what you're seriously asking me to do?' I was absolutely furious at what had been suggested, and told the other players to keep Warhurst away from me. Then I went to speak to Trevor and told him I was not going to play centre back in the FA Cup final against Ian Wright, or anybody else. I said that I played number nine, and that was the only place I was going to play. I felt sorry for Trevor, because he should never have been put in a situation like that. I think he tried to explain to Paul in a calm, matter-of-fact way that if David and I played up front we had a better chance of winning the game.

It took a while but Warhurst eventually came around to the idea that he was going to have to play at the back and not the front. I couldn't believe how selfish he was, not to mention the fact that it was complete madness. If Ian had seen me lining up at centre back to play against him, he would have licked his lips. I think he would have actually apologised before the start of the game for what he was going to do to me, and then he would have proceeded to turn me inside out for the following ninety minutes.

The next day I lined up in my usual position alongside David Hirst, and we both knew we were facing not only a very good defensive unit, but a very good team. We knew what to expect and knew what a difficult afternoon it was going to be. Nobody liked playing against them and, as a forward, you knew you were going to get clattered on a regular basis during the course of the game. Not only were their defenders very good, they also let you know they were there from the first minute to the last. Tackles from behind were not uncommon then, and it certainly wasn't the same as it is now for a striker in the Premier League. We were two very evenly matched teams and at the end of ninety minutes it was 1–1. Ian put Arsenal ahead in the first half and Hirsty equalised in the second. We went to extra-time, but there were no more goals. Another FA Cup final replay. I'd been there before.

Arsenal once again had Tony Adams and Andy Linighan playing as centre backs, and it didn't take Tony long to let me know he was there when, very early on in the game, he came clattering into me from behind as we wrestled for possession of the ball. I knew it was going to be another tough physical encounter with the two of them, just as it had been in the first game five days earlier. A little later in the half Paul Warhurst won a header in our half and the ball came looping towards me, and I knew that as soon as I jumped, Andy Linighan was going to come steaming in to try and win the header. As the ball dropped towards us, I had a quick glance over my shoulder to see exactly where Andy was, and then as we both jumped, I stuck out my arm and smashed him in the nose with my elbow. He fell to the ground clutching his face, and it soon became obvious that he'd broken his nose. I'd done it deliberately. I hadn't set out to break his nose, but I did want to lay down a marker to let him and Tony Adams know they weren't the only ones who were capable of dishing it out. When the referee, Keren Barratt, came over I thought I was gone. For a split second it looked as though he might send me off, but he didn't. I got away with it.

Ian worked his final magic once again by scoring to give them a first-half lead. Chrissie Waddle levelled it for us in the second half, I had a good chance but hit the post and we found ourselves having to go to extra-time. The match was so close, it was one of those games where you felt a mistake or a set-piece might decide it, and that's exactly what happened. It looked as though we might be heading towards penalties in order to decide who was going to win, when Arsenal won a corner on the left with literally seconds remaining of the match. Paul Merson went to take it and I took my position in the penalty area ready to mark Andy Linighan. Merson curled his cross into the middle, I jumped to try and make contact and clear the danger, but Andy Linighan jumped higher and made perfect contact with the ball, heading it through the fingers of goalkeeper Chris Woods for the winning goal. There was no time for us to come back from it. Linighan had outjumped me and scored the winner. Some would call it poetic justice. I'd broken his nose, and now he'd broken our hearts. We'd played good football throughout the season and got to two cup finals, so to end the season with no silverware to show for our efforts was cruel. That empty feeling of losing a final at Wembley swept over me again. It was horrible.

A couple of days later I phoned Ian. We both knew how close the games between our two sides were, and the results might easily have been different. We'd gone close, but not close enough, and although I was really disappointed at missing out, I was pleased for Ian. He'd won his first two trophies with Arsenal and I knew how much that meant to him, and I congratulated him. I also needed his help.

'Can you do me a favour? Could you get Andy Linighan's number for me?' I asked him.

'Are you sure?' he said.

'Yeah, what I did was out of order,' I explained. 'I want to talk to him.'

Ian got the number for me and I rang Andy.

'It's Brighty,' I said when he picked up the phone.

'Hello Brighty, how are you?' he asked.

'I'm fine. Listen, it's about your nose,' I started to say, but Andy just began laughing and told me not to worry about it. I said I wanted to apologise personally and told him what I did was out of order. He was really good about it and said that when it came to dishing out a bit of punishment, he was way ahead of me in the game. It wasn't an easy call for me to make but I knew I wanted to make it, and the way Andy reacted was great. When it was time to say our goodbyes, he began to chuckle.

'Brighty,' he said, 'see you at the far post next season!' We both laughed.

16

Vegas

My first season at Wednesday might have ended in disappointment, but I knew I had made the right decision in going there. I grew to love the place and the fans were very good to me. I'm sure it helped that I scored goals and formed a really good partnership with David Hirst but, looking back, I realise at that time in my career, the club was right for me and I was right for the club. It was a good fit. I'd liked the place almost a decade earlier when I had gone to see Howard Wilkinson, but instead went to Leicester.

The group of players we had in the first few years I was there was very good indeed. Not only were they experienced, we also had a very good team spirit, and we all loved football. On Tuesday nights, if the reserves had a home fixture at Hillsborough a lot of the first team would go to watch the match and then, after the game, we'd all go to a bar called Hanrahan's. We'd have a few drinks because we used to have Wednesdays off, but the main reason for going was to talk football, nothing else, and we loved it. We would talk about tactics, about players, about teams, about matches, about our own experiences in the game: it was a regular football forum. Nothing formal, we just used to turn up and talk, and then some of the reserves who had played would come along and join in. They were always great nights and I think it helped us as a team.

After missing out on those two cup competitions, we took a few months to get going in the 1993–94 season. Perhaps it was a bit of a hangover after the two finals, but I think it had more to do with the fact that David Hirst got injured after a handful of games at the start, and spent much of the season out of the side. Once we did get going, we climbed up the league and eventually finished in seventh place, the same as the previous season, and we also got to the semi-final of the Coca-Cola Cup but lost both legs to Manchester United, going out 5–1 on aggregate. On a personal level I had a very good season, finishing with nineteen goals in the league and four in the cup competitions. The fans had really taken to me and despite the fact that I'd spent so long at Palace, I had quickly begun to feel at home following my move to Wednesday.

One of the goals I got that season came in a 2–0 away win at Everton just after Christmas. Howard Kendall had resigned as their manager a few weeks earlier and, in January, Mike Walker took over from him. There were a few rumours flying around that they might be interested in signing me. It was the usual newspaper speculation, which I took no notice of, but clearly some people did. Around the middle of January, a letter arrived at Sheffield Wednesday's ground. There was no such thing as social media then and players often got letters sent to them from fans, usually asking for things like autographs or a signed photo. This was not one of them.

Delivered in a brown envelope, it contained a note written in capital letters, with a short, sharp message for me: 'LISTEN YOU HORRIBLE BLACK TWAT, COME ANYWHERE NEAR EVERTON AND YOU'LL GET YOUR FUCKING BACK BROKE YOU SLUT SHAGGING BAG OF NIGGER SHIT BE WARNED'

Maybe I should have done something about it and told the authorities, but I didn't. I just shook my head in disbelief at the thought that morons like that existed and that they could get so angry about the rumour of a black man like me joining their club. If that person is still around today, I wonder what they will have made of all the black players who have since played so well for the club. Probably the worst concentrated racism I'd felt as a player was, at that point, during my time at Leicester, when I could hear the monkey chants from a certain section of the crowd.

I have to say that I think the whole racism thing has got better in this country since I received that message, but it has clearly not gone away. You only have to see some of the abuse black players get, even now, to realise that it is still a problem, and having the platform of social media makes it easier for people to make those comments and remain anonymous. The person who sent me that note back in 1994 would probably have a field day now, posting the same kind of stuff, just using a phone instead of having to go to the trouble of finding a piece of paper, getting an envelope and finding a letterbox. It is depressing to see that racial abuse of players still goes on, but it's great that people like Raheem Sterling have a big enough profile within the game to be able to make a stand and speak out about it. The trouble is that a player in the lower leagues, or from non-league, will not have that profile, and their voice might not be heard in the same way. Of course, it's better now than it was in my day, but in many ways when you hear about abuse in the current game it's even more shocking, because society has moved on and you just can't believe some people are still so prejudiced and blinkered in the way they think.

I was top scorer again in 1994–95 with a total of thirteen, but Hirsty was again troubled by injury and we struggled as a team to reach the level of consistency we'd previously had in the side. We finished thirteenth in the league and the board decided to sack Trevor after four years in charge. I liked him and was sorry to see him go. He'd given me the chance to join the club and I was grateful to him for that. He also managed me well as a person and treated us all as adults. He'd wanted Hirsty and me to form his main strike force, and it was unfortunate that David had injury problems which kept him out of the side for long periods during two consecutive seasons.

When Trevor left the club, I was thirty-three years old, the sort of age where the media will often put the word 'veteran' in front of your name. I'd looked after myself physically, which meant I was still able to perform at the top, but even back then, players in their early thirties were considered to be coming to the end of their careers, and there was probably added pressure to perform well in every game to prove that you still had something to offer and were not over the hill. In general, players in today's game look after themselves better than they did twenty-five years ago, but I had started to pay attention to my diet and what I ate during my Palace days. I would prepare food for myself at home and then eat it after training instead of having the canteen lunches that most of the players had. I also never drank alcohol once the season started, and I think the regime definitely had an effect and allowed me to maintain decent fitness levels when I got into my thirties, but I realised I had more seasons behind me as a player than I had in front of me. However, I was a fit and experienced proven goal scorer in the top flight of English football.

I don't really have regrets about my career, but I do wonder how things might have gone if I'd made a different decision during the summer of 1995. My contract with Wednesday was coming to an end, and Jamie Redknapp phoned to ask whether I would be interested in talking to his dad, Harry, about the possibility of going to play for him at West Ham. I arranged to meet Harry at a hotel in London's Swiss Cottage. We sat and chatted about football for about two hours and he told me that I was just the sort of player he was looking for. I liked him a lot and I liked what he was saying. I should have signed for him, but I didn't. I knew I could still do a job in the Premiership, as it was known by then, and I still believed I could do that job for Sheffield Wednesday. I was happy at the club, and it seemed as though they were happy with me. I knew the set-up and the players, and had a reasonably successful time there so when I was offered another contract, I decided to sign a new two-year deal with them. In Trevor's last season in charge I played thirty-three full league games, and I finished as the club's top scorer, so with a new manager coming in I was confident I could do a job for him and for the team.

Unfortunately for me, the new manager who came in was David Pleat, and it was pretty clear during the course of his first season that he had other ideas about my ability to perform on a regular basis in the team. By the time the season was over I'd made just fifteen full league appearances for Wednesday, and the writing was probably on the wall for me, even though I'd still managed to score fourteen goals in all competitions. My days as a Wednesday player were numbered. That season the club finished in fifteenth place, two places below the finish that had seen Trevor get the sack, and it was their lowest position since getting promotion five years earlier. Chris Waddle and Chris Woods left the club that summer, as did a player called Marc Degryse, a Belgian forward David Pleat had brought in a year earlier from Anderlecht, but it hadn't really worked out for him. In that same summer the club also spent £2.5 million on a young player named Andy Booth from Huddersfield. He was a striker, and the writing on the wall probably got bigger for me. I had always backed myself to score goals, and still did, but that means nothing if the manager of a club just doesn't fancy you to do the job.

I had enjoyed my time at Sheffield and settled into life up there really well. Being in the north also meant that I was able to see more of Gran Davies, simply because the travel involved was a lot easier for me. I would often finish training and pop over to have a cup of tea and a chat with her. When

I was in London I would go up and see her for a couple of days at a time whenever I could, and she enjoyed coming down to London for a long visit on one occasion when I was able to spend a week with her and show her around town. She loved it and she really liked the girlfriend I had at the time.

Sometime in 1995 Wednesday had an away game and I was rooming with Chris Bart-Williams. We were watching television on a Saturday morning before a game. A girl appeared on the screen singing her latest single and I couldn't take my eyes off her.

'I'm going to marry her,' I said.

'What?' said Chris, looking at me as if I was mad, but I was serious. The girl in question was Michelle Gayle, and about a year after I got to meet her, we were married.

We met in a place called the Spot in Covent Garden on a Saturday evening. A lot of players would go there after games to listen to music and have a drink before going on to other places. Michelle was there with a friend and a guy called Dennis Lewis, who was the brother of the heavy-weight world champion, Lennox Lewis. I knew Dennis and Lennox and recognised Michelle, so I introduced myself and chatted to her. The next day I phoned Dennis and asked him for Michelle's number. He said he couldn't give her number to me without asking her first, but promised to contact her for me and then get back to me. When he did phone back, he had a message from her for me.

'Tell him, if he was a man, he'd have asked me for it on the night!' she'd said.

Dennis explained that Michelle would be going to a party Lennox was having in central London that summer, and knew that I would be going to it as well, so it meant I would get the chance to have a chat to her again. Michelle was already there with a friend when I arrived wearing a Panama hat and white shirt.

'Who the hell does that guy think he is?' asked Michelle's friend when she saw me.

'He's the one I've been telling you about,' she answered sheepishly.

I hadn't set out to look flash, or outrageous, but despite the way I looked that night, Michelle and I chatted away happily before I had to leave because I was driving up to Sheffield that night for the start of pre-season training the next day. On the way up we spoke again on the phone and the conversation lasted for about two hours. We talked about anything and everything. It was a happy, easy conversation and we began to see more of each other, with her sometimes taking the train up to Sheffield and staying, or me going down to London when I could.

One evening I was sitting with my gran watching television. *Top of the Pops* came on and I knew Michelle was going to be singing on it, so I made sure I watched it with Gran. Michelle appeared on the screen, singing and moving around the set. Halfway through it, I turned to Gran and pointed at the television.

'Gran, this is my new girlfriend,' I told her, nodding towards the pictures of Michelle.

'Oh, that's nice, Mark,' she said. 'Is she a go-go dancer?'

The way she said it was hilarious, but little did she know at the time that it wouldn't be too long before Michelle stopped being my girlfriend, and instead became my wife.

As the 1996–97 season began it was pretty clear I was being eased out as a first-team player. I didn't really get a look in. I came on as a substitute for a home game against Leicester at the beginning of September, but there seemed to be no chance of me playing regular first-team football for Wednesday again. I wanted to play games, but it wasn't happening. David Pleat's assistant was Peter Shreeves, and I got on well with him, but when training came around, he had the unenviable task of letting players know if they were part of the first-team plans each day.

'Right, if I read your name out, stay here. If I don't, go up and train with the reserves,' he would say.

'Pete, why don't you just say, "Brighty, go up and train with the reserves"?' I asked him.

'Mark, don't shoot the messenger,' he told me, and we both laughed. I knew it wasn't his decision to have me training with the reserves, but it did start to feel as if the only way I was going to be playing regularly was in the first team of another club. He probably knew it, and so did I.

During November there was an international break, which meant that I would have a long weekend off. I'd been training but not playing. The situation was getting worse for me and it was a really frustrating time. I wanted to play matches. Training and having no real end product was no good to me, especially as I was well aware that I was now coming towards the end of my career, with probably less than a handful of seasons in front of me. There had been some interest from other clubs and I knew I might have to go out on loan for a while just to get some game time and put myself in the shop window for a possible permanent move somewhere. Before all that happened, I had something much more important to do. Michelle and I had decided to get married and have the wedding in Las Vegas. Knowing that the international break was coming up we decided to do it on that particular weekend. Michelle was already in Los Angeles, doing some recording, so after training in Sheffield on the Friday, I drove down to London and caught a plane to Vegas. We got married on the Saturday, and then on the Sunday she went back to LA and I flew home to England, but the flight was delayed and I ended up missing training on the Monday. I phoned the club to tell them that I wouldn't be able to make it, but there would be consequences for missing the training session, which of course I knew I would have to accept. That was perfectly fair and reasonable. What I wasn't prepared to do was tell anyone where I'd been and the fact that I was now a married man.

When I went into training the next day David Pleat asked to see me. He said he was going to fine me one week's wages for missing training, and I told him I understood and had been delayed getting back from a trip. He asked me where I had been, but I refused to tell him, then he said that if I did tell him, he wouldn't fine me, but I still said no. I think he was baffled by the fact that I was prepared to pay the fine and not reveal where I'd been. It seemed to intrigue him, especially when he made the offer again, and

I once more refused and said I'd accept the fine and pay it. I just didn't want to share the secret of me getting married with a guy who didn't seem to rate me as a player, and who was easing me out at the club. Years later, we met at a match and David reminded me of the incident, and asked where I'd been that weekend, expecting me to finally tell him, but once again I refused to say, and the two of us laughed about it.

David wasn't the only person kept in the dark about what had happened, because neither of us had told our families and friends about the Vegas trip. The reason was that Michelle was about to release an album and we didn't want publicity surrounding our marriage to overshadow it, but a newspaper found out and said they were going to run the story. They basically gave us a day to let anyone we wanted to tell know about the wedding, and then they were going to print with it. I knew I had to tell my gran, and I also knew she wasn't going to be happy about being kept in the dark. I went across to see her and took some pictures of the ceremony with me. I sat down and had a cup of tea with her and then produced the pictures.

'What are these?' she asked, and then slowly realised what they were. I tried to explain why we had gone to Vegas to get married and not told anyone, but I could see just how upset she was because she was physically shaking.

'How could you do this to me, Mark?' she asked.

I felt terrible. I knew how much family and family events meant to her, and being at my wedding must have been something she had thought about quite a few times, and to not go and not be told hurt her more than I had imagined. She was still in a bit of a state when I suddenly had a thought.

'We're going to have a blessing, Gran,' I said.

'What?' she asked, looking at me.

'We're having a blessing. We'll go through it all again and then have a get-together for family and friends next summer.'

I was thinking on my feet. I knew I had to say something because I could see how upset she was, and I hated seeing her like it. Happily, the idea of a blessing did the trick. She immediately started looking forward to it, even though it was going to be months away.

As soon as I left Gran's I phoned Michelle. She hadn't exactly had a great reaction from her parents either, but then I told her about the blessing and party idea I'd come up with and we both agreed it would be a nice thing to do. From that moment, when we told family and friends, we also mentioned the fact that we would be doing something for everyone in the summer. Phil and my sisters were surprised, because they knew nothing about the wedding either, but thankfully they weren't upset in the same way Gran had been, and were just pleased for me and Michelle.

Having come back from a whirlwind few days in Vegas and the happiness of getting married, I was soon back to the reality of contending with a football career that was stagnating. There was no hope of me getting my place back in the team and I wasn't even involved as part of the squad. It had come to the point where on Saturday mornings I had to train on my own with one of the fitness coaches at the club. The thinking was that although I wasn't playing matches on a Saturday, I still had to maintain my fitness, so I would run in the morning and then jump into my car and head down to London to see Michelle, and if Arsenal were playing at home, I would go to Highbury and watch Ian. I did this one day and found myself caught up in a nasty incident with an Arsenal fan. I'd parked my car and was walking to the ground. I walked past a pub on the way and an Arsenal fan stepped in front of me.

'You're a cunt. You broke Andy Linighan's nose,' he said.

I couldn't quite believe what was happening. The incident with Linighan had happened years before, Arsenal had won the game and Andy had the last laugh by scoring the winner, when he climbed above me to head the ball into the net. I explained this to the guy, but it was obvious there was no reasoning with him, and it also became clear he wanted to whack me. I kept calm and just stared at him, wondering how to try and defuse the situation, before one of his mates came over and pulled him out of my way. It was a crazy situation, and it could so easily have ended badly. I love football and I love the passion and commitment that supporters show, but I couldn't believe the sort of twisted thinking the guy displayed that day. It showed how quickly things can escalate out of nothing and end in possible violence. Happily, I haven't been involved in an incident like that since, but I suppose it is one of the perils of being recognised. These days if someone recognises me it's usually just a quick nod of recognition, maybe some friendly banter or someone wanting a selfie.

I desperately wanted to kickstart my career and in order to do that I had to be playing first-team football. Clearly, I wasn't going to be doing that at Wednesday, so I needed to go to another club. There were a few clubs who were interested in taking me on loan, and one of them was Millwall. I wondered how it would go down with their fans with me having played for Palace, one of their local rivals, but in the end it was a chance to play some games and it was in London, so I agreed a one-month loan deal with them. They were in Division Two, but I was grateful to be playing again and scored on my debut in a 1–1 draw at Bournemouth.

I knew going to Millwall was not going to be a long-term solution for me, but it was a step in the right direction, a step towards accepting what was now inevitable. Sadly, I had to leave Sheffield Wednesday.

17

Alpine Adventure

The idea of one day playing abroad was something that had always appealed to me. When I was at Palace, I spent a year learning Spanish at night school. I thought if ever the opportunity came to join a club in Europe one day, being able to speak Spanish might not be a bad idea, and having another language appealed to me. I'd seen how Gary Lineker and his wife at the time, Michelle, had enjoyed their time when he went to play for Barcelona. The two of them helped me with the language when I was doing the course. As things turned out, I might have been better off learning French, instead of Spanish, because early in the New Year I got an interesting call from my agent at the time, Struan Marshall.

He'd been contacted by a French agent who was acting on behalf of a Swiss club called Sion. They were looking for a number nine, I had come up on their radar, and they wanted me to go to Switzerland and meet them. Struan thought it would be a good idea. After all, what did I have to lose? The obvious answer to that was not a lot, so we flew over to meet with them at a hotel in Sion. The president of the club was a man called Christian Constantin, who was a big, imposing figure, and he spoke to us through the French agent who translated everything he said into English.

'I like strong players,' he told us. 'I like your record. Do you want to come and play for my team?' It soon became apparent the guy was unlike any chairman or owner I'd ever come across in England, and it was also obvious that he was very much in charge of everything that went on at his club. The more we talked the more I liked the idea of signing for them. He showed me around the club, and I liked the look of the place. After more discussion about what was expected of me and the contract they were offering, I decided to sign. As always when you make a move, things seem to happen very quickly. I got back to Sheffield, packed a trunk to be shipped over to Switzerland, and was off. Having only just got married, it probably wasn't great for Michelle, but I knew she had her career and I think we both kind of understood that there would be times when we would be away from each other. She also realised that I badly needed to get my career going again, and at the age of thirty-four, I didn't have too many years left as a player.

It was exciting for me as a player and as a person, and it just seemed like too good an opportunity to miss. I'd had so many happy times at Wednesday since joining them, but my life as a footballer had become miserable after David Pleat's arrival. He was the manager and it was his decision not to play me, which I understood and respected, but as a senior professional and someone who had scored a lot of goals for the club during the little more than four years I had been there, I just felt I hadn't been treated particularly well. Moving on was the right thing and the best thing I could have done at that time. I assumed when I agreed to go to Sion that it was a clean break from Wednesday and a fresh start for me, but that didn't quite prove to be the case.

When I made the decision to go, one of the people I spoke to was the Sheffield Wednesday chairman, Dave Richards. I'd always had a very good relationship with Dave and I liked him, so I thought it was important to let him know that I liked Sion and wanted to move there.

'You've been brilliant for us, Brighty,' he told me. 'If that's what you want, we're not going to stand in your way.'

It was just what I wanted to hear. I was going to open a new chapter in my footballing career in a new country. It all started well enough. I went there as a proven Premiership goal scorer and they clearly seemed happy to have me at the club, and made me feel very welcome. I only spoke a handful of French words, but most people there spoke English to some degree or other, which made the whole process of settling in a lot easier for me. They also made sure I took French lessons three times a week, which was great from my point of view, because I gradually felt more confident using the language, even if most of it was used for football-related things. They sorted out an apartment and a car for me, and I soon settled into life in what is a beautiful part of the world.

It was different to anything else I'd experienced before as a footballer. Let's face it, there weren't too many mountains in the Potteries or south London, but it wasn't just the fantastic scenery that was different, it was the whole way of life. The pace was so much slower than in London and Sheffield, which I loved. I wanted to play abroad for the experience as much as anything else and I quickly immersed myself in Sion life. It was a small place with a population of about 27,000. I'd played in front of more people in matches for Palace and Wednesday, but I very quickly felt good about being there and the players made me really welcome. The coach was an Italian guy named Alberto Bigon, who'd been an attacking midfielder and striker in his time as a player, and was in the same very successful AC Milan side as Fabio Capello.

Bigon obviously liked me as a player and thought the way I played in England was something he could use for Sion, but as I mentioned, the club was controlled by the president, and in my meeting with him he came across as the sort of guy nobody messed with. While I was at the club, he once strode into the dressing room to let the players know exactly what he thought of them. The team were drawing or losing a game at the time. He spoke to a player in French, but one of the other lads translated the exchange for me.

'Your wife wears nice clothes?' he asked the player.

'Yes, Mr President,' the player replied.

'Your kids go to nice schools?'

'Yes, Mr President.'

'You live in a nice house?'

'Yes, Mr President.'

'You drive a nice car?'

'Yes, Mr President.'

'Then don't fuck with me!' screamed Constantin. 'Don't go and play like that, you're insulting me. If you don't improve in the second half, I'm going to stop your money.'

He then pointed at two or three other players, speaking in German and French, and threatened to sack one of them. I couldn't believe it and told the other lads that he simply wasn't able to do what he had said.

'Oh yes he can,' they informed me.

I was told that there was no such thing as the Professional Footballers' Association that we have in England. As crazy as it might sound, the players all seemed to accept this as the way of life at the club, and to be honest, I never felt it had an adverse effect on team morale.

I joined Sion just as they were having their mid-season winter break, and that meant that before we resumed playing competitive matches, there was a kind of mini pre-season when we played some friendly matches. The training regime was different to the sort of thing I'd experienced in England. I found it new and fresh, which I liked. It was what I'd looked forward to when I decided to go to Switzerland. Something which was familiar was the changing room. By that I mean the jokes and the general 'banter' that seems to be universal among players, and it helped me to settle in. Just like any player going to a new club, I was going into the unknown and, in some ways, you have to win your team-mates over. Not just by becoming a part of everything as quickly as you can, but also by showing the rest of the squad that you can play and will improve the team. They knew my background, but I was starting from scratch in many ways. I very quickly became part of the group, although I did manage to unwittingly get in their bad books on one occasion when I was chatting on the phone to Michelle and lost track of the time. We were all due to have dinner together and I walked in late, not thinking very much of it, but it was a big deal within the group, and the management soon put me straight, telling me that we all had to eat together at the agreed time. Then they told me to apologise to everyone and shake their hands. I thought they were joking at first, but could soon see how seriously they took it, and I was genuinely sorry for keeping them all waiting. When I thought about it I could see it was an important part of building team unity within the group.

One day I turned up for training and there was a buzz about the place. I was told there was another player who would be joining the club, or to be more precise, re-joining the club. He had been playing in the Portuguese leagues, but was with Sion before that and had obviously made a favourable impression.

'His name's Roberto,' one of the players told me. 'Roberto Assis.'

'I've never heard of him,' I said. I wasn't trying to be rude, I was just stating a fact. It wasn't a name I was familiar with, but they were all very excited about the prospect of him coming back to the club.

'You wait, Bright,' they said. 'You will see what a great player he is and what a fantastic left foot he has.

He takes great free kicks, you will not believe how good they are.'

A few days later this quite short, plump figure with wavy black hair turned up at the training ground. It was Roberto. I found out that he was from the great footballing nation of Brazil, but in all honesty, he didn't look too impressive when he wandered in. In fact, he didn't really look like a footballer, or any sort of athlete. He was clearly carrying a few pounds and was out of shape, but he was pleasant enough. Even though he only spoke a few words of English and my Portuguese was non-existent, we got on fine and somehow managed to communicate. He offered to do some crossing for me over a static wall and into the penalty box when the other players had finished training. It was just him and me out on the pitch, and I would meet the ball with either my head or foot and knock it into the net. As soon as he began to hit the crosses for me, I could understand what the other boys were saying about him. His left foot was unbelievable, and when he moved the wall and started prac-tising his long range free kicks, he looked world class.

He got himself fit during the pre-season training period and one evening when we were all having dinner, Roberto told me how tough it had been having to leave all of his family back in Brazil in order to try and earn a living as a professional footballer in Europe. I discovered there were lots of players who took a similar route, and they would play for various clubs in different parts of the continent, often staying for just one season or even less. Roberto said that he had a younger brother back in Brazil who was really talented.

He said the kid was only about sixteen, but was sure that if his brother got a break in Europe, he could make it as a professional. Roberto had tried to get the club he'd played for in Portugal to give his brother a trial, and he'd offered to pay his air fare for him to come over to Switzerland to have a trial with Sion, but the president wasn't prepared to take him up on his offer. I felt sorry for Roberto. He clearly thought the world of his kid brother and, more to the point, he believed in him, just as Phil had done with me when I was trying to make it as a professional.

Quite a few years after I had this particular conversation with Roberto, I got a call one day from an old friend named Andy Ansah. Andy was a former professional footballer and when he'd retired from the game he got into acting, and he also choreographed various football-related routines that were used for adverts and promotional material. He'd worked with all sorts of well-known players from all over the world, so when he called, I naturally asked him what he was up to, having not spoken to him for a while.

'I'm doing a video for Nike,' he told me. 'I've also got someone here who wants to say hello to you.'

Andy passed the phone to someone and a couple of seconds later I heard a voice that immediately took me back to my time at Sion.

'Bright, Bright! It's Roberto Assis,' said the voice on the other end of the phone.

I could hardly believe it. His English was better than it had been at Sion. When he'd found out that Andy was a former English footballer, he told him about meeting an English player in Switzerland. He said his name was Mark Bright, did Andy know him? When Andy told him he knew me well, Roberto asked him to call. It was great to hear from my one-time teammate once again and, after a brief chat with him, he handed the phone back.

'Andy, how do you know him?' I asked, intrigued at the thought of him working with Assis.

'Who, Roberto?' said Andy.

'Yes,' I replied.

'I'm doing a video with his brother,' he explained. 'His brother's Ronaldinho!'

I couldn't believe it. The kid brother Roberto had told me about, the one he claimed was a great little footballer, and who both Sion in Switzerland and Sporting Lisbon had passed up on, was now a genuine world superstar, and his big brother, Roberto Assis, was his agent. I was stunned. It was an unbelievable story, which you just could not have made up. I was so pleased for Roberto, who was not only a really good footballer but a really nice guy as well. I was also pleased for the kid brother he'd had so much faith in, and who finally made it as a professional footballer in such spectacular fashion.

When I went to Sion, I thought I would be going there on a free transfer, with no fee involved. My contract with Wednesday was due to end that summer and I was clearly not in any plans David Pleat had. I'd done well during my time at the club and scored a lot of goals for them. Not having to pay a fee for me obviously made it a more attractive proposition for Sion. They got a proven goal scorer and all they really had to worry about was my salary for the one-year contract, but then things suddenly got complicated. I discovered Wednesday were asking for a fee. I thought there was some mistake, because I believed they didn't want a fee, so I decided to speak to Dave Richards again. He told me he paid David Pleat to manage the club and he had decided he wanted £60,000 for me. I couldn't believe it. I thought it would hold the whole thing up, but I signed and was told that the situation would be sorted out, but it never really was. Instead, I entered a frustrating period where I could train and play in friendly matches, but not in league games. I played in one friendly and clattered into the opposition goalkeeper, which prompted a mini punch-up on the pitch. It wasn't really anything too heavy, but I think the referee suggested to our coach that it might be better if he took me off, just to help take the sting out of the whole situation. It was the sort of challenge that wouldn't have raised any eyebrows in England, but it wasn't something they were used to seeing out there. The president liked it though.

'See this guy,' he said to the other players as he pointed at me. 'He likes to fight for my team!'

I think he liked me as a player, but not enough to pay a fee, and when he realised there was another striker who he already knew and could bring in, he did just that. It was obviously disappointing and the way it all ended wasn't great, but there is an old cliché that says nothing should surprise you in football, and after being told what was going to happen, my first thought was making sure I didn't dwell on the situation. I had to put it all behind me and move on.

My experience of playing abroad had lasted a matter of weeks, and despite the way it ended I had enjoyed my brief time at Sion, but I was aware that I quickly needed to find myself another club.

18

Happy at the Valley

When the decision was made not to go ahead with my transfer to Sion, it left me very little time if I wanted to find a club in England. At the time, the transfer deadline day was the last Thursday in March, and there was no such thing as designated transfer windows as there are now in the summer and in January. In those days players could be bought and sold throughout the season but that last Thursday in March marked the cut-off point and no permanent business could be done after then, so I literally had days to try and fix myself up with a club because that deadline was fast approaching.

I spoke to a few people, including a couple of friends who happened to know the Charlton manager, Alan Curbishley. He had done a fine job at Charlton, gradually building a team and squad of players in an effort to try and get promotion from the First Division. My friends had a word with Curbs, and explained the situation I found myself in. He liked the idea of taking me to the club for the last few weeks of the season to see how it worked out, but he didn't want to jump into anything without checking on me first with a few people in the game. One of them was my old Palace boss, Steve Coppell.

'Take him,' Steve apparently said. He knew me as a player and a person, had seen me play and train, and knew what I was like around a football club. Curbs must have got other similar feedback from people he asked, and I soon found myself back in English football, and back in south London. I was relieved and grateful to get the chance, but went there knowing they were only going to sign me until the end of the season, which was fair enough. From my point of view, I just wanted to be able to play some games, hopefully score some goals and put myself in the shop window. By the time the new season started I would be thirty-five years old, but I was really fit thanks to all the work I'd done in Switzerland, and as a forward I would back myself against anyone to score goals.

I started the first two matches as a substitute, but in my first full game I scored a goal in each half at the Valley, as we beat Portsmouth in a home match. I played the last three games of the season after that, and then it was decision time.

I knew Curbs wanted to have a real crack at promotion and that he thought having someone with my experience and goal record around could only be a good thing for the squad. My contractual problems were finally settled with Sion, and he offered me a one-year contract and I was happy to sign. I liked him as a manager, liked the set-up at the club, and liked the club itself. I never felt unwelcome, even though I'd had a long association with one of their south London rivals, Crystal Palace. I felt happy and settled there, even though my daily commute to the training ground in New

Eltham in south-east London was a bit of a nightmare at times, because Michelle and I had bought a house in Harrow, which was in north-west London. It was where we had the blessing and party we'd promised everyone and, despite the journey, it felt good to be back and settled at a club that had ambition, and I felt I could play a real part in helping them get to the Premiership.

I was very comfortable with the situation. Curbs needed more experience in the squad, the team had young legs and I found myself at a club that had ambition and wanted to achieve things so, far from winding down towards the end of my career, I was part of something that was full-on, which was exactly how I liked it. I never wanted to go into a bad situation at some club just for the money; that wasn't ever in my thinking. I wanted to continue to play, but play for the right club who had a purpose about what they were doing, and Charlton were perfect for me.

The nucleus of the team was already good when I got there for the final few weeks of the season, but in the summer before the 1997–98 season, when Curbs had told me that the club were going to go for promotion, he brought in some more experience in the shape of defender Mark Bowen, Matty Holmes from Blackburn and, perhaps most importantly, Clive Mendonca from Grimsby. I soon discovered what a great finisher Clive was, not just in matches, but also in the way he scored in training. He was a natural, a really nice guy, and remained totally unaffected by the praise he got during the season as his goals helped Charlton into the play-off places.

Having gone through the drama of the play-offs before with Palace, I never thought I would be doing it again nine years later. Getting into the top flight changes a football club. It was certainly true of the time Palace went up after that two-legged victory against Blackburn. Not only did we get to play in what was the old First Division against the best teams in England, but financially it meant so much to the club. By the time Charlton reached the play-offs in 1998 it was estimated that going up into the Premiership was worth around £10 million. An incredible amount of money at the time, especially to a club like Charlton. We beat Ipswich over two legs in the semi-final, which meant we were going to meet Sunderland in the final. They had finished third in the league and we had ended the campaign a place behind them. Unlike my last experience of the play-offs, the final was no longer on a home and away basis over two legs. It was a one-off game played at Wembley, and the stakes were enormous.

It was the seventh time I'd played at Wembley. I'd been involved in FA Cup finals which had gone to replays, a League Cup final, and that ZDS Trophy, and knew how intense one-off games at the stadium could be, and how they could go by in a flash without the people involved being able to fully take in the day. I was determined to make sure it wouldn't happen on this occasion, and decided to record a lot of the day with a video camera. I'm not sure what Curbs made of me getting on the team bus with a camera in my hand, but when I explained the reason behind it, he let me carry on, and I know he thought my experience of playing at Wembley on some big occasions could benefit the team.

The match itself turned out to be an absolute classic, and one of the most memorable I played in during my career. It had pretty much everything in it, but perhaps the biggest ingredient was drama. We opened the scoring through Clive, they equalised with a Niall Quinn goal, they went ahead thanks to Kevin Phillips, we equalised with another goal from Clive, Quinn made it three for them, and centre half Richard Rufus forced the game into extra-time when he made it 3–3. It was an amazing ninety minutes and there was even more drama to come.

I came off after a few minutes of extra-time and was replaced by Steve Brown, and shortly after that the game took another twist when Nicky Summerbee made it 4–3 to Sunderland, and the game started to look over for us, but there was a tremendous spirit in the side and a desire not to be beaten. It was Clive who once again hit the back of the net, and the game went to penalties. Having taken five each, the sides could still not be separated. It went to 6–6 and the tension inside the stadium was unbearable. Both sets of fans could not really believe what they were seeing. Neither side was cracking and when we went 7–6 up, it still felt as though we were never going to settle it, especially as the next man up to take a penalty for them was Michael Gray. He had a superb left foot, and if ever any player looked a certainty to score from the spot in those circumstances, it was him. He didn't because our keeper, Saša Ilić dived to his left and saved Michael's shot. The £10 million save, some of the newspapers later called it, and suddenly Charlton Athletic were in the Premiership. The club had endured some terrible times in the 1980s when they almost went under, and they had been forced to leave the Valley and ground share at Selhurst Park and then West Ham's Upton Park before returning to the Valley. In just five and a half years since that return, they were in the top flight of English football.

It was an incredible story, and I had only come in at the end of it, but I was so pleased and proud to be part of it. They were a good club, with good people who ran it, and good players in the squad. The fans had suffered, but they never stopped supporting Charlton, and although they had no way of knowing it on that hot and sticky Monday afternoon in May 1998, under Alan Curbishley they were to go on and have the ride of their lives in the eight years that followed.

The match left everyone dazed and drained. You also had to feel sorry for Sunderland. They had put everything into the game and ended up with nothing. It was cruel, but I was pleased that a year later they did make it, winning the league and getting automatic promotion.

We had a reception at a hotel near Heathrow, and everyone just seemed to be knackered after what had gone on. We were all delighted but it had taken so much out of everyone, both physically and emotionally, and as pleased as we all were, it was hard to get going in many ways because I think we were still all coming to terms mentally with what we had done. I'd been to Wembley and lost in FA and League Cup finals, so being involved in such a remarkable game and ending it as a winner was a fantastic experience.

In many ways it had felt like a Cup final, but it was also so much more, because it meant the club would be playing in the top flight of English football. Getting promotion with Palace nine years earlier had been incredible, but I think the change to making the play-off final a single game, instead of over two legs, just added to the whole thing, and the drama of the day made it very special.

It was a strange day for Clive Mendonca as well. He had played brilliantly and scored a hat-trick, but he had been a Sunderland supporter since he was a kid. It was funny seeing all of his family at the reception, because they had been to the game and supported Sunderland. I was pleased for Curbs and for Les Reed, who was his coach: they had both put a lot of work in during the season and their planning for the final had been meticulous. It was a great day for everyone, but I knew that in a matter of days I was going to be out of contract once more. I felt fit and able to play in the Premiership again, but knew the decision wasn't down to me.

Curbs had a conversation with me in the summer. I was thirty-six years old and we both knew I was coming to the end of my playing career. He said he wanted me around the place, but was straight with me as well. He told me he was going to be bringing players in and that I wasn't likely to get that much playing time in the first team, but felt I was the sort of player who could help the squad in what was going to be a massive challenge for them. It made me think about whether I should pack in playing at that point, rather than start to feel frustrated at not being in the first team. I told

Michelle about what was on offer for me if I signed another contract.

'If you want to pack it in, then pack it in,' she told me, 'but if you want to carry on playing you've got to embrace the whole situation and go for it, even if you are out of the team.'

I knew she was right and I knew I wanted to still be part of the squad. I agreed another one-year deal, but played most of my football in the reserves. I still trained as hard as ever and it was good to be there and part of a special season for the club. I also enjoyed talking to some of the younger players and giving them advice if they needed it.

As expected, it soon became a tough learning curve for the team and it wasn't long before we were fighting for our Premiership lives. About halfway through the season I played in a midweek reserve fixture alongside another striker named Kevin Lisbie. He was about twenty years old at the time and although he'd played in the first team for Charlton before that season, like me he wasn't really in the side at the time. During the course of the game he had the chance to square the ball to me a couple of times when I was in a good position to score, but he didn't.

'Lis, you've got to pass the ball, you can't score from there,' I told him.

'Fucking shut up!' he shouted at me.

It stunned me a bit, and I suddenly thought, This is what it's come to. I've got a twenty-year-old kid telling me to f-off. Gary Stevens was the reserve team coach and at the end of the game he could see I was a bit fed up. He asked what was wrong, but I didn't say anything. Instead, I got showered, changed and drove home to Harrow. I told Michelle I was going to sleep in the spare room that night because I had something to think over. I got up early the next morning to go to the training ground, and knew that I was going to call it a day on my playing career. I told Michelle what I'd decided to do, and said I felt better having sorted it out in my own mind.

'Mark,' she said, 'have you ever quit at anything in your life?'

I knew what she was saying, and we both knew the answer was no, but this was different. I'd already made the decision to stop playing at the end of my contract and try to move into media work, but the Kevin Lisbie incident just made me think it wasn't worth hanging around for another six months. On the way in I phoned Curbs, because I knew he always got in early, and asked if I could pop into his office and see him when I arrived, which was what I did. I told him I wanted to retire there and then and explained why.

'Brighty, no, don't pack it in now. I'll talk to Lisbie,' he said.

'It's not just the Lisbie thing, Curbs,' I told him. 'I can't do what I used to do. I don't feel as effective, and if I go it will leave a space for you to bring someone in.'

Curbs was adamant that he wanted me to stay for all the reasons he'd outlined to me during the summer. He wanted my experience and knowhow around the place. The age thing obviously meant I wasn't going to be involved too often, but I think he valued experience, and underlined that point a few months later when he signed John Barnes from

Newcastle on a short-term deal until the end of that season. I agreed to stay on and not hang my boots up at that point. Sometime later Kevin Lisbie came to see me to say sorry for what had happened.

'Lis, does it take the management to tell you to apologise, or do you really feel bad enough about it to want to say sorry?' I asked him.

Either way we shook hands and moved on. I just thought what had happened showed a lack of respect for a senior professional. I wasn't getting all high and mighty about it, but it was something I would never have done when I was his age and still making my way in the game. Maybe times had changed, but I found it disappointing nevertheless. I'm glad I did change my mind and decide to stay, and it was nice to hear Curbs say that he thought I could be of use at the club, even if my first-team chances were going to be limited. I found him to not only be a good manager, but a fair one. I told some of the younger players that they were lucky to have a manager like him, because he'd give them a fair crack at being in the team. I also told them that if they weren't playing or they were on the bench, they shouldn't mope around the place, they just had to accept it and work hard at getting their place back. Like Steve Coppell, he treated the players like adults, and I think everyone felt they could always go to him if there was a problem or something in their personal life that they had to deal with. In January 1999 I spoke to him and asked for some time off. Gran Davies had cancer and was very ill, and it was clear that she didn't have much time left.

I travelled north not really knowing what to expect. She did not want to be in the hospice any longer and instead was staying at my Uncle Malcolm's home. I met Phil there and the two of us spent all day sitting with her. It was getting late when Uncle Malcolm came in to speak to us.

'Why don't the two of you shoot off, and I'll see you in the morning? There's no point staying here all night.'

We drove back to Phil's place and within about two minutes of getting there, the phone rang. Both of us just knew it was Malcolm, and both of us knew what had happened. At the age of eighty-four, Gran had passed away.

Both Phil and I knew she was ill, we both knew she didn't have long left, but nothing quite prepares you for the shock and wave of emotion that hit you when the person you've loved, and who has loved you for so many years, is no longer there. She and Grandad had given the two of us so much. Without them our lives could have been so different. We owed them an awful lot. She had dedicated most of her life to looking after children who were not her own, making them part of her family, giving them the love and care that had been missing in their lives. She left Phil and me with lots of great memories, happy moments from when we were kids and then later on when we were adults. For years Phil would go across to Gran's every morning to make sure she was all right and give her a cup of tea. I was pleased that I'd managed to spend more time with her during my time at Wednesday, and that she enjoyed coming to stay with me in London. I was grateful that she'd been around to see me play in those finals at Wembley; it meant a lot. After giving so much of her life to the two of us, I think we both enjoyed trying to make her happy and making sure we included her in our lives as much as we could. She was an incredible person.

After Gran's death I knew I only had a matter of months before I became an ex-professional footballer. I was pleased that she had lived long enough to see me realise my dream and make it as a player. I knew she was proud of me and it was lovely to have her around to share the highs and lows I'd experienced. The thought of my professional career coming to an end seemed strange but, at the same time, I felt I had started to prepare myself for the next stage in my life. I'd tried to do as much media work as I could, getting experience on radio and television, trying to learn all the time. I'd started doing a regular slot on Mondays with Johnny Vaughan on Channel 4's *The Big Breakfast*, and although I was still fully focused on playing football, I knew it was important for me to prepare for a future outside the game.

I was involved in the squad but wasn't really part of the first team. That season I made five appearances as a substitute and scored once, when I came off the bench in a 2–2 home draw with Newcastle. I also played one full game against Everton at Goodison near the end of the league campaign. The team drew at home against Blackburn in the next game as we battled to avoid relegation. With two matches remaining it looked as though we were down, but the boys managed to pull off a 4–3 win at Aston Villa to keep things alive going into the last game of the season, a home match against my old club, Sheffield Wednesday. I desperately wanted to be involved in the game. I knew I wasn't likely to play, but it would have been nice to have been one of the three substitutes. It was an important game for the club, and there was a chance that, against the odds, we might be able to avoid relegation. In order to do that we had to beat Wednesday, and Everton had to stop Southampton from winning. By half-time Southampton were already ahead, and then news came that they'd scored another in the second half. Things looked bleak for us and, with eleven minutes remaining, Wednesday scored what proved to be the winning goal. There was no fairy-tale ending as there had been a year earlier with that fantastic play-off win, and after one season in the Premiership, Charlton Athletic were relegated. It would have been great to have pulled off the great escape, and it would have been nice to have made an appearance against my old club just before the curtain came down on my career, but it would have been a bit hypocritical of me to have had a moan after what I'd said to some of the other players about not kicking up a fuss if they weren't in the team.

The time I spent at Charlton holds a lot of happy memories for me and I was grateful that I was able to be part of something that was very special in the club's history. My final training session as a professional footballer was memorable as well, because at the end of it the boys all chaired me off the pitch. I knew they were a good group of players, and that once they got over the disappointment of being relegated, they had the ability to bounce straight back into the top flight. My playing career was over, but they still had so much to look forward to. Before I left, I stood in front of them and gave a little speech.

'My time has come to an end,' I told them. 'You lot can get promotion next season, because there's enough talent in this group to bounce back first time. Go away, have a good summer, then come back, be fully committed to each other and the club, and you can get back up. You all know now that the Premiership is the best place to play.'

I said my goodbyes, walked to my car and drove out of the training ground. I was no longer a professional footballer.

19

Feels Like Home

Iknew I would be retiring in 1999. I'd made the decision during the course of the season and began the process of opening a new chapter in my life by doing some TV and radio work, trying to prepare for what was to come, for life as a former footballer, but nothing really can.

When you stop playing there's a void and you can't fill it. You get up and don't know what to do. For so many years you have got out of bed in the morning knowing that as a professional footballer, there is a purpose and plan to everything you do during the week. Training, and playing matches, becomes a way of life. Then, suddenly, it's gone. You're finished as a player and there's nothing. It really gets to you. I found it difficult to begin with. There's no pre-season training, and then when the season actually starts, you're not involved, not playing. It's a strange, empty feeling. I can quite understand why some players say to themselves, 'I'm just going to give it one more year.' When Robbie Savage retired in 2011, he called me and asked what I did to cope with packing it all in. I told him how important it was to create a new routine for himself, to make sure he did things, and that his time was occupied each day. There isn't exactly a group of ex-players who keep in touch and give support and advice to each other, but football is a small world and you inevitably see each other at various things involving the game.

I knew it was the right time for me to retire. My body was tired, I didn't have any speed or zest. The last season had been a bit of a slog for me. I'd called it a day and had to live with the decision I'd made, and as strange as it felt to begin with, I told myself that it would get better. Apart from working on getting jobs in the media, I also knew I had to do regular physical stuff like going to the gym and doing half marathons. I needed the discipline of training for a run and having something to aim for, and I wanted to stay fit. As a player you take fitness for granted; you feel great and healthy because it is part of your way of life. When you stop playing, you have to make an effort to keep fit. Nobody organises training for you each day, you're not kicking a football any more.

I tried to put it all into perspective, because I knew that although I missed playing, it was the start of something else in my life. I was lucky enough to start working for the BBC, doing a variety of football-related things for them, including programmes like *Football Focus*, and co-commentary for live games. Having a job with the Beeb not only kept me involved in football, it also allowed me to move into a different career. I'd worked so hard to fulfil my dream of becoming a professional footballer, and when I'd finally made it, I gave football everything I had. When it came to an end, I had no regrets, because I knew I could not have worked any harder in football, and I took that sort of work ethic into trying to build a media career. I knew nothing could replace playing, but I'm not the sort of person who lives in the past. I knew I had to move on, I knew my life would be different, but instead of being depressed about not playing, I became excited about the work I was doing for the BBC, and I think I was fortunate to be able to step straight into something like that. There were no real gaps. I didn't have periods of inactivity, I was busy, and that's how I liked it.

At the start of the new millennium I had a lot to look forward to in my professional life, but in April 2000 it was something which happened in my personal life that brought great happiness: Michelle gave birth to a baby boy. It was an incredibly special moment for both of us, and we called him Isaiah. The name itself was special too. When we'd talked some years earlier about one day having children, I'd told her that if it was a boy, I had one particular name that I liked. Michelle told me she had a name as well and then asked me what mine was. I said Isaiah and also told her how I was spelling it. She jumped up off the couch we were both sitting on.

'I don't believe it,' she said. 'That's the name I'd thought of as well!'

Poor Michelle suffered after the birth because she contracted pre-eclampsia, which was pretty serious and made her body swell for a time, and she felt terrible. At the same time nothing could spoil the fact that we were now the very proud and happy parents of Isaiah, and we gave him the middle name of Philip after a very special person in my life, my brother. Phil and I shared so much together, and we were always there for each other as kids. We went through the whole fostering process together and I'm not sure how either of us would have coped without each other. There is no doubt we have a special bond and the belief he had in me as a footballer was a major factor in helping me eventually make it as a professional. When I needed support and encouragement he was always there, and having him in my life was so important to me.

Neither Michelle nor I were concerned about whether it was a boy or a girl, and we didn't know the sex until our son was born. Becoming a parent is an incredible feeling and it carries a huge responsibility. From my own point of view, the one thing I realised was that I knew exactly how not to be a dad, because of my own experience. I was lucky to have someone like Grandad Davies in my life, who acted as a role model to some extent and made up for the lack of having a relationship with my real father.

My dad was terrible, and the worst possible example of a dad you could ever imagine. An out-and-out awful parent. He just up and left when it suited him and started a new life, and I just don't know how anyone could do that. Over the years, and through social media, I've discovered that he's got kids all over the place. He was totally irresponsible and selfish, and an absolute lesson in how not to be a good father. Having been to the Gambia and traced some of his family, spoken to uncles and cousins, I found out that they are nice people, but for some reason, my own father was different. After travelling to England, he just left a trail of unhappiness behind him for so many people. He affected the lives of a lot of people, and didn't care about them, or what happened to them. When Marie and I went to see him, he acted as though he was so pleased to see us, but he hadn't once made any effort to be part of our lives, other than sending the letter to me when he'd seen I'd become a professional footballer. I have a really good relationship with Phil and my sisters. Despite all that happened to us, we have thankfully come through it and enjoy being a family, even though we spent so much time away from each other during the years we were kids. Our father did nothing for any of us, and wasn't worried about the consequences of his actions.

So when Isaiah was born I knew I was always going to be there for him, be part of his life, and not run away from him or the responsibilities of being a parent. It really was love at first sight when he was born, and that love for him has never changed. We have a great relationship and he knows that I am always there for him when he needs me. I'm his father but I also hope I'm his friend as well, and I think I am able to understand better than most people just how important having a dad in your life is, simply because I never experienced it.

I was finding my work with the BBC challenging and really interesting. I got asked to do all sorts of things, and I was literally learning on the job sometimes, which made it exciting and a bit scary at the same time. One day Bob Shennan, who was in charge of Radio 5 Live, told me about an idea he had for a new Saturday morning show he had for the station, which involved me and Ian. It was going to be called *The Wright and Bright Show*, with the two of us presenting it. We'd speak to players and people in the game, give our own opinions about what was happening in the world of football, as well as taking calls from fans. It was a great opportunity for me and Ian, who had also moved into the media and was involved, not just in sport, but in variety shows as well.

Ian and I had always stayed in touch. We would speak to each other on the phone or sometimes socialise together. Whenever we did meet or talk it was just like old times and we never lost the rapport we used to have when we were both playing in the same team for Crystal Palace. The banter and chat was second nature and we had a great time with the shows and were lucky to have a brilliant producer named Simon Cross. He guided us through the shows, offering advice and encouragement, and used his experience to make sure everything went as it should, but on 1 April 2001 he was faced with a unique situation. Ian was going to tell the nation, live on air, that his great friend, David Rocastle, had died. 'Rocky' had passed away the day before. His wife Janet had spoken to Ian and broke the terrible news, saying that she wanted him to make the announcement. Ian and Rocky had been friends since their days as kids in south London. They had a real bond that went beyond just being mates; both of them had dreamed of being footballers, and both had been spectacularly successful, earning legendary status as Arsenal players.

Ian was absolutely in bits when he heard the news, but agreed to carry out Janet's wishes. Nobody knew about David's passing and when I was told the night before the show, I was in shock. It was Janet's wish that the news would not become public until Ian announced it, and the atmosphere in the studio on the morning of the show was understandably sombre and tense. It was decided Ian would use a script to break the news, and it was going to be down to me to introduce him. We had a pre-recorded interview, and then Simon indicated it was time for me to speak.

'Ian Wright just has a little announcement,' I said nervously.

'Yes,' said Ian, trying to hold back his emotions. 'Something that's been absolutely killing me, Brighty. News that will sadden football fans throughout the country. My best mate and former teammate, Arsenal winger, England winger, David Rocastle, lost his battle last night with non-Hodgkin's disease . . .'

Ian then started sobbing and just couldn't go on. He pushed the script across to me and I tried to carry on, managing to finally get to the end of the announcement.

'He leaves behind his wife and three children. Our hearts go out to his wife and family.'

It was all I could do to just finish the sentence. Ian was crying, there were tears in the eyes of everyone involved in the show. Rocky was just thirty-three years old, and had been diagnosed only five months earlier. It was a horrible, cruel way for him to lose his life, and it left Ian totally devastated. Somehow, we managed to get through the rest of the show, and I apologised at the end for us not being our usual upbeat selves, but there was really no need. Everyone understood just how difficult and upsetting the day had been, and the whole of the football world were united in grief at the terrible news we had broadcast that morning.

Apart from that horrendous day, the two of us really enjoyed the show, and Bob Shennan was happy with it, but Ian's work commitments meant that it became difficult for him to carry on, and in the end, we had to stop. It was a fantastic opportunity for me and a brilliant learning curve, and I'll always look back on my time doing the show with great fondness.

Like any normal dad, I wanted to be involved in Isaiah's life as much as I could. I wanted us to do things together and I wanted him to be able to look back on his childhood in the years to come and say he had a great relationship with his dad.

My father might have been a lost cause as far as I was concerned, and although I didn't have the easiest of relationships with my mother, I thought it was important for her to see Isaiah. When he was just a few months old I told Michelle that I was going to take him up to see his grandmother. Michelle thought it was the right thing to do as well, and after that we would go up and see her from time to time, and Isaiah obviously got to meet other members of the family as well over the years. Both Michelle and I thought it was important and it was nice for him to get to know his uncle, aunts and cousins. Through those visits I suppose I re-connected with my mother to some extent. Nothing could make up for her not really being in my life when I was a kid, but I didn't want any hate in my life, and there was probably a lot of sadness in her because of what had happened in the past. If there was a family gathering or some sort of party, she would have a bit to drink and then sing the song 'My Way', with particular emphasis on the line that says, 'Regrets, I've had a few'. I'm sure she had regrets. In fact, I know she did. In July 2011 my mum passed away. I went up to see her when she was very close to the end and sat with her as she lay in her bed that had been moved into the conservatory of her home.

'I've made mistakes, Mark,' she told me, and there was a genuine sadness when she said it. We both knew she was right.

When my mum died, I was once again a single man. After eleven years together Michelle and I divorced. The marriage just came to an end, but there was no acrimony. To this day we have maintained a very good relationship with each other, and both of us were determined to be the best parents we could for Isaiah. Despite the divorce, I believe we've done that. Both of us have always been there for him, and always will be. In 2011 Isaiah was asked at school to write about someone they admired in their family and he chose me as the subject. He brought it home from school and Michelle gave it to me. His words remain one of my most treasured possessions.

The person I admire in my family is my dad. I admire him because he became a footballer and I want to be one. My dad helps me practice by helping me with my ball control and letting me take shots with him in goal. We normally play at Battersea Park because my dad lives in Battersea. I usually go there on the weekends. The park is one of the highlights of when I am there.

My dad has an interesting job he is a football commentator. My dad and I think it is exciting. He works at the BBC and sometimes I get to go as well, which I really think is entertaining. I have met all the people that work for Match of the Day. I think I will always enjoy meeting them. When I practice my dad often gives me tips. I always have a lot of fun with my dad.

My mum and dad married in Las Vegas in 1996 but divorced in 2007. My mum and dad are still friends, which I think is amazing. My dad is probably the most considerate person I know that is why I admire him.

I haven't remarried but have had other relationships since the divorce, including one which could have had disastrous consequences for me. About ten years ago I was invited to a birthday party. It was an enjoyable night, everyone had a good time, including me, but what I didn't realise was that party would become the starting point of a personal nightmare.

During the course of the evening, I got chatting to a Brazilian girl who was living in London. We exchanged numbers and soon after meeting we began seeing each other, but I quickly realised that something wasn't right. I started to feel uneasy about the whole thing and decided I wanted to stop seeing her. I tried to let her know how I felt, but she didn't seem to want to listen. She bombarded me with texts and would call me all the time. I ignored her, hoping she would get the message that any relationship we'd had was over, but that just seemed to make things worse. The calls and texts became more frequent and she refused to accept how I felt. I didn't know how to stop her.

My sister Maureen was a police officer at the time, so I phoned her for advice. She told me to arrange a meeting with the girl in a public place and to bring along a couple of people who would be witnesses to any conversation we had. She also told me to spell out the fact that I wanted the relationship to come to an end and to make sure that the girl understood this, then I was to follow up with a text to confirm what had been said at the meeting. Hopefully, she would then understand our relationship had come to an end, but still nothing changed. In fact, the whole thing reached a new level. Not only did she continue to try to contact me, she also began to make threats.

One night, another of her texts arrived. This one was much more sinister than anything I had previously received from her. She told me that if I didn't answer her calls, she was going to go to the police to tell them that I had raped her.

I panicked. I knew I had done nothing wrong, but the thought of her accusing me of rape sent a chill down my spine. I phoned my sister again and she told me to call the police and report what had happened – and that's exactly what I did. The next morning, they arrived at my home to take a statement. They were very good about the situation and I showed them all the texts that the girl had sent me. It became clear that they had also interviewed the girl and got her version of events, as she then sent me a vile text raging at me and generally being really nasty.

The whole episode was overwhelming and scary. I lived in fear of a story breaking in the newspapers, knowing that just the allegation would be enough to ruin my reputation, end my media career and finish me in football. I knew it didn't matter if my name was eventually cleared and I was proved innocent, the damage would have been done. I didn't sleep for about three weeks.

The police clearly felt I was telling the truth, because the girl eventually had to agree to some kind of restraining order preventing her from contacting me. But three months to the day after this happened, I got another text from her asking to see me again. I went straight to the police and showed them the message. Happily, that turned out to be the last time I heard from her, but not the last time I saw her. Some months later I was walking along Fulham Road in London, when someone called my name. I turned around and it was her.

'Come and speak to me!' she shouted.

I ran as fast as I could.

As well as working for the BBC on a national basis, including covering things like the World Cup and the Africa Cup of Nations, I also began presenting a regular Friday evening sports slot for BBC London. It was very enjoyable and I covered all sorts of sports during that time including, on one occasion, having to go down to Brands Hatch to interview a driver who was taking part in a touring car championship. My producer told me that the guy I would be talking to knew me, and was a big Crystal Palace fan. I went to Brands Hatch, met the guy, got on really well with him, and did the interview. During the course of the day he told me that we'd met before, and the meeting was way back in 1990, at Brown's nightclub. I was there with Andy, Finn and Wrighty and he was there with Gary Crowley, the broadcaster and DJ. I remembered him immediately when he told me. He was the skinny kid who never really said a word, and now he was a successful businessman and he was taking part in the touring cars event as a hobby. His name was Steve Parish, and he really was a big Palace fan.

The club obviously meant a lot to him, as it did to me. That's why I'd agreed to go there for free and help coach some of the young strikers they had coming through the academy. I would spend some time in midweek and enjoyed doing it. After meeting Steve Parish, we'd stayed in touch and one day I got a call from him. He told me he was leading a consortium that was going to buy Crystal Palace. He said they needed a spokesman and asked if I'd like to do it. I said I was happy to, but when I told my bosses at the BBC they said I couldn't do it because it would be seen as a conflict of interest. So instead of speaking on behalf of the consortium, I ended up reporting on the fact that Steve and his partners had gone ahead with the purchase of the club.

That was in 2010 and three years later the club won promotion to the Premier League after a play-off final win at Wembley against Watford. I was obviously delighted for the club and knew Steve and everybody at Palace would be looking forward to the new season, just as I was. Unfortunately for me, quite literally on the eve of it starting, I was told by the BBC that they could only offer me work for one day a month. After working for them for fourteen years, the news was delivered to me by the head of sports talent, Mark Cole, over a chicken sandwich and a cup of coffee in a Pret a Manger near Oxford Street in London.

With the new season about to start, I had little time to try and get fixed up with work. It was a big blow and a poor way to do it. A story about what had happened appeared in the *Daily Mail*, and the chief executive of the Premier League, Richard Scudamore, read it. He called and invited me along for a chat. He was really helpful and had a word with the people who ran Premier League TV, an organisation that sends matches all over the world. I started to do some work for them. I also did some ambassadorial work for the Premier League, and it was all thanks to Richard. He was brilliant and I will always be grateful to him for the help he gave me.

I stayed in touch with Steve Parish and went to a lot of Palace games. I enjoyed going to Selhurst on a regular basis and watching the matches. The club meant a lot to me and I had very happy memories of my time with them as a player. Steve suggested I become a club ambassador, and I was genuinely honoured to take on the role. Then in January 2015, my old Palace teammate, Alan Pardew, was appointed manager, and later that year Steve spoke to me about taking on a new full-time role at the club. He asked if I'd be interested in being the loan manager, the person who had responsibility for young players who had been loaned out to other clubs as part of their development. I was a little bit apprehensive about saying yes, even though the job appealed to me. I asked Steve if it was a role both he and Pards wanted me to take on, and he said it was and I was delighted to say yes to the offer. I have to say the way Steve has treated me since we first met has been incredible. He has included me in family holidays and I've spent Christmas with him, his mum Doreen and his daughters Jess and Izzy.

The job has evolved over the last few years to include things like scouting, and I thoroughly enjoy it. I like the degree of involvement I have at the club and, having been around football for so long, I know I would have missed not being part of it in some form. It's really interesting to see the way some of the younger players have developed, and it's funny to think that many of them weren't even born when I was at the club and scoring goals. The game has moved on so much and overall I think the changes have been for the better. The education of young players and the way they are looked after in the academy system is excellent, and the training facilities are a world apart from those I experienced as a player. When we trained at Mitcham during the winter the place could often resemble a mud heap, but the pitches the players train on these days are absolutely immaculate all year round.

The most obvious difference in the game today is the money that washes around. It is quite incredible, particularly at the top end in the Premier League. Players can become millionaires overnight when they sign a contract, and the money isn't confined to first-team players. Youngsters at a Premier League club can earn an awful lot even before they play a first-team game, and that can sometimes be a problem.

Having money always sounds great, but having a lot as a youngster can pose problems for some players. The old saying of have too much, too soon, can be very true and that's why having good advice and good people around you from the start of your career is so important.

I've always been the sort of person who is happy to have a chat with young players and offer advice if they ask for it. I always try to let them know that I'm simply giving them the benefit of my experience, and never insist they act on what I say. It's there for them and then it's up to them whether they agree with me or not. Everybody has to make their own choices in life and all you can hope is that you make more good ones than bad.

I've loved football all my life and I was fortunate enough to achieve my goal of becoming a professional. The era I played in wasn't as prosperous or high profile as the one modern-day players inhabit, but I loved my career, even if there were some bumpy moments here and there. I earned good money and had a good lifestyle, thanks to football, and I also had a lot of laughs along the way. It's been said before, but earning a living for doing something you love so much is pretty special. I enjoyed playing for all the sides I was a part of, but Palace provided some of the happiest memories I have from my playing days. It's the place where I really blossomed as a footballer and as a person.

I'm back at a club that feels like home.

Acknowledgements

To my sisters, Marie, Sharon and Maureen. Although we missed out on a conventional brother–sister relationship, it doesn't matter. I love you all the same.

To 'our kid', my brother, Fizzer. It's hard to measure the impact you have had on my life and career. The unwavering support and endless encouragement. I appreciate everything you have done. And to my sister-in-law Jane, my nephew Taylor and niece Georgia.

To two of my dearest friends, Robbie and Sandra Earle, apologies for my awful godparent skills with your daughter, Saffy.

John Rudge. Without question, I would not have had the career I had without you. Thank you.

I'm eternally grateful to Steve Coppell for turning my career around and changing my life. Thanks also to Ian Wright Wright Wright for being such a great playing partner and friend, and to Tony Finnigan for thirty years of friendship and support.

Steve Parish, thank you for your generosity and friendship.

I'd like to express my thanks to all the managers, coaches

and teammates from all the clubs I've played for, and to Mr Arkle, Jan Matthews and the teaching staff at Maryhill School.

To Kevin Brennan, someone who has been part of my journey from day one at Crystal Palace. Thank you for your time, patience and attention to detail. Not an easy story to tell, but I think we got there in the end.

My thanks also go to Gary Lineker, for writing the foreword to this book and for being a good friend ever since we first met at Leicester City all those years ago. I must also thank Tim Bates for believing in the book as well as Andreas Campomar, Claire Chesser, Howard Watson and everyone at Constable for making it happen.

Dee, best of the best. X

Lastly, to Isaiah Bright. From the moment you took your first breath, it's impossible to measure what you mean to me. I hope reading this book will give you some perspective on my journey. It's not always been easy, but it's been worth it. Love you, Dad. X

Index

Adams, Tony 239
agents 192, 221
Anderson, Viv 229
Ansah, Andy 264–5
Arkle, Mr (teacher) 3–4, 7, 59, 195
Armstrong, Chris 227
Arsenal 207, 213, 231, 234–6, 238–40, 255
Assis, Roberto 262–5
Aston Villa 151, 161, 181, 219, 280

Baldwin's Gate 66
Barber, Ian 196
Barber, Phil 196, 200
Barker, Richie 230
Barnes, John 188, 277–8
Barratt, Keren 240
Bart-Williams, Chris 229, 249
Bathpool Park, Kidsgrove 53, 54
Benn, Nigel 173–4
Bert, Phil 24
The Big Breakfast (Channel 4) 280
Bigon, Alberto 260
Birmingham City 153, 154
Blackburn Rovers 152, 153, 154, 156–9, 219, 231, 280
Booth, Andy 248
Bowen, Mark 271
Bowles, Paul 83
Bradford City 75, 77, 154
Brands Hatch 294–5

Bright, Edwin (father) 9–11, 12–14, 17, 20, 23–4, 47, 208–12, 286–7, 290
Bright, Isaiah (son) 285, 287, 290, 291–2
Bright, Mark
  abuse from fans 114–16, 119, 126, 132
  birth of son 285
  bond with brother 17–18, 21, 68, 79, 104–5, 285–6
  career record x
  club career see Charlton Athletic; Crystal Palace; Leicester City; Port Vale; Sheffield Wednesday; Sion
  depression 120–2
  divorce 291
  engineering apprentice 66, 67, 72, 85, 88–90, 92
  experience of racism 37–40, 44, 45, 114–15, 245
  false rape accusation 292–4
  fitness and stamina 64–5, 135–6, 247, 284
  foster care 10, 14–15, 17–27, 30–6, 47–57, 65, 67–9, 72
  Golden Boot award x
  gun incident 169–72
  injuries 173, 174, 176–81
  marries Michelle Gayle 252–4

media career xi, 280, 283, 284–5, 287–90, 294–6
non-league player 66–7, 69–71, 74–5, 81
osteitis pubis 135
partnership with David Hirst 228–9, 243
partnership with Ian Wright ix–x, 145, 146, 151–2, 163–4, 196–7, 213, 214, 220
pay 84, 90, 104, 138, 224
professional debut 82–3
properties 108–9, 139–40, 271
retires from professional football 281–2, 283–4
role at Crystal Palace academy 295, 296–8
schooldays 1–5, 22–3, 36–44, 63–4
Serginho nickname 116–17
Sunday league football 70
visits Gambia 211–12
young player 1–2, 4–5, 24, 40–1, 59–67, 69–72, 74–5
Bright, Maureen (mother) *see* Davies, Maureen
Bright, Philip (brother) 9, 13, 14, 17–18, 21, 22, 23, 24, 25–6, 27, 28, 29, 30, 34, 35, 36, 37, 39, 48–9, 53, 54, 55, 56, 65, 67–9, 73–4, 75, 76–7, 79–80, 82, 104–5, 140, 185, 279, 285–6
Brighton & Hove Albion 206
Brissett, Trevor 124, 125, 147
Bristol Rovers 206
Bromage, Russell 70, 71, 83, 88
Brown, Steve 273

Cambridge United 173, 174, 175, 176
Cannon, Jim 143, 152–3
Cantona, Eric 229

Capello, Fabio 260
Cardiff City 151
Cascarino, Tony 146, 152
Cegielski, Wayne 88
Chamberlain, Mark 62, 83, 87
Charlton Athletic x, 269, 270–9, 280–2
Clarke, Wayne 62
Clough, Brian 62
Clough, Nigel 133
Coca-Cola Cup 231, 244
  see also League Cup final (1993)
Cole, Mark 296
Coleman, Chris 217
Collymore, Stan 217
Constantin, Christian 257–8, 260–1, 266
Coppell, Steve 131–4, 135, 136, 137–8, 143–4, 146–50, 151, 153, 154, 155, 162–3, 166, 167–8, 173, 176–7, 178–9, 184, 185, 186, 187, 188, 190, 194, 196, 199, 201, 205, 214, 215–16, 217, 220–1, 222–3, 227, 229, 269–70
Cork, Alan 232
Coventry City 164
Cross, Simon 288
Crowley, Gary 295
Crystal Palace x, xiii, 131, 132–8, 140, 141, 143–203, 205–8, 212–21, 222–3, 227, 229, 231, 295, 296–7, 298
Curbishley, Alan 269, 270, 271, 272–3, 274, 275, 277, 278
Dalglish, Kenny 146
Davies, Bob and Irene 31–3, 34, 35–6, 38–9, 43, 47, 49–53, 55–6, 67–9, 72–3, 85–6, 201–2, 248–9, 250–1, 253–4, 278–80, 286
Davies, Malcolm 56–7, 72, 73, 279

Davies, Maureen (mother) 9–11,
　12–14, 15, 20, 23, 24, 25, 27,
　30, 47, 49, 290–1
Davies, Tom (Tommo) 24, 27, 49
Defoe, Jermain 93
Degryse, Marc 248
Dennis, Mark 163
Derby County 176, 216, 217
DeWitt, Doug 173
Dodd, Alan 82
Dyer, Alex 153

Earle, Robbie 87, 91, 93
Eustace, Peter 101, 102
Evans, Ian 153
Everton ix, 109–10, 123, 167,
　206–7, 244, 280, 281

FA Cup final (1990) xiii, 5, 6–7,
　189, 192–202
FA Cup final (1993) 236–40
FA Cup final record 192–3
faith healing 176–80
Ferguson, Sir Alex 200
Finnigan, Tony 139–40, 149, 153,
　208–9, 218
First Division play-off final (1998)
　272–5
Football Focus (BBC) 284
Foote, Andy 99
Francis, Trevor 220, 221, 225,
　227–8, 229, 236–7, 238, 246

Gabbiadini, Marco 216–17
Gambia 11, 211–12, 286
Garner, Simon 157
Gayle, Howard 157
Gayle, Michelle 249–51, 252, 253,
　254, 258, 271, 276, 277, 285,
　286, 290, 291
good-luck telegrams 5, 6–7, 195
Graham, Arthur 94
Graham, George 234

grandmother (maternal) 10, 14, 23,
　27–8, 29–30, 33
Gray, Andy 134, 139, 146, 149–51,
　161–3, 185, 187, 188–9, 201,
　217, 218–19
Gray, Michael 273
Greenhoff, Jimmy 87
Grobbelaar, Bruce 187
Hall, Eric 192, 193
Hamilton, Bryan 123, 124–5,
　126–7, 147
Harkes, John 235
Hartlepool United 231
Henry, Lenny 45
Hereford FC 87–8
Heysel Stadium disaster 207
Hirst, David 225, 228–9, 231,
　236, 237, 238, 239, 243, 244,
　246
Holmes, Matty 271
Hopkins, Jeff 153, 155
Horton, Brian 129–30
Huddersfield Town 172
Hughes, Mark 196, 197
Hull City 129, 145
Humphrey, John 205

Ilić, Saša 273
Ipswich Town 136, 231, 272

Johnson, Paul 70
Jones, Robbie 116–17, 118

Kelly, Robbie 116–17, 118
Kendall, Howard 244
Kerby (ballgame) 24
Kidsgrove Athletic 74–5
Kilcline, Brian 164

Langford, Rob 65–6
League Cup final (1993) 234–6
Leeds United 167
Leek Town 70–1, 74, 80, 81, 84

Leicester City ix, 97–8, 99–100, 101, 103–30, 134, 138, 140–1, 231, 245, 251
Lewis, Dennis 249–50
Lewis, Lennox 249, 250
Leyton Orient 206
Lincoln City 95
Lineker, Gary ix–xi, 99, 106, 107, 108, 109–10, 111, 123, 257
Linighan, Andy 239, 240, 241, 255
Lisbie, Kevin 276, 277, 278
Liverpool FC xi, 165–6, 168, 176, 183–4, 185, 186–9, 207–8
Love Thy Neighbour (TV sitcom) 44
Luton Town 126

McAllister, Gary 117
Macclesfield Town 124
McFarland, Roy 75, 76, 77
McGoldrick, Eddie 153, 157, 158, 180
McGrath, John 71–2, 81–2, 83, 88, 90–1, 95, 105
McGrath, Paul 94
McGregor, Barry 64–5
McMahon, Steve 187
McVey, John 127, 135–6
Madden, Dave 153, 158, 194
Manchester City 152, 153–4, 191
Manchester United 94–5, 163, 168, 184, 186, 190, 191, 196–8, 200, 201, 205, 229, 235, 244
Marie (sister) 9, 13, 14, 17, 20, 21, 23, 28–9, 80, 209, 210, 211, 287
Mariner, Paul 81
Marshall, Struan 257
Martin, Lee 200, 201
Martyn, Nigel 167
Masons Arms 70, 71, 74, 83, 84
Matthews, Sir Stanley 203
Maureen (sister) 20, 293
Mendonca, Clive 271, 273, 275

Merson, Paul 235, 240
Millwall 152, 256
Milne, Gordon 99, 100, 103, 104, 109, 110, 113, 114–15, 123, 127–8
Morrow, Steve 235
Moss, Ernie 93
Mühren, Arnold 94

Neilson, Donald 54–5
Newcastle United 107, 280
Newton, Bob 87, 88, 93
Nicol, Steve 165
Noades, Ron 131, 135, 136, 138, 144, 190
Norwich City 184, 206, 229
Nottingham Forest 62, 133, 167, 206, 227

Oldham Athletic 184, 190, 191, 213
O'Neill, John 99
O'Reilly, Gary 143, 144, 166–7, 186, 187, 196
osteitis pubis 135
Oxlade-Chamberlain, Alex 62

Palmer, Carlton 235
Pardew, Alan 144, 148–9, 165, 173, 186, 189, 296–7
Parish, Steve xi, 295, 296–7
Parker, Scotty 93
Parton, Helen (Nana) 18–19, 20, 21, 22, 24–5, 26, 27, 28, 47, 73, 117–18
Pearce, Jonathan 159
Pearson, Nigel 229, 236
Pemberton, John 166, 187, 232, 234
Pennyfather, Glenn 151
Phillips, Kevin 273
Philpott, Alan 62–3, 64
players' pool 192

Pleat, David 248, 252–3, 258, 266
Port Vale x, 60, 62–3, 71–2, 74,
    75–6, 77, 81–5, 86–8, 90–5,
    97, 98–9, 100, 104, 106, 107,
    111, 123, 124, 126, 130, 138,
    140
Portsmouth FC 172, 270
Premier League TV 296

Queens Park Rangers 161, 163,
    231, 236
Quinn, Niall 273

racism 11, 37–40, 44–5
  in football 114–15, 155–6,
    245–6
Ramsey, Paul 105, 106, 118–19
Redfearn, Neil 146, 153
Redknapp, Harry 247
Redknapp, Jamie 247
Reed, Les 275
Rennie, Dave 105, 106
Richards, Dave 259, 266
Richardson, Dave 98, 112
Robson, Bryan 94, 196
Rocastle, David 288–9
Rochdale AFC 172
Ronaldinho 265
Rooney, Wayne 225
Rudge, John 71, 77, 86–7, 91, 92,
    95, 97, 100–1
Rufus, Richard 273
Rush, Ian 146, 186

Salako, John 143, 187, 197, 207,
    213
Savage, Robbie 283
scouts 60, 61, 297
Scudamore, Richard 296
Serginho 116
Shankland, Andy 87
Sharon (sister) 15, 17, 22, 28
Sharp, Graeme 146

Shearer, Alan 228–9
Sheffield United 231, 232–3, 234
Sheffield Wednesday x, 101–2, 219,
    221–2, 225, 227–41, 243–8,
    251–3, 254–5, 258–9, 266,
    280, 281
Shennan, Bob 287, 290
Sheridan, John 229, 230, 232–3
Sheringham, Teddy 146, 152
Shirtliff, Peter 229, 236
Shreeves, Peter 251
Siddall, Barry 126, 129, 138
Sion 257–8, 259–64, 265–7
Smith, Alan 99, 100, 106, 108
Smith, Bobby 119
Southall, Neville 110
Southampton FC 167, 206, 281
Southend United 206
Southgate, Gareth 217–18
Staffs Hydraulics 66, 85, 88, 89–90
Stapleton, Frank 94
Sterling, Raheem 245–6
Stevens, Gary 276
Stoke City 70, 87
Stringfellow, Olga 177–9, 180
Suckling, Perry 151, 167
Summerbee, Nicky 273
Sunday league football 70, 159
Sunderland AFC 272–4, 275
Swindon Town 154, 155–6

Tartt, Colin 93
Ten-Em-Bee 144
Ternent, Stan 153
Thomas, Geoff 146, 164, 165, 169,
    175, 188, 207
Thomas, Mitchell 169, 170, 171,
    190
Thompson, Bill 89–90
Thorn, Andy 168, 186, 189
Till Death Us Do Part (TV sitcom)
    44–5
Torquay United 83

Tottenham Hotspur 112, 169, 173, 218, 231
transfer deadlines 269
transfer and signing fees 104, 111, 138, 167, 216, 218, 227, 248, 266
trials 60–1

UEFA Cup 208

Vardy, Jamie 71
Vaughan, Johnny 280
Venison, Barry 187
Vickers, Alan 70, 80
Virgin Atlantic 169

Waddle, Chris 221, 229, 230–1, 232, 240, 248
Walker, Mike 244
Wallington, Mark 99
Walsall FC 130
Warhurst, Paul 236–7, 238, 239
Warzycha, Robert 207
Watford FC 153, 154, 156, 295
Watson, Gordon 229–30
Webb, Neil 200, 201
West, Dave 134–5, 137, 179, 180
West Ham United 247
Whelan, Ronnie 165

Whiteside, Norman 94
Whittle, Leslie 54–5
Wilkins, Ray 94
Wilkinson, Howard 100, 101–2, 103, 243
Williams, Paul 227
Wilson, Danny 229
Wimbledon 95, 126, 164, 168, 184
Wolverhampton Wanderers 62–3
Wood, George 143, 151
Woods, Chris 229, 240, 248
Worthington, Nigel 229
Wright, Carl 36, 51, 55, 56, 73, 85
Wright, Ian ix–x, 133, 134, 136, 139, 144–5, 146, 149, 151–2, 155–6, 158, 159, 163–4, 169, 170–1, 172, 176, 183, 186, 189, 190–1, 193–4, 195–7, 198–9, 200, 201, 205, 206, 207, 212–16, 217, 218, 220, 224, 231, 234–5, 237, 238, 239, 240–1, 287–8, 289–90
Wright, Nesta 174–5, 201, 223–4
The Wright and Bright Show 287–90

Young, Eric 205

ZDS Cup 206–7